Until the
Lion
Speaks

Billy Moore

PAGE PUBLISHING, INC.
Conneaut Lake, PA

First originally published by Page Publishing 2021

ISBN 978-1-6624-2900-2 (pbk)
ISBN 978-1-6624-2901-9 (digital)

Printed in the United States of America

To all the young men who have sacrificed
their lives in the cycle of ignorance,
never having the benefit of living to realize their full potential

Until the lion speaks, the tale of the hunt will always glorify the hunter!

—African Proverb

Contents

Foreword

To BE IN Chicago's South Side in the 1980s was to be in an unfolding story about race, violence, and hypersegregation in urban America. Twenty years earlier, Martin Luther King Jr. came to Chicago to confront the institutional persistence of racism through restrictive covenants, redlining, and police brutality. By the 1980s and through tactics realtors dubbed as blockbusting, most working-class white families had fled from the neighborhoods King and the Chicago Freedom organizers marched through as did many of the middle-class jobs associated with the factories that once employed them.

It was the era of legendary street organizations. The Black P. Stone Nation, the Gangster Disciples, and the Vice Lords and their various offshoots dominated the streets, and within a few years, crack cocaine would create more bloodshed and desperation and drive a new regime of mass incarceration in cities like Chicago across the country. Amid white flight, factory closings, and the first wave of middle-class black flight to the suburbs, the young black men from working-class families who were left behind were confronting an increasingly narrow set of options and opportunities. Sports, and especially basketball, was one of the few avenues left.

Before the reign of Michael Jordan and the fame of hoop dreams, a young up-and-coming superstar from Simeon high school on Chicago's South Side represented the hopes and aspirations for an entire community. His name was Benji Wilson, and his brief but tragic encounter with the man whose story is at the center of *Until the Lion Speaks* would cost him his life and thrust the city and espe-

9

cially the African Americans in the city into a state of shock, grief, and anger directed to the sixteen-year-old who pulled the trigger that day: William "Billy" Moore.

For years, Billy, like so many young black men before and after him growing up amid similar circumstances, was known exclusively by the tragic violence of one terrible moment. The results of his encounter with a highly aggravated and upset Benji Wilson on a cold fall Chicago day would go on to define Billy for an entire city and a criminal justice system that had already systemically devalued young black men's lives. Yet beyond those in the criminal justice system that literally attempted to take his life, political icons and cultural celebrities in the black community absorbed and internalized many of the same sentiments. Even cultural forces like Common who grew up idealizing Benji would go to pejoratively reference Billy in one of his tracks as "the marks that shot Benji."

Until the Lion Speaks and so much about Billy's life before and after that fateful moment tell the courageous and difficult story from the perspective of a young man who refused to bow to that narrative. I met and worked alongside Billy years after that fateful day and met a man determined to do everything and anything he could to work toward reconciliation, opportunities, and hope for a new generation of young men whose lives were even more ravaged by a system that had fully failed them at every turn. I interviewed and hired Billy to work as a case manager for these young men in IMAN's Green ReEntry program a few days before his own and only son was shot sixteen times and left for dead sitting in a car.

I sat with a grieving father in that moment and told him I fully understood if he needed to defer the decision to work with us or needed more time off and was floored by his response. "My son's murder has left a gaping hole in my heart, and nothing will ever fill that. But there is nothing else I'd rather do and nowhere else I'd rather be than doing this work here with you all," said Billy in response to my suggestion that he take time to grieve the loss of his son.

While working with Billy, I had the privilege of working along-side a man who never once shunned owning the consequences of his actions as a young man but who also never accepted the logic that any young black man growing up in these circumstances is only as good as his worst moment. As news came to us of young men in our program who were shot or tragically killed, I saw Billy respond with even more heart-crushing sadness than the day I saw him after losing his own son. Reading this book gave me a greater appreciation of all the things Billy was confronting in those moments.

Themes of redemption, reconciliation, and resistance are woven into this vivid story that captures so much of what we rarely hear in the thirty-second news sound bites and often dehumanizing story of violence and black men in our inner cities. The story of these very same men settling difference, working toward greater change, and committing their lives to changing the systemic and structural factors that have created and sustained the conditions for that violence is a nuance that doesn't get as much coverage. In *Until the Lion Speaks*, we are provided powerful and complicated portraits of such moments, even one with Common, who visited our center while Billy was conducting a session with a group of young men and publicly embraced Billy and apologized for the demeaning way in which he portrayed him in his lyrics many years earlier.

Yet the moment of reconciliation between Billy and the brothers of Benji Wilson more than three decades after his death is perhaps the most stirring of such examples. Sitting at the table while that conversation happened will perhaps be the single most profound illustration of forgiveness and reconciliation I've ever witnessed.

There are ultimately many things anyone will take away from reading this book, and I hope among them will be a call to action, a call for all of us to consider what acts of courage, sacrifice, and reconciliation we are willing to lead in radically transforming and improving the life trajectories of young black men in our urban centers across this country.

Dr. Rami Nashashibi
Executive Director of the Inner-City
Muslim Action Network (IMAN)
2018 MacArthur Genius Award Recipient

"BILLY MOORE'S LIFE story is one of the most powerful lessons in humanity I have ever known. Heartbreak and hope, rage and redemption, pain and purpose, fury and forgiveness, and war and peace.

The early chapters of Billy's life are beyond painful. The current chapters are beyond inspiring. And I have every confidence that the best chapters in his life are still to come.

A warrior can be a warrior for many causes. We are so lucky that Billy is a warrior fighting to save the lives of our city's young men. Tragically, no one knows better than him the staggering cost of gun violence to our families, our communities, and our city. We can't win this war without him."

Arne Duncan,
former Secretary of Education
for the Obama administration.

Introduction

"MAN, AIN'T YOU going to say 'Excuse me'?"

"Nigga, fuck you. I don't owe you an excuse. Now what?"

"Fuck you, nigga. You pushed me."

"Ah, so you got a gun, huh? Whatchu going to do, shoot me now?"

"Man, don't walk up on me." *Bang, bang.*

This was my first and only encounter with Ben Wilson.

Chapter 1

Kid

ON JANUARY 13, 1949, three and a half years after World War II ended, my father was born to William Moore Sr., my grandfather, and Ola Bell Moore, my beloved grandmother. My father was the third oldest of nine children. He had six brothers and two sisters. Although he was not the firstborn son, my grandfather chose to name my father after him. I later learned the reason why he may have been chosen to be the namesake of my grandfather although he was the third son born.

As the decade of the forties was coming to an end, according to my uncle Gary, the approaching new decade was not looking too bright for my grandparents. Gary told me that just like the ending of that old decade, it may have been my grandparent's marriage that also was on the verge of ending, and possibly, they were living in separation. With so much on the line for my grandparents trying to raise children in the forties and up against all the other social challenges and societal norms that African Americans were facing in this country, like the institution of Jim Crow laws, it benefited them more to fight for their marriage to better stand against everything that made it hard for them to live in America at that time.

It was during this time of their separation that my father may have been conceived. I could only assume that their separation had resulted from a culmination of issues that I mentioned earlier that probably put stress on their marriage that had made them consider ending it. At some point, they decided to reconcile and face the fight together, I would like to think, but it could have been just the simple fact that they decided to get with each other, and as a result, my father was conceived, thus prompting my grandfather to name my father after him to symbolize the new beginning of my grandparents' marriage.

I had many reasons of why I looked up and admired my father. As a son, I'm sure I was bias. But in my assessment of what I thought a father should be, he shaped my opinion of fatherhood, and there is no biasness in that. Boys need that resource, and who is better to provide it than their own fathers? My father was responsible, a hard worker, lived up to his responsibility to me, and supported my mother although they weren't together. I never saw any demeaning or disrespectful behavior from him toward my mother or women in general. I've always known him to work, and he stressed education. He was handsome and tall, and his intelligence was beyond average. He respected his mother and loved his family. He had principles and was a man of integrity. Even when I didn't realize it at the time, I credit so many lessons I've learned from him as I look back.

One thing I remember him telling me was, "Men isn't measured from head to toe but from head to sky, brains to heart!" I cannot quite explain it in words, but there was a presence about him that communicated to the senses that, clearly, he was a man. What I mean by that is this: When he walked into a room, you could feel that his energy was different. He was noticed even if he was not trying to be. Even in his absence over all these years, his presence has left a lasting impression on me, thirty-five years to be exact after he departed this life.

I know my father was only human and certainly not perfect, but I also believe he was very intentional in his effort to be the best representation of himself to me. He left within me this myth-like image of himself. It was not a false sense above any scope of reality that can easily be created and conjured up in the mind of a young boy's imagination, but because of the way he consistently set examples of what a man should be like, those examples had such a great influence on how I remember him.

I know in this world there are plenty examples of what real men are and examples of what they are not, but for me, my father was one of a kind. He was consistent in his realness. Fatherhood and manhood were what he was for me! He was my superhero, and never have I looked up to another man in the way I looked up to my father. No matter what I do in this life or achieve, I don't think I could ever live up to the legacy he left for me to remember him by. If I ever found a pair of his shoes, I would never put them on. I know there's no way I could fit them. They are simply too big for me!

Since I became conscious and my awareness began to manifest an understanding of the world around me, I was impressed with him. It was everything about him—from the way he walked, talked, and carried himself—that personified the perfect image of what I wanted to be, especially how I saw the way other people treated him, as if he was special. To me, he just seemed to be a step above. He always seemed to take it all in stride, never appearing to act arrogant or self-centered but humble around those people who treated him in that way. He would just smile at their compliments as if he never took them too seriously. I rarely saw my father get upset, and on those rare occasions I did, his anger didn't last long.

It did not matter what we talked about—from school to baseball to everyday life. He was the first of only a handful of people in my life who seemed like with every conversation, I learned a lesson. When he spoke, he taught, and I listened and learned. I felt like I always walked away being schooled from what he had to say. I may not have realized it then as a kid, but looking back now, it was an honor for me to be his son and to have him as my father.

I remember when he told me he won his union election and became president of his local, he said, "The position does not make a man. It's the man that makes the position. If you give a man power, you will see a man's true character!" Obviously, I never forgot when he told me that. Throughout my life, I've seen people in positions of power; and based on how they handle their position, I would think about what my father had said. His words would ring out in my mind every time I saw how people allowed their position of authority to rule their character and expose them for who they really were. "Position of power," he said, "is not meant for everybody. Some people just don't know how to handle it. Don't be that way!"

When I was born, my father was nineteen years old and living on the South Side in Bronzeville on Forty-Third and Lake Park. To those from Chicago, this area was known then and still to this day affectionately as the Low End. The Low End was a big area on the South Side that went from Forty-Seventh Street as far north and to Thirty-Fifth Street as far south—from State Street to the west and the Lake to the east. "From State to the Lake!" as many Low End people would say!

This time in Chicago, while my father was growing up and living out his teenage and young adult years, was also the era in which the major street organization of Chicago had started establishing themselves as a strong and prominent presence in the urban communities on the south, west, and north sides of Chicago. Because of where my father lived, he, his brothers, and his friends were being heavily recruited by the BlackStone Rangers, later becoming Black P. Stones (BPS), and El Rukn.

The BlackStones was one of the largest and most recognized street organization in Chicago. The BlackStone Rangers pretty much had a stronghold on the neighborhood. But where my father attended high school—DuSable high school, which was located on Forty-Eighth and State Streets, right across the street from the then Robert Taylor Homes, North America's second largest project complex that only the Queensbridge projects in New York was larger— was Disciples territory, and they ruled the neighborhood with an iron hand. The Disciples, being the other major organization on the South Side and maybe the largest in Chicago, was rivals to the Stones. I guess home was where the heart was for my father because, apparently, he made his choice. It was the BlackStone Rangers.

As these groups began to grow in numbers and spread throughout the city, they became more organized and started forming coalitions as the smaller groups were absorbed by the larger ones. These organization began referring to themselves as Nations, not gangs!

They structured themselves through rank and file, functions, and responsibilities. Positions and authority were highly respected. This became so much of Chicago urban culture and way of life that it would have a lasting effect on the city until this very day.

The legacy of gang life is at the heart of Chicago's urban culture. It was no different for my father and his friends and not unusual for them to be influenced by it. My father was a natural leader, whether it was his street life or his professional life or among those close to him, his brothers and friends, who were his crew. His people looked to him for his leadership, so when he joined, they did too. Jeff Fort became the undisputed chief of the BlackStone Rangers, but initially, Eugene Bull Harris was the leader. Jeff Fort was well-respected throughout the city by everybody, but my father held down his set. I was told that as an infant, my father put a red tam on me and took me in my stroller to the Big House, a place where the Stones held their meetings.

I must go back a few years before when my mother and father started dating, maybe around 1966, a couple of years before I was born. My mother was an attractive young woman. From what I was told, every young cat in the hood wanted to date her. But according to her and my father, it was one dude who caught her eye and attention. You guessed it—Kid, Billy, aka my father, William Moore Jr.

Kid was my father's nickname affectionately called by close friends. My mother and father lived around the corner from each other. My mother, Vennetta Eileen Harvey, was the second oldest daughter to my grandparents, Relton Harvey Sr., aka Big Harvs, and Alfreda Harvey. My mother had two other sisters and a brother, and they lived on Forty-Fourth and Oakenwald. As I stated earlier, my father and his family lived on Forty-Third and Lake Park. They fell in love and became teenage sweethearts.

Young and in love, nothing mattered. My mother said they spent every moment they could with each other. She admitted to me that looking back on those times, she said she was too young to be that serious about someone but said my father was her first love and that she fell hard for him. She fell so hard for him, and eventually, my mother got pregnant with me. She said getting pregnant with me was not in the plan. She said clearly that was a mistake but also told me I was the best mistake she ever made!

My father told me that when he found out he was going to be a daddy, he told my mother he wanted to marry her and the next day asked my grandfather for his permission to marry my mother, which my grandfather granted. My father dropped out of school in his senior year at the age of eighteen. As much as my father may have felt it was a decision of necessity, it was not an easy one to make. See, my grandparents Ola and William instilled in their children the importance and value of an education. They wanted their kids to not have to struggle in life and achieve more than what they did. So I'm sure the decision to drop out of school was not something my grandparents were happy about and were definitely not happy about their eighteen-year-old son getting someone pregnant!

Nevertheless, he made the decision to drop out of school, but he promised my grandparents he would go back and get his diploma. He got a job to help support my mother. So although my father felt like he disappointed his parents, he believed what was most important at the time was to take care of his responsibilities and support me and my mother. After getting a job at the post office, he took night classes and would eventually get his GED, thus fulfilling the promise he made to his mother and father.

I was told that around the time I was one year old in 1969, my father's social conscience started convicting him. There were a lot of things going on during the time my parents were growing up in the 1960s. The civil rights era was in full swing, and it was this time in America that had given birth to a generation of young people who were the first generation of the Northward Migration.

Unlike a lot of their parents who had been born and raised in the racist and oppressive south that Jim Crow laws dictated how life was, there was a revolutionary spirit inside my parents' generation that compelled them to rebel against the status quo. For them, it was about fighting the fear that compelled those who came before them to flee the south. They weren't going anywhere. There was nowhere to run! They stood up to challenge the system and fought against what life was about in the urban cities across the north.

It was the Power to the People movement that resonated with my parents' generation. There were many movements that had awakened the consciousness of black people to stand up and challenge the system that had an impact on the quality of life supported by the discriminatory laws designed to oppress black people, so I can safely assume as he became more aware of the plight and struggle of the times that he was compelled to align himself with the movement and join the fight of his generation that was taking place in America during the 1960s in urban cities across this country.

He started feeling he had more of a responsibility to get involved in being a part of the solution and not contribute to the problem, so he and some of his friends decided they were no longer going to be BlackStone Rangers and decided to join the Black Panther Party, who was headed by the extraordinary and dynamic young leader Fred Hampton, the chairman.

My uncle Rico, who is my mother's younger brother, told me he was there the day my father and three of his friends—Willie Tatum and Johnell and Ronald McClendon—told Jeff Fort they were quitting the BSRs. Rico said Jeff and a small army confronted them, and when my father told Jeff they quit, Jeff Fort said, "Nobody quits us." He told my father and his friends they'll be back before driving off as if to say, "This isn't over," but Rico said Jeff never came back. Make no mistake about it. Jeff Fort could have come back and made his point, but I think it was out of respect that he didn't. Truth be told, I'm sure my father expected Jeff Fort to come back and was glad when he didn't!

The reason why I think my father was drawn to the Black Panther Party was because of its political agenda, its conscious movement, but more than anything else, the way the party empowered young black people to take control of their communities and not allow anyone to bring harm to it. They were prepared to defend themselves, and unlike the peaceful movement led by the courageous Dr. King, they had no problem with going to blows if it came to that! Because of this, the Black Panther Party was emerging as the voice of many young African Americans across urban America. Apparently, the agenda of the Panthers held more weight with my father than the

BSR's (BlackStone Rangers) did. His involvement with the Panthers lasted only a few years and came to an end around the time Fred Hampton, the chairman, was assassinated by the Cook County State's Attorney, Chicago police, and the FBI.

I know my father was a good person and family man. He had a few jobs after he left the post office. Eventually, he landed his job at ARGO Cornstarch, a place that produced cornstarch in Summit, Illinois, on the far southwest side of Chicago. I'm not sure when or what year he began working there, but I remember when I was thirteen years old in 1981, my father was elected as the president of his local union at his job.

One of the things I remember from that time is when unions in the country came together during the National Solidarity March in Washington, DC. It was the Solidarity Day march, September 19, 1981, and he took me to it. Me and him along with the members of his local hopped on a bus and rode to DC to join the march! That was a long ride. I didn't understand at the time the importance of why we were going there. Neither did it matter to me. The only thing that mattered was that I was with my father traveling to DC.

The trip to DC was the first time my father and I took a trip out of town together except for going to Peoria, Illinois, where my father's younger brother Gary attended Bradley University. Although Gary is my father's baby brother, Gary is one of the smartest people on this planet that I know. Gary is one of the other few people who no matter what the conversation is that I have with him, I always walk away feeling more educated and informed. I consider him a mentor whom I have looked up to and has admired my entire life. Gary was, before his recent retirement, the voice of Central Illinois by anchoring the news and urban radio for over thirty years there. I looked forward to these trips to Peoria with my father to visit my uncle while he was attending Bradley University.

My father and I bonded on this trip to DC. The solidarity march only lasted a few hours, then it was over. My father decided we should go and venture out and take in the sights and sounds of DC. As my father went about trying to school me on the politics and the importance of the need for unions for the American workforce, I think he picked up on my lack of interest. The talk was a little above my head. Honestly, my attention was drawn to the historical and majestic monuments and statues that decorated the landscape that has for decades identified the nation capital.

As the sun began to set over Washington, DC, and casted its shadows over those historic monuments, I remember my father looking toward the setting sun and saying to me, "Can you believe a black man helped to design this great city?" I wasn't going to doubt what my father was saying. He tended to know what he was talking about! He told me about Benjamin Banneker, a black man whose father was a slave. He said Banneker was a mathematician and was one of the people who helped designed the city of DC. Whenever he talked to me about something like this or anything that's historic, he would tell me to go do my research on it. He would say, "Never let somebody just tell you something and you just believe it without finding out if it's true or not for yourself."

We ended up going to a show while we were out sightseeing. The movie we went to see was *The Elephant Man*. It was about this guy named John Merrick who was born with this rare deformity. Before we went into the show, my father explained to me what disease John Merrick had. He said it was called neurofibromatosis. I remember in the movie, John Merrick was being exploited as if he was a circus attraction and how he was being treated. One line I remember he said was, "I am not an animal. I am a man," slurring with every word he spoke. That movie made me think about how grateful I was I didn't have to go through life like John Merrick.

I wondered how my father knew so much about the condition of this man. My father was a knowledgeable cat. He was like the real-life Furious Styles, the character Lawrence Fishburne played in *Boyz N Da Hood*. My cousin Cindy told me that the first time she saw *Boyz N Da Hood*, Furious Styles reminded her of my father.

I wouldn't visit Washington, DC, again for another twenty-seven years, March of 2018. What brought me back was a march organized by the students of Marjory Stoneman Douglas High School in Parkland Florida, who lost seventeen of their fellow students to a former student armed with an AR-15 assault weapon. The March for

Our Lives was organized with people from all over the country coming together to speak out and rally against gun violence. This march was far more significant for our times.

We took busloads of traumatized youth from Chicago who daily had been witnesses and victims to gun violence. We joined forces with people from around this country who had suffered from the same trauma that gun violence was inflicting not only in urban communities but also in places like Parkland. We came to unite, sympathize, and comfort the survivors. I know my father would have been proud to see me rallying and committing myself to a fight that I believed in by joining forcing to effect change just like my father did when he took me to Washington twenty-seven years earlier.

The place where my father worked was a hazardous and unsafe work environment. It was believed that the exposure to the chemicals used to produce cornstarch put the workers there at high risk. Employees there were getting sick and dying. I remember my father telling my mother that he was going to way too many coworkers' funerals who had died from cancer. Because of the hazardous pollutants that poisoned the work environment where he worked, my father's employer sent him to school to develop a filtration system to filter out the harmful pollutants to make the work environment cleaner and safer. Although he learned how to filter the pollutants and created a safer work environment, it wasn't before the effects of years of working in that toxic place caught up with him.

My father was diagnosed with cancer in March of 1983, a year and a half after marching in DC. Although my father was a resilient man, his condition was terminal; and on September 22 of that year, my father died at the young age of thirty-four years old. I was only fifteen years old. I had never known life without him been alive, and now I must learn how to live without him. I didn't know what life was going to be like without my greatest mentor and role model. There was no longer my perfect example to emulate and the example of what I should be striving to be like. The day he died became the first of a few of my worst days.

Chapter 2

Mama

IT WAS THE winter of 1968 when my mother gave birth to me. She was sixteen years old, only a junior at Forestville High School where she attended at the time. Forestville later became King High School on the South Side of Chicago. The original Forestville she went to has been torn down. My mama told me she was watching *The Bozo Show* when she went into labor with me. It was seven hours of pain she endured that proceeded my inevitable entry into this world on a cold New Year's Day in 1968. The temperature was negative nine degrees that New Year's Day, but according to my mother, my birth brought nothing but warmth to her heart. She told me that from the very moment she knew she was pregnant with me, it started a life of love deeper than she would ever feel for anyone. I could not understand or know the depths of a mother's love, but as the recipient of that love, I felt it every day of my life.

I was the second grandchild born into the family on my mother's side of the family. Two months earlier, my cousin Fats, Edward Charles Thompson, was born on October 29, 1967, to my mother's older sister Vicky, who we affectionately call Poo Poo. Fats was more like a brother to me than my cousin. For the first few years of our lives, we were literally inseparable. We slept in the same bed and spent almost every waking moment together. During this time, we lived with my grandparents until my father and mother got their own apartment.

My father worked to support us while my mother went on to graduate from Calumet High School in 1970, a year and a half after giving birth to me. After high school, my mother got a job at the post office. My parents and I, from what I was told, lived together up until the time I was around two years old. I couldn't remember ever living with my parents. I was just that young. My mother told me very little of what caused their separation. She had confessed that after my father died, her greatest regret was that she did not go back to my father. Early on in my life, I've been taught how hard it is to live with regret and to try do more of what can be done to live without them. Of course it's easier said than done. What I also have learned is that people make mistakes, hold on to resentment, and let their pride get in the way of letting them do sometimes the right thing. I remember my father occasionally telling me how much he loved my mother and how he would do anything to have her back despite the fact he had plenty of women.

As a kid, my father would come and get me and take me around his old neighborhood on the Low End, Forty-Fifth and Cottage Grove. There was a pool hall and liquor store his friend Johnell ran next door to the Caesars Palace Lounge owned by this dude named Richard Cain. I can remember that on many occasions, beautiful women would come around, and my father would either approach them or they would walk up to him. Next thing I knew, he would tell Johnell to watch me for a minute before leaving. Those minutes always turned into hours before he returned. That was the one thing I didn't like when I was with my father, when he would leave me in the pool hall.

I remember one time while waiting for my father to come back on one of these occasions, a fight broke out between two dudes who were gambling and shooting pool. I knew one of the dudes. He was a friend of my father named Rat. Rat was a big man and scary-looking. Honestly, it really wasn't a fight because Rat chased the other dude around the pool table a couple of times before he escaped out the door. This dude came back with the police and said Rat had taken his money. Johnell told the police, "That motherfucker lying. Get the fuck outta here with that shit." The police told the other dude, "Don't bother us with this shit!" Then they left out the door. The guy ran behind them, and everybody started laughing. I heard Rat tell Johnell, "When I catch his ass, I'mma fuck his stool pigeon ass up!"

When it came to my father and those women, for some strange reason, I admired that about him. I went home and told my mother about what had happened with Rat, and my mother told me Rat was a bully. She said he had been one all his life and that when they were younger, my father had to beat Rat up. After seeing the type of fear I saw Rat put into that other man and then to hear my mother tell me my father had beaten him up, this same man who made that other dude run for his life, it made me feel a sense of male pride only a son could feel for his father knowing Pops will whoop some ass.

Unwittingly, not only did I tell my mother about what Rat had done but I also told her about all my father's pretty girlfriends I had seen him with and how he would leave me with his guys to dip off with these women. Not really understanding that I was tricking on my Pops, I naturally underestimated my mother's feelings she apparently still felt for my father; so the next time we were together, my father said to me, "Hey, listen, man. If you are going to be hanging with me, you can't be telling your mama everything you see, especially about my cutie-pies, bet?" I said, "Bet," and then we dapped on it. After that, I never tricked on him again, even when my mama asked me if my daddy had me around his "bitches!" See, what I came to realize later was that even though my parents were not together, they, too, occasionally would dip off too. So Mama was still feeling Pops when I was a shorty.

Let's go back to why I think my mother left my father. She told me one day that when I was about two years old, my grandma Ola called to tell my mother she wanted to take me to church and that she needed to get me ready by a certain time. Like most grandmothers, mine was no different. She was a faithful churchgoer and that it was her duty to make sure her grandchildren were getting their proper Christian teachings. My mother told me she didn't like the tone in which my grandma Ola spoke to her in, and an argument started. My mother said she hung up on my grandmother and out of anger called her a bitch. She did not go into details, but she said my father at that moment made her feel fear inside of her that she had never felt before or since then.

What I knew about my father and my uncles, his brothers, was, they had this type of love for their mother that if necessary, they would kill somebody about her if she was ever disrespected. My mother never told me exactly what had happened that day, but whatever it was made my mother leave my father, and they never got back together. They lived as separated until the day he died, and my father regretted also what he did that led to their separation. He never discussed with me what that was. He did tell me that he was ashamed of himself for what he did. I really believe they loved each other despite them never getting back together. I know they had a close friendship, and my mother was at the hospital every day with my father until he passed.

As a child growing up, I felt the love of my mother. She did the best she could to raise me. I can remember how my mother worked during the day and went to school at night. She went to school for administration assistance. She could type so fast. I remember her showing me how to write in shorthand. My mother was smart and would always pass her exams with As. But she would tell me that the smartest person she knew was my father. She really looked up to him. She played a role to reinforce my feelings of love and respect for my father and didn't negatively talk about my father in front of me as the classic baby mama often did. I don't know if she realized it at the time, but when she spoke about my father in such a way, it validated my love for the man he was. Although I saw him through my own eyes and loved him through my own heart, she was able to strengthen and reinforce the positive image I had of my father. I appreciated the fact that if she did harbor any negative feelings for him, it wasn't expressed in front of me.

I saw firsthand how hard my mother worked. The drive to have more for us sometimes meant I wouldn't see her for an entire day. During the day, she would be at work; and after work, she would go straight to school in the evening and wouldn't get home sometimes until after I had already gone to sleep. So there would be times I wouldn't see her until the next morning while getting ready for school. As a self-confessed mama's boy, I couldn't understand at the time her sacrifice; and selfishly, I held it against her. I just missed her. I always had an uneasy feeling when I didn't see my mother. That feeling only went away after I laid my eyes on her. Looking back on the sacrifices she made gives me a greater appreciation for who she was. Although she always bragged on how smart and great she thought my father was, she, too, showed she was equally as smart and great in my eyes!

When I was around twelve, I remember she landed this job she really wanted. I was glad for her as well, and because it paid better than what she was making before then, she started giving me an allowance in addition to the allowance my father was giving me. Up until that time, since I was two years old, my mother and I had lived with my grandparents on Eighty-Fifth and Bishop, 8522 S. Bishop. My grandparents bought that house in June 1968. I was only six months old when we moved there. We were the second, maybe third, black family who moved on the block. I practically grew up in that house.

This is the Auburn Gresham area on the southwest side of Chicago. It was on the next block from Foster Park. Foster Park was also the park where Michael Jordan occasionally played pickup games on Saturday mornings in the field house early on in his NBA career. Foster Park was where I saw for the first time in person the first and other GOAT (greatest of all time) Muhammad Ali when I was around nine or ten years old. That has to be one of my fondest memories as a kid, to be able to meet one of, if not the greatest, dude ever to put on boxing gloves! He came to Foster Park with the then mayor of Chicago Michael Bilandic. The entire neighborhood seemed to be up at the park that day. It seemed like a thousand people were there, and believe it or not, I got right next to the champ, close enough to get into an exaggerated shadowboxing sparring match with Ali while he playfully hit me in the jaw.

Actually, this was the second time I was in the presence of the champ. The first time was when my father and mother were walking along the beach while my mother was pregnant with me. My mother told me Ali said she was a beautiful woman, and just as with me ten years later, the champ and my father got into a shadowboxing match. Therefore, Ali was also considered by many to be the people's champ. He made people feel special in his presence. That was how I felt, and that was the feeling my parents had felt also. It was a special moment for them as well. Living on Bishop was where I had so many memorable moments in my life.

By the time I was five years old, all the white people who lived on Bishop had moved except one white dude who still lived on the block across the street from our house. For whatever reason, he decided he was going to stay. I always remember him mowing his lawn. He would speak to the neighbors but mostly kept to himself. He was the last of the Mohicans, so to speak. He lived on Bishop until the day he died. He was the only other white person I saw on an everyday basis until I started school. Then it was the teachers at school.

As the block began to take on its new look, everyone started developing friendly relationships. We had a tight-knit group of neighbors. Everybody knew one another and basically got along. I enjoyed living on Bishop. We lived in a tan brick bungalow that was classic to the look and that identified Chicago's urban neighborhoods across the city. It blended beautifully into the Chicago landscape that looked like the millions of houses that provided shelter to the residents of our great city.

When my mother started working her new job, she decided to get her own apartment and, of course, expected me to live with her. Her new apartment was in the same neighborhood, only four blocks away on Eighty-Second and Ashland, an apartment building my grandmother's brother, Uncle Lonnie B, aka Uncle LaLa, owned. My mother's younger sister Valerie lived there too with her husband at the time, Willie. I would go between both places, but I preferred to spend most of my time at my grandparents' house because all my friends lived on the block. Also, the other reason why I spent more of my time on Bishop was because my mother ended up meeting this dude named Ronald.

Honestly, I didn't like him at all at first. He didn't fit into the image I envisioned for my mother. The perfect picture in my mind for my mother was my father, not Ronald. No matter how much I wished, prayed, or tried to will Ronald out of my mother's life, it didn't work. This dude wasn't going anywhere. He stayed around like an irritating cough that wouldn't go away. Although I had seen my father with other women, I just felt different about seeing another dude around my mama. But the more I came around, the more I opened up; and eventually at some point, I started coming around to liking Ronald.

Honestly, Ronald was a good guy, and he always treated me with respect no matter what type of attitude I displayed when I was around him. He was a smart man, but Ronald had been through a lot and wasn't prefect. I blamed him for some things that I thought he was responsible for, like me feeling like my mother had changed, but over all, the dislike I initially had toward him disappeared. We would talk sometimes when I spent time at my mother's apartment. I wasn't disappointed when my mother and Ronald broke up, I want to say. My mother and Ronald dated for about two years, and then one day, he was gone, no longer around.

Looking back on it, I didn't realize just how young my mother was. To me, my mother was just my mama. I never considered that my mother was a young woman even though she was only sixteen years older than me. I had this thing that my mother wasn't a woman. She was just my mama. But the reality was, Mama was a woman who just happened to be my mother. I didn't fully embrace that thinking until I got in trouble. Getting in trouble forced me to mature fast, so I had to start seeing things differently. My eyes opened to the fact that my mother was also a woman!

Chapter 3

Living in the City!

THERE WERE A lot of fun times I shared with my mother, like when she would take me to the neighborhood theater on Ninety-Fifth and Ashland. It was called the Beverly Theater. The building is still there. It's a church to this present day. We had gone and watched a bunch of movies there. When I was about five years old, there was one movie I begged my mother to take me to go see. It was the movie *The Exorcist*. Man, I begged and begged her until she eventually gave in and agreed to take me to go see it. That movie turned out to be the scariest movie I ever saw. Everything about that movie scared the shit out of me! But strangely enough, I fell in love with scary movies.

We would go downtown to places like Ronnie's Steak House and theaters like the Oriental to watch movies like *The Bingo Long Traveling All-Stars & Motor Kings* and old-school martial arts movies at the McVicker's. I remember going to the Rhodes Theatre on Seventy-Ninth and Rhodes and watching *J.D.'s Revenge*. We took countless trips to the Museum of Science and Industry, then always visiting the ice cream shop in the basement there where she would buy me sundaes and banana splits. I remember cobblestone floors and taking black-and-white pictures in the Model T car. My mother was always taking me places and exposing me to things the city of

Chicago had to offer. My mother instilled in me an adventurous nature to get out and see things beyond my neighborhood.

One day, I was standing on the front porch of our house on Bishop. As I looked north past Foster Park, I noticed the majestic structure of the then named Sears Tower. Its imposing presence looming in the backdrop of Chicago's skyline could clearly be seen, the largest building in the world at the time standing tall in my city, the beacon of the Midwest. It could be seen from every vantage point in and surrounding the city. I noticed as I started going places that no matter where I went, I could see it, even from the suburbs. This erect monstrosity could be seen from almost everywhere.

Not just satisfied from being able to see this skyscraper from afar, I wanted to see this behemoth up close, to touch it, to go inside all the way up to the top, conquer this symbolic mountain. As I began to get bigger and older, my adventurous spirit began to awaken inside of me. I saw symbolic towers in other places that led me to begin to venture off the block and out of the neighborhood. I wanted to see more, and so I did. But just as the Willis Tower could be seen for all to see, for some people from where I was from, it was hiding in clear sight. It represented something that was unattainable for those in the hood. It was like a mirage in the desert.

Chicago is like *A Tale of Two Cities*. There is this phenomenon of self-isolation that is present with our urban youth, who are skeptical to venture outside their self-imposed boundaries of what they know and are comfortable with. Usually, at best, their limits extend no more than maybe a four-block radius of their neighborhood. Rarely do they extend themselves beyond these peripheral boundaries. The Sears Tower can only appear as an oasis to some young people who seem to be dying in this urban desert. Believe it or not, there are some people who have grown up and lived their entire lives in this amazing, beautiful city and have never been downtown. For some, although the Sears Tower could be seen, it might as well be like the moon—unreachable! It's like the make-believe Emerald City of Oz, but in this real-life scenario, they never have to seek out the wizard to get home. Home is somewhere they never left.

I eventually made it to the Emerald City and got a chance to walk on the moon. One day, a friend of mine named Fuzzy and I cut school. Since it was early in the day and being outside with nothing to do, we decided to jump on the bus and take the train downtown. We made our way and found ourselves standing right next to this iconic landmark standing tall on Jackson and Wacker Drive, the Sears Tower. Looking up at it was amazing. I was finally standing right next to it, up close and personal, and reflecting on all those times I had seen this monolithic giant in the distance. Now I was standing directly under its wing and shaded by the projected massive shadow, a shadow that must cast out a few miles away from itself and that shaded distance things that would never stand underneath it.

We didn't go inside. Everybody I saw moving about, going in and coming out, looked like they had business there. It looked like they had a small portion of ownership of this building and as if it was for them. I feared I had no business to enter because it wasn't for me, so we didn't go inside. Plus, in the back of my mind, I didn't want to be stopped by the security or harassed by the police since I was cutting school. After that day, I saw the Sear Tower from a different perspective. It was no longer sitting in the distance appearing to be unattainable as if I was looking at the moon or the stars in the sky—to be seen but never touched. Now it was there within reach for anyone to touch and explore.

The next time I went to Sears Tower, my grandmother took me and my cousins Fats and Cindy. We did go in and went to the top. The city looked vast. That was the highest I had ever been up. I could remember trying to see where I lived. Obviously, the block didn't stand out from above the perch of a hundred stories up the way my view was in reverse seeing this building from almost everywhere I went. That's another hidden truth. From that vantage point of being all the way up, where I come from was easily overlooked from high places! What I did remember being able to see from my vantage point was Comiskey Park where the White Sox played and where I had watched them play a hundred times. I had always wondered what the town looked like from up there. That day, I finally got to see.

Chapter 4

Only Child?

MAYBE AROUND THE time I was fourteen, I started hanging out more with my cousins who lived in Englewood. I was usually on Eighty-Sixth and Ashland at the game room called S&R with my friends. We would spend hours in there playing games like Pac-Man, Galactica, and Galaxy or just standing outside in front of Ma and Pop's liquor store that was on the corner of Eighty-Fifth and Ashland. Sometimes, I would and see the bus coming and jump on it and head north to Englewood a couple of miles away. At that time, they lived on Fifty-Ninth Street in between Ada and Throop.

My cousins were Pook, Daniel, Steve, and their little sister, Lachelle. Sometimes, Fats would go with me; but most of the times, I would go by myself. I saw Pook more like an older brother whom I looked up to. He was two years older than me but far wiser beyond his years. Pook was street smart and fast in the game. He was someone everybody respected. His brother Daniel called him the Godfather. Daniel was the one who was smooth and got all the girls. It wasn't hard for this dude when it came to females. They loved Daniel, and because of this, we gave him the nickname Macafee! He was a real player from an early age.

Steve was the younger brother, and he was super hyper and energetic and quick-tempered. Fats was more laid back than I was and would probably be game to do anything I would. My cousin Cindy, Fats's sister, was nice and sweet but wasn't a punk. She would fight a damn tiger if she had to at the drop of a hat but also would give you the shirt off her back. Then my little cousins Phil, Big, Kenya, Sherri, Naughty, Rocky, Shaun, and Donald Moe were all like my younger siblings. Donald Moe was a younger cousin of mine on my father's side who was so close to me. We were like brothers. I am regressing just a bit as I must give a shout-out to all my unofficial brothers and sisters who are my family. With all this love for my cousins, I was the only child to my mother. Except for Pook, Daniel, Steve, and Lachelle, my cousins and I all at some point lived in my grandparents' house together.

One day, my father came by the house and asked me to take a ride with him. It was more of a demand than a request. He told me there was someone he wanted me to meet. Having no clue and without any suspicion, I left with my father. As he drove, his demeanor was pretty much as it always was, making small talk about what was going on with school and stuff like that. So I wasn't expecting anything major from his statement: "I want you to meet somebody!"

After we pulled up to this house and parked, he told me to sit tight for a minute right before I attempted to get out of the car, so I sat back. He said "I'll be right back" and then exited the car. I watched him walk up the stairs and ring the doorbell, and maybe a minute later, someone, who I couldn't make out or recognize, came to the door. He went in and disappeared behind the door. A few minutes later, he came back and gestured for me to come inside the house. I got out of the car and walked up the stairs and through the door as my father held it open for me.

There across the room was a lady, and standing next to her was a pretty-faced, skinny little girl. What my father said next caught me totally off guard. He said, "Lil Billy, this is Felicia. She's your sister. And this is her mother, Denise!" I didn't know how to respond to that or what to think of what I had just heard. For thirteen years of my life, I thought I was the only child. I was confused and speechless. Once my mind began to absorb this revelation, standing there face-to-face with my new six-year-old little sister, I just walked over

38

and hugged her. I always wanted to have siblings, but I guess on my terms if that makes any sense. I say that jokingly. Siblings don't come on your terms. They just come, and you don't have shit to do with it! After embracing my little sister, from that moment on, I loved her as if I'd known her all her life.

The strange thing about this situation of finding out I had a younger sister was how my mother and that side of my family embraced her and her mother Denise as if they were family. The relationship that was established with my mother's side with my sister and her mother became close, maybe even closer than it was between my father's side and with my sister and her mother. Don't get me wrong. My father's side loved my little sister, but I know the love my mother's side of the family had for my little sister and her mother, they felt it! Felicia wasn't just known or referred to as Big Billy's daughter in public or private. She was referred to as family without any explanation beyond that!

My mother and Denise were as close as friends could be also. My granny and granddaddy called Felicia their granddaughter, and she called them Granny and Granddaddy. All my aunts and my uncle called her their niece, and she called them her aunts and uncle. All my cousins called her their cousin—not in the affectionately played cousin sense but as real family as if their blood was the same as her blood—and she called them all her cousins. The day I found out I had a sister was when my family found out we had another member added to our family. I'm not sure if my mother knew about Felicia before then, but from that moment, we all have loved Felicia ever since. That was my family. They embraced the good even if it came out of unusual circumstances. My sister was an innocent kid, and my family, despite this not-so-normal circumstances, believed she deserved to be loved.

Chapter 5

The Chicago I Know

As I STARTED venturing outside my neighborhood, not wanting to be just another local dude, I would go to different places on the CTA, both bus and train. Although I would go to many places, I was respectful of those known boundaries that was clearly defined in Chicago. Chicago, as great of a city it is, is one of the most segregated cities in America not just along racial lines but also gang lines! Chicago has had this underlining gangster heritage going back to men like Al "Scarface" Capone, Tony "Joe Batters" Accardo, and Sam "Momo" Giancana, even Teddy "Robin Hood" Roe, the black policy king in Chicago. These men are less relatable to the generation of my time, but to the overall community I come from, men with the same pedigree as those I just mentioned are more relatable, men like Larry "the Chairman" Hoover, King David Barksdale, Jeff "Chief Malik" Fort, Henry Mickey Cogwell, Willie "Utha" Lloyd, Minister Rico Johnson, and King Gino Colon.

Chicago's gang legacy is now an institution within the urban landscape that has deep roots. These men inherited this legacy, reinvented it, and passed it down to a great degree. This has defined this city and the way of life for most of African American and Latino males who have grown up in Chicago over the last fifty, sixty years. Because of this gang culture, black and brown males knew where they were safe and where they were not, where they could go and where they couldn't. The lines have always been drawn and the boundaries clearly understood. To violate them was hazardous! So with that in mind, I strategically navigated as I moved around, making sure not to go to places that would be dangerous.

What I learned about gang life was that it was seductive. The spirit of camaraderie and brotherhood was strong in places of not so strong communities with weak environmental infrastructures. It was acceptance, the feeling of power that was embraced by the propaganda of doctrines of the particular organization. For some, the gang organization was the first thing that they had ever been a part of that had some sort of meaning for them.

At that time, to be considered an upstanding member of any particular group, you had to have an understanding of the literature that governed the organization, among other things—being together, posturing and campaigning, the spirit of fraternity, the paradox of territorial claim to ownership of a block you have no real equity and investment in, the oxymoronic professed love for self and others that is displayed in the destruction of the community we live in.

People wonder why people join gangs; these are some of the reasons why. There are many other groups that men are drawn to. These brotherhoods, fraternities, organized teams through sports, and even law enforcement all have some common elements that are present in why young men join gangs. The sense of belonging and knowing you are a part of something that protects you and those with you having your back.

Just like most of my peers, I found myself drawn into it for some of the aforementioned reasons. Even though at this time in my life my father was alive and present, we still didn't live under the same roof, and Mom was working full-time. This made for limited supervision and idle time on my hands. So as a young teen hanging out, the influence of popular street culture put its arms round me, hugged tight, and wouldn't let go.

There are levels of gang life and involvement—like the youngsters say, "Its levels to this shit." You have hard-core dudes who see their entire existence dedicated to their organization. They actively look for the oppositions (opps) to engage in hostile conflicts, i.e., to fight, hurt, and eliminate. Everything they do is to represent the group they are a part of. They take every opportunity to solidify the reputation they've worked for and earn to establish them as the one that's serious about that life. It gives them the identity of being all about what they represent. Then you have the guy that's just a member because of associations with people and neighborhoods. They don't go out of their way to actively participate in high-risk behavior. Although they have a real commitment to the group, they're not hard-core in their activity.

   This level of activity makes up most of the memberships in street organizations. I fell into the latter category with my involvement. It was something to do because everybody was basically doing it. Looking back on it and seeing it for what it's worth now, gang life is a negative aspect within the urban community. It was all about a self-imposed division among our youth and community. Street organizations are the result of greater issues that are present in urban communities suffering from fractured families, social and economic instability, and deterioration of the community. Young people can't see those things. You're not just going with the flow. In so many ways, you are the flow. This is the vulture above the clouds system. What I mean by that is, in the wild, it's all about survival; and being in survival mode, nothing is fair, but everything is fair game. The strong generally dominates the weak, and this cycle continuously plays out daily. Only the strong survives!

   In urban communities weakened by the suffering of poverty, high unemployment, direct and vicarious trauma, neglect, disinvestment, drug abuse, overcriminalization, subpar education, mass incarceration, and high rate of gun violence, this creates the circumstances that gives birth to a level of ignorance that devalues everything around and within it, human life being no exception. People living under these circumstances are imploding through self-destructive behavior while structurally there are systems and other communities prospering because of the plight of those things mentioned. Unlike in the wild, you see the vultures circling overhead waiting to scavenge the dead; but in the hood, you can't see the vultures. It's like they hide above the clouds, and it becomes too late when they start to eat their prey alive.

I felt safe in Englewood, especially in the neighborhood where my cousins lived. I had fun hanging out there with them and their friends. This wasn't my introduction to the exposure of gang life, though, but this was when my involvement was ratcheted up. Hanging out with Pook and his friends had a great influence on me, from the way they dressed, talked, and carried themselves. All that was influenced by gang life. Around where I lived on Bishop, the organization that was present there was the Renegade Disciples, and on the other side of the park was the Black P. Stones. The side of the park I lived in was given a nickname in honor of a brother who had died when I was a kid in the late seventies. It was called Jermaine Town after Richard Jermaine, who was an old-school Renegade Disciple whose reputation outlived him. He was killed when he was seventeen years old, and after his death, he seemed to still be bigger than life for a lot of people in that neighborhood.

This tradition proceeded neighborhoods today in Chicago that are still being christened in honor of the names of dead homies who will be honored by the next generation who eventually will be renamed by yet another young man who will be raised in the hood who unfortunately died young in the hood. Since I lived in Jermaine Town, I aligned myself with the Renegade Disciples. But as I started spending most of my time in Englewood around Pook and Daniel where the whole neighborhood was Gangster Disciples, GD for short, I eventually became a GD.

I wasn't just accepted in because I chose to claim GD or because I was Pook's cousin. Of course I had to have demonstrated traits of being a qualified and stand-up dude. There was no getting jumped in or made to go and carry out some stupid mission or some unrealistic ritual of initiations to be allowed membership in. You had to have showed you had heart and wasn't a punk. You didn't necessarily have to know how to fight, but being nice with the hands was highly respected. Even if you couldn't fight, at least you were expected not to be scared to fight and have your boys' back. I was blessed in by Pook and accepted by everybody in that immediate area because they knew I had heart, which had already been displayed on several occasions I had to display it. Also, they knew I wasn't scared to throw them hands if I had to.

One of those times came one day when we were hanging out in the Copernicus playground on Sixtieth and Ada, now named after the esteemed alderwoman, the late Anna Langford, Englewood's finest. It was in the fall season. I remember because the brown leaves were blowing over the ground. There was a crisp fall breeze whistling through the trees. The length of the day was decreasing by the early darkness that had robbed us of the short sunlight. There were about twenty of us hanging out, females too, so the testosterone was thick in the air.

I think it was my cousin Steve who had a boom box. I could remember hearing house music blaring through the speakers, and the bass line was heavy like it was the heartbeat that kept the crowd alive. There was nothing special going on, just young people hanging out while being young and foolish, cracking jokes and signifying on each other. There was one dude in the crowd from around there by the name of Bruce, whom I knew for a while. Ever since we met, I had known Bruce didn't like me, and I didn't like him either. The reason why I didn't like Bruce was because it seemed like he was always fronting and putting on this facade, an image he projected as a tough guy that I really didn't think was authentic. He was a bluffer! He also was very loud and wanted everybody to notice him.

Anyway, somebody decided to make Bruce the punch line of a joke, and everybody started laughing at him, including me. I guess Bruce wasn't flattered by what was said and didn't see the humor in it, but instead of addressing the crowd with his displeasure, he turned directly to me and said, "Who the fuck you laughing at, nigga?" Honestly, when he said that to me, for a second, I had no response. He caught me off guard with his question to me, but it was really more of a statement he wanted to make. I wasn't going to let him make one at my expense, so as the shock of what he said quickly disappeared, I responded, "You, nigga!" As soon as I said that, it seemed like everything got quiet, including the wind, which seemed like it stopped blowing. The music stopped blaring through the speakers, and no more laughter could be heard from the crowd. The focus of everybody out there was on me and Bruce.

After a long moment of awkward silence and an intense stare down between the two of us, neither of us wanting to blink first, everyone, I'm sure, could feel the tension. The silence was broken by my cousin Macafee when he said, "If you niggas got a problem, square up. Ya'll can slapbox, or leave that shit along!" Immediately, Bruce started unzipping his jacket and said, "Let's go!" Now moments like this can define you and leave impressions in the minds of others for life of how they see you and what they will think of you based on the way you handle it. As faith would have it, I was in one of those moments. I had no choice but to deal with this situation as bold as the way it was brought to me. Bruce was not backing down. I was being challenged, one I couldn't afford not to accept. I was being put on the spot in the hood in front of everybody. I knew some of those people I still needed to solidify my reputation to of who I was, and what I was made of. But make no mistake about it. I was up for any challenge Bruce was offering me.

I had every intention of whopping Bruce's ass! Plus, I had a psychological advantage over him. The way I figured it, only Bruce's underestimation of me was what made him so quick to want to challenge me. By him underestimating my potential, my ability and skill to beat him had everything to do with his character of being a bluffer. This turned out to be an epic fail for him. I remember my father asked me one day, "You know how to win every fight you ever have?" I responded, "No, how?" He said, "By never starting one!" "That's it?" I asked. "That's it," he said. Man, I thought he was about to drop some ancient philosophical martial art hidden secret information on me, but that was his advice to me, basic and simple. And as I thought about it, it made all the sense in the world to me. I saw the truth in it. So in my mind, Bruce had started a fight I wasn't going to win!

For those who may not know what slapboxing is, it's a style of sparring in which you swing using an open hand to slap with instead of a close fist to punch with. It's all about the skill of speed, precision, and heart. Generally, if you are slapboxing with someone, the fight isn't real, but the contact is. This style of fighting has been around in the hood since the beginning of hood time. It's a rite of passage.

As I took off my jacket, I started jumping around a little bit to get loose so I could redistribute some of the nervous energy I was feeling. The adrenaline that was rushing through my veins felt like it had the force of a hurricane! I won't lie. The thought in the back of my mind was what if this dude got out on me. Everybody out there, including all those females, would witness it. That would be the most embarrassing thing that could happen, but there was no turning back now.

We squared off, standing toe to toe, both of us doing our best to mask any sign of uncertainty in the moment of truth. When we finally got busy, Bruce started to swing wild like he had no technique. I swung a few times, both of us exchanging a few elbow blows. Bruce kept on swinging wild, so I just leaned back as far as I could so he couldn't hit me. This was something I picked up from a friend of mine who lived around my house whose name was Smitty. Smitty had the fastest hands I ever saw, and his style I tried to emulate. I timed it perfectly. It was like I saw it before it happened. Time seemed to slow down, and everything was right there in front of me. The way in which he swung, he telegraphed his move.

As he missed, I came forward at the same time with my right hand and caught the whole left side of Bruce's face flush. It sounded like I had just shot a gun. The sound my hand made smacking the side of Bruce's face reverberated off the bricks of the school, the bunkhouse, and every structure that stood in the playground that shouted out the loudest echo! The moment was surreal. You could hear the sound of that smack on repeat like a broken record. It was the repeated echo that made the spectators snap out of the shock of witnessing what had just happened.

I heard a voice yell out, "Shit!" I didn't realize just how hard I slapped Bruce until I saw my whole handprint appear across his face in a red silhouette like I had just tattooed it on him. Bruce's eyes had betrayed him with the look of defeat in them! He was now struggling to not let the blood trickle down from his nose by trying to hold his head up. The blood pooling in his nose gave him the only reason to hold his head up in that moment when he had every reason why he probably should have dropped his head. It was obvious he was finding it hard to deal with the embarrassment of being slapped like that. That moment fed my self-esteem a high level of confidence that only a victory like that could give. Bruce was done and didn't want to continue. The towel was thrown in. I had won the day and also the hearts and minds of those who were there to witness it. My cousin Daniel still jokes about what happened then right now today.

Unfortunately, the mentality of acceptance from others being a priority in seeking out their approval to feel validated, that's one of the biggest problems in a community of young people who still are unclear of their identity, especially in communities that are socially anemic! Other people's perception too often defines the reality of how some young people see themselves. The challenge is to defy those perceptions that others hold against them. One of the challenges I see prevalent in our community among young African American males is that they tend to measure and equate their manhood with their egos. This is especially true when they in any way have felt like they have been disrespected or when they see the disrespect as what they think may define who they are if they don't address it as boldly as it was made. It becomes more reckless and potentially deadly if the disrespect happens in front of others.

Prisons and graveyards across this country are filled with men who allowed their decisions to be influenced by their egos in order to validate who they think they are or trying to prove who they are in front of others. These actions can be detrimental to individuals and community that can easily lead to a loss of freedom or, even worse, a loss of life. This is such a great challenge we struggle to overcome due to the way we are conditioned to not think. So many times, we put the feelings in front of the thinking, which always leads to later regrets. Although I realize there is a level of maturity that one must grow into so that the ego's influence is minimized in the decision-making process, we have to teach our young men how to start using a higher degree of self-control, self-assurance, self-identity, and self-security over insecurity, a lack of self-respect, and doubt so that they don't have to suffer a life full of regrets that will be hard to come back from.

It's been proven that young people, particularly before the age of twenty-five, will not make wise decisions. The development of the mind is scientific! It's believed that before the age of twenty-five, the frontal lobe of the brain is not fully developed. The frontal lobe plays a role in future planning, including self-management and decision-making. According to Health Encyclopedia, "Good judgement isn't something they can excel in, at least not yet. The rational part of a teen's brain isn't fully developed and won't be until the age of twenty-five or so." Now with this being the case, and add to it that young people haven't been raised with positive influences to help mold and groom them into making sound decisions, then more than likely, the odds for making major mistakes will be great.

The reason why mistakes can end up being made on major levels is because of the exposure to negative influences. Ignorance never sheds light on ignorance. Only when knowledge is introduced is when ignorance is realized, and unfortunately, in life, the lessons learned usually comes after the tests have been failed. The one thing I've realized working with high-risk youth who have been through a life of trauma, which took me thirty years to figure out, is that it has become so hard, if not impossible, to push the fast-forward button on their understanding to get them to figure certain shit out earlier in life. Certain lessons I guess must be learned the hard way, but the hard way for us is sometimes the lessons that we might not come back from.

Hopefully, these young men will take heed of the mistakes I've made so that it won't take thirty years of their lives to understand how to do things the right way. I'm committed to giving them the keys that will unlock their ignorance and help them elevate their thinking, understanding, and behavior so eventually they begin to demonstrate and see the value in themselves and value in the lives of others.

Although there are lessons in life that can only be learned through personal trials and tribulations, I wish it were easier getting young people to see the benefits of learning from the mistakes of others so they don't have to suffer the grave consequences of their own mistakes. If we could help young black and brown people understand that their chances to mess up may be broad and them having the chance of being excused or fairly handled are narrow, then maybe we could reduce the number of young people dying early and going away to prison for long periods of time out of their life. Lesson learned in life that may come with major consequences should not always have to be learned from firsthand knowledge. True wisdom is when you can learn the crucial lessons in life from what you have observed from other people being made to be the example instead of you becoming the example.

In life, mistakes will be made, and lessons will be learned; but for some, the stakes are big, and the margins are small. So while we exist inside these small margins, we can't afford to continue to make big mistakes because society is less forgiving and designed to capitalize on them. We can't keep touching the fire and getting burned up!

Chapter 6

Baseball

GOING BACK TO the early days of my childhood, the first thing I fell in love with outside my family was baseball! My father introduced me to the sport and passed along his love for it to me. My love for baseball was cultivated and injected into my blood by him. If you check my DNA, baseball would be coded in it! As far back as I can remember, my father took me to baseball games—to White Sox games, then at the old Comiskey Park directly across the street north of the stadium they play at now, watching players like Bucky Dent turn double plays with Jorge Orta, sitting in the bleachers in right field as Claudell Washington ran down fly balls and Chet Lemon commanding center field.

I'm such a fan of baseball. I would actually watch games on TV and still do today. I religiously watch WGN Cubs games. Iván DeJesús, one of the best defensive shortstops I've ever seen, was my first favorite ballplayer. Shawon Dunston stepped into the shoes of DeJesús at shortstop for the Cubs and had the strongest arm ever. The fans at Wrigley Field would track his batting average with the Shawon-O-Meter! Bill Matlock, Hall of Fame third baseman, and the Hawk, Andre Dawson

My father said shortstops was the best player in the infield. Most shortstops were savvy. It's the cool position. My father was a shortstop, and so was my uncle Lawrence. So, of course, when I started playing, I had to be a shortstop. My father would take me to watch him play softball, 16-inch clincher. He started out playing league ball, but as he got older, he transitioned into playing softball. He was a really good player. He played for a team called the Tigers. He was a part of that elite class and rich culture of Chicago's historic 16-inch clincher softball legacy that was just as popular during the late 1970s and 1980s as anything that the city of Chicago could claim as its own.

As far as I could remember, I've always had a baseball, a glove, and a bat. All I wanted to do was play shortstop like my father. My father's love for the game was passed down to him from his older brother Lawrence. Lawrence played professional baseball. In 1953, he took Ernie Banks's spot on the roster of the Kansas City Monarchs when Banks left the Negro league to play for the Chicago Cubs. Lawrence played in the Negro league in Panama and overseas in the United States military.

After getting my first baseball glove, I would get my cousin Fats to play catch with me. It was like getting my first bike for Christmas, having to wait for the weather to break so you can finally enjoy the gift you waited a season to ride. But I couldn't wait. If I couldn't get Fats to play catch with me, I played catch with myself by throwing a rubber ball against a wall to catch the rebound. When I would go see my father play, I would take my glove and a ball with me. Either before or after his games, he would always spend time hitting the ball and pitching to me. He would tell me, "Charge the ball. Keep it in front of you. Don't be scared of the ball. It won't hurt you. Choke up on the bat. Keep your eye on the ball."

He never, never let me take swings at a softball. He said it would throw off my timing. So I didn't. I wouldn't touch a softball. I focused on learning how to hit fast-pitching. Before I ever played an organized game, I started playing strikeout when I was around eight or nine years old. Strikeout was the hoods version of the batting cage. We would vandalize somebody's property by spray-painting a box with an X inside the box on a garage or the side of a building or a fence or played on one we found already on some existing structure. The painted box was the strike zone. I played strikeout with my friends in the summertime while the sun was up until the sun went down. We developed our hitting skills through playing strike out.

We also played Over the Plate, which was a real game of pickup baseball. At that time, in urban communities across the city of Chicago, baseball was a very popular sport. This was before the "I want to be like Mike" era, who would eventually have everybody wanting to be a basketball player! A little-known fact is that baseball was Michael Jordan's preferred sport. Back then, we built our youthful reputations through sports like baseball, basketball, and football. We played 21, which was a basketball game that was basically every man for himself, and the first person to score twenty-one points wins the game. We played football and Kill the Man with the Ball, a football game where everyone focused on trying to tackle the guy who had the ball. Slap boxing was a passive-aggressive way of challenging one another sometimes without fighting. It was a sport we participated in with the undertone of establishing a pecking order within your crew.

At eleven years old, I tried out for my first Little League team at Foster Park, the Phillies. Mr. January was the coach of the Phillies. He was not an easy man to impress or play for, but everybody wanted to play for him because the Phillies was good, and he wanted to beat the other dominant team at Foster Park, the Cubs. It was hard getting on the Cubs. In the era I grew up in playing Little League baseball, you really had to know how to play and try out to play on a team. If you weren't good enough, you weren't going to make a team. Tryouts was a grueling weeklong drills that Mr. January and his coaches put the hopefuls through. After each day of tryouts, cuts were made.

The first day of tryouts, we had a scrimmage, and everybody got a chance to play the position they wanted to play and also where Mr. January wanted to see you play at. At the end of the first day, I did pretty good and was told to come back to the park the next day. I was so excited. I fantasized about wearing my first Little League uniform for the Phillies. I made it to the last day of tryouts. It came down to Mr. January putting everybody on a defensive drill. He started telling everybody on the last day of tryouts to go to the position they were trying out for. He started hitting ground balls to the infielders and line drives and fly balls to the outfielders. He started going around to infield, starting with the third baseman. Everyone had ten balls hit to them. If you fielded every ball, you made the team; but if you missed or booted the ball, you got cut right then and there. Mr. January would tell you to get off the field and go home.

I saw two third basemen dreams shatter and sent home. I immediately became very nervous. Up until this point, I was having fun, and my confidence was sky-high. But now all I could think about was how nervous I was and how I should not mess up. Mr. January was not being nice or patience during this drill. For those who failed during the drill, January said things like, "Get the hell off my field!" "Who told you you could play baseball? They lied to you!" "Come back next year. Maybe then you would have learned how to play." That was Mr. January. I guess Mr. January didn't care about hurting your feelings. Apparently, it didn't matter that we were kids. He didn't spare our feelings!

Now it was my turn. He hit a shot right to me, and I fielded it clean, but the next one that came wasn't right at me. I tried to backhand it. I remember it as if it were yesterday. It hit the heel of my glove and rolled up my arm. I missed it. I felt the intensity of my error like a five-hundred-pound weight landed on my brain. I couldn't move. All I saw was the dust of the dirty diamond blinding me of my immediate surrounds. I didn't want to hear what I knew was coming next, but the sound of January's voice I couldn't help but hear as every word brought with them the end of my dream and fantasy of playing for the Phillies and wearing the white and red pinstripes by saying, "Get yo ass off my field!"

I was cut! My hope, desire, and dream that had lived inside my heart, body, and soul and that I carried over the winter, through the spring, and into the summer had been killed with those words. I felt like a failure. My self-esteem was damaged. I was embarrassed because I didn't know what I was going to tell my father. I couldn't tell my pops I got cut. I knew I was better than that moment, than that error. I went home feeling dejected and depressed. I knew my father was going to call me later that day wanting to know when my first game was going to be. I dreaded the thought of that inevitable phone call.

But as faith would have it, I was sitting on my front porch with a few of my friends—Donnie, Boogalu, and Rib—and my cousin Fats, talking about me getting cut. As we were talking, two of our other friends, Chucky and Kevin, and their father, Chub, whose grandmother lived next door to me, drove up.

Chub just started coaching a Little League team at another park not far from where we lived, just the next neighborhood southeast of where I lived, Brainerd Park on Ninety-Second and Throop. Chucky and Kevin were on their father's team, and Chub, who knew we could play, asked us if we wanted to play for him. We all said yes! We went up to Brainerd the next day, and we all made the team. I made sure from getting cut to play like the player I knew I was, and I did. We were now the Brainerd Park Cubs! Brainerd Park had a good and competitive Little League baseball program. In no way was it a step down. Brainerd Park baseball was just as good as Foster Park baseball!

Early on, some of the dudes from around Brainerd didn't like us at first because, one, they didn't know us, and because, two, we took some guys' spots on the team. But as everybody got to know each other, we eventually became friends with everybody. It only helped when we quickly became the best team at Brainerd. I started at short-stop. All our families came to watch our first game. Every game we played became a family affair. The first team we played against was the Pirates. They were good. This dude name Leander, who was one of their best players, pitched against us that first game. We got them that first game, though. My first at bat, I hit an opposite field triple to right. I went 3 for 4, and we won by a blowout. We won our first six games by blowouts. Coming from Foster Park and being as dominant as we were, some of the coaches of the other teams decided to start looking to see if we were all the right age.

When the season started, Donnie, who came to Brainerd Park with us to play, was twelve years old, but his thirteenth birthday was in the beginning of July. For him to be eligible to play Little League, Donnie couldn't turn thirteen before September. He did turn thirteen in July, which made him ineligible. Donnie could no longer play once they found out, and those six games we had won with Donnie, we had to forfeit. I was devastated. Our team was devastated. Despite our setback, I still managed to have a fun summer playing baseball at Brainerd Park. Although we finished third place, I knew we still had the best team. I played the next summer at Brainerd for the Cubs. That was the last summer I could play Little League Baseball. When I turned thirteen, Fats and I went back to Foster Park and played phony league for the Astros, who was coached by Mr. Crawford and Mr. Mosley. We weren't that good as a team at first. I got the chance to play every position in the infield except pitcher as I had done in Little League. I played mostly at shortstop and back catcher. I played some at first base too. I made the all-star team, and we had the best record of the second half of our first season. I played two seasons with the Astros too and then aged out.

Mr. Crawford was a good man. He cared deeply for the young people he coached. He wanted to see us succeed in life. He didn't want to see any of the kids he coached end up in trouble. For his day job, he worked for the Cook County Juvenile Temporary Detention Center, the audie home, the place minors who found themselves in trouble with the law went to. I'm sad to say, out of all the kids Coach Crawford coached, I was the only one to go to jail. I messed up his prefect record, but that should tell you about the positive impact he had on the youth he encountered through the game of baseball. Mr. Crawford is still coaching youth baseball at Foster Park until this day.

That was the last time I played organized league ball. Also, that was the last time I felt safe being at Foster Park, the park maybe only a hundred yards from my doorstep. One of the reasons I chose not to play baseball in high school was because Calumet home park, where they practiced and played most of their games, was at Foster Park. I knew I was not welcomed there any longer.

Chapter 7

No Longer Chasing the Dream

AROUND THE TIME I started getting involved in Chicago's gang culture was also when my interest in playing baseball started to fade. I mean, I never stopped loving the game. I just lost my interest in playing it. I stopped chasing the dream. My interest in females spiked around this time. I started really focusing on the opposite sex more intensely, constantly thinking about them. My hormones were kicking into overdrive. The way my mind was operating, my thoughts provided no empty space that the image of a female didn't occupy. For me, when I started appreciating the beauty of creation, I realized it in the female form. There was nothing I loved more. Everything about females I fell in love with. This started around eighth grade and the start of my freshman year in high school.

Although I had gotten my first piece about a year before when I was thirteen with a neighbor whose name was Donna, I lied to my father out of embarrassment when he asked me one day riding in the car if I had been with a girl yet. I looked out of the window, contemplating if I should tell him the truth, but I didn't think I was ready to have the conversation that might have followed if I had said yes, so I lied and said, "Naw!" I felt he sensed my embarrassment and didn't take the conversation any further but did tell me that no matter what it was, I could talk to him about anything. I appreciated him giving me the way out so I didn't have to face my embarrassment, but looking back on that moment, I should have given him the benefit of the doubt because he really was smooth enough to talk to me about anything without me having to feel ashamed or embarrassed.

The first girl I could claim as a girlfriend lived across the street from me. Her name was Pixie. Before she became my girlfriend, I never paid any attention to her until one day when my cousin Cindy told me that Pixie liked me. As soon as Cindy told me that, it was like Pixie came alive to me. My eyes saw a different girl. It was as if I was seeing her for the first time, like she had a halo of a sunray hovered over her head suddenly. Of course I knew her, but when Cindy brought to my attention that Pixie liked me, I didn't realize until then just how pretty she really was. It was innocent, our little time together. It was a puppy love infatuation that never became too serious. One reason why was because Pixie's father was a real strict dude and didn't let Pixie out of his sight. She would come outside, but rarely could she leave the block. Pixie and her family ended up moving soon after we started going together. That was the other reason why it didn't last long. It seemed like just as fast as we became boyfriend and girlfriend, that was how fast it was over. I never saw Pixie again after she moved away.

During the time my father was battling his sickness, I needed some distractions to help me to deal with the reality of watching my father, my best friend, slowly slip away from the sickness that every day was stealing his life away. The wrong direction seemed like the right path to go down for me at the time. I was looking for anything to take my mind away from what we were dealing with. I was with my boy name Reg one day when I saw one of those distractions walking down the street while we were coming from a store on Eighty-Sixth and Ashland.

I saw her before she saw me, a young lady who was a bit too developed to be fifteen years old as I would learn later. I had never seen her before that day, so she had to be new to the neighborhood. She was walking toward Laflin, about to turn on the block. I asked Reg if he knew who she was, and he said he had seen her once but didn't know her. We both looked at each other, and without saying it, it became a challenge to see whose mack (*mack* means, for lack of a better term, who was more persuasive) was the strongest and who would win her interest. *I got to have her*, I thought as we started walking in her direction until, eventually, we caught up to her.

She was pretty and, as we would say in the hood, thick! There was no way I was going to let Reg get this victory! I was sure Reg felt the same way. As we approached her and started talking to get her attention, she turned around and waited for us to catch up. I asked what her name was, and she said, "Mona!" She told me she had just moved to the block. I asked her how old she was, and she said she was fifteen and a half. I guess she must have assumed that adding "and a half" to her age would make her seem more grown. I introduced myself, and so did Reg. The conversation was going well, so good that it was only me and her talking. Reg, I'm sure, didn't like it.

As my and Mona's conversation continued to flow, Reg looked more and more like the proverbial third wheel. I'm sure it became uncomfortable for him to see I had won through every word he had to hear between me and Mona! His voice took my attention away from her when he said before he left, "Man, I'll catch up with you later." Reg turned around and walked away. As we continued walking and talking, she told me she was living in a foster home and really didn't like the people she was living with.

My situation with Mona quickly turned out to be just a physical situation. We were young and servants to our hormones. Physically, Mona was experienced beyond her years. It got so crazy between me and her that she would do outlandish things to try and get my attention. For example, one day, as I was sitting in the house chilling in the early evening, the sun just set to close out the day, as if on cue, the porch lights in front of every house on the block popped on in unison to illuminate the neatly manicured lawns that made the block appear more like some quiet suburban neighborhood rather than an inner city, middle-class section of Auburn Gresham. The front door was open with the screen door closed, protecting me and my family from the bloodthirsty mosquitos and annoying flies as I sat inside in my living room watching TV.

From my peripheral, I saw Caesar's, our German shepherd-collie mix and the craziest dog I've ever known, ears rise to attention. The next thing I knew, Caesar bolted toward the screen door, barking out warnings to whoever was approaching the front door. I was forced to jump into action to see who was coming up the front porch steps and to try to contain Caesar from charging through the screen door to attack whoever was encroaching. Once I was able to grab Caesar by his collar, I looked out the screen door and saw a small dog running for its life back down the steps.

I had seen this dog before. It didn't take long for the dog to leap into the arms of its savior for me to recognize that it was Mona standing there clutching this frightened dog with a look of shock on her face as if she just realized her little ten-pound pooch damn near got eaten up. How selfish can one be? She had sent that little dog on a damned suicide mission just to get my attention! I ended up walking her and her scared dog home. She snuck me into the basement and did what we did whenever we were together. Later that fall, Mona's foster parents put her out, and I never saw her again.

One of my closest friends at the time was my boy named Issie. We called him that because Issie was short for Israel. Issie had lived in Israel with his father as a kid. When he first moved back here, Issie spoke with such a heavy accent that it was very hard to understand the shit he was saying. He had these scars on his arms from cutting himself. He told me he did that while he was locked up in an Israeli jail. I asked him about his scars, and he explained that when he was a kid living there, he was locked up and, while being detained, started cutting himself.

At the time, my understanding of the world around me was at best very limited if not totally ignorant. So I had no idea what life was like in other countries, countries like Israel. This was the Holy Land where the Yahshua, the Messiah, was crucified and where the prophets walked and taught the kings of Israel, where great men like King David and his son the wise King Solomon ruled the people of the Most High, Yahweh!

I had no understanding of the politics of the day with Palestinian and Jewish people over in the Holy Land and of how life must have been for blacks living in Palestine/Israel at the time. He said black people were treated badly and this treatment was why he started cutting himself. For me, I couldn't understand the struggle and trauma he had been through. I had no idea; it took a while for me to understand Issie.

We didn't start out as friends, though. Actually, our first encounter was a brutal one. It was the same summer of '83. A bunch of us from the neighborhood were sitting on my porch, enjoying the hot summer day. My grandfather had just made me cut the grass that morning, so I was a little possessive about anybody walking, stepping, or standing in the grass. It kind of seemed like Issie had just popped up like out of nowhere on the scene in the neighborhood. He came walking up the block with Nard. Nard was Reg's little bother, my friend and competitor for Mona. They came and stood in front of my house to hang out with us on the porch. At the time, I didn't know Issie, but I had seen him a few times in the neighborhood prior to that moment.

Issie walked right up and stood in the grass. So without putting any thought to it, I asked him in a nice way not to stand in the grass. Without any resistance, he stepped off onto the sidewalk. I had no idea that he felt some kind of way about me asking him to not stand in the grass. He may have felt a certain type of way because there were a few females on the porch with us, and so he probably thought I was trying to front him off in front of them. The relationship between the male ego and a perceived affront in the presence of females can be volatile. I made a mistake by not taking into consideration the audience that was within earshot of me simply asking a brother not to stand in the grass. Of course this is only an assumption on my part, but it's a safe assumption because of how this situation turned out.

Apparently, his ego did get in the way because later that day, I was walking up to Eighty-Sixth and Ashland on my way to the store with my boy Barry, who was also on the porch earlier, when I heard someone yelling out. I didn't know who he was talking to, me or Barry. So we slowed up so he could catch up to us. When he reached us, he started talking, but since I couldn't understand what the hell he was saying, I really wasn't paying too much attention to him until he started getting loud and aggressive and directing his attention toward me. At this point, he had my full attention. I asked him what was up once I realized he was talking to me. Eventually, I was able to make out what he was saying. He basically said I was trying to act like a tough guy in front of the females on my porch when I asked him not to step on the grass. I thought, *Is this nigga serious?* That couldn't have been further from the truth. It was never my intention to be disrespectful.

I tried to explain to him that that wasn't the case, but Issie wasn't hearing it. We were standing in front of Adams Bicycle Shop on the corner of Eighty-Sixth and Ashland. (The building is no longer there.) So since I saw he wasn't trying to hear what I had to say, I tried to walk away several times. My last attempt to walk away ended with him grabbing me by my shoulder from behind and yanking me around. Immediately, everything around me became blank. I lost my sense of reasoning, and now I wasn't trying to hear anything Issie had to say. All I saw was Issie's mouth while my other senses became null and void to my immediate surroundings. Time seemed to slow down until it eventually stood still. The only thing that was clear to me was his mouth talking that broken English. I was in total reaction mode, and without any hesitation, I unleashed three precise punches directly into Issie's face.

It sounded off like a three-gun salute. He fell back into the building with his back to me. I didn't realize how bad I had hurt him until he turned around bleeding profusely from his nose and mouth. There were a lot of people out there who had witnessed it. One person in particular who was out there was this dude named Joe. I later found out that Joe was Issie's cousin, but at the time, I was unaware of that. As soon as I attempted to rush in to finish Issie off, somebody from behind grabbed me and started to punch me in the face from the back. It turned out to be Joe. Joe was a big dude. He played high school football for Harlan HS. At the time, I may have weighed around 135 lbs. Joe was every bit of 185 lbs if not more. Issie was slightly bigger than me too but was in my weight class.

I tried to turn around to defend myself, but that was when Issie came in and started punching me too. As I swung back to try and free myself from the onslaught of punches being thrown at me, I eventually got free before it turned bad. I immediately went at Joe, but now motherfuckers wanted to come and break it up. I was bleeding from the nose and mouth, and I had a little ring under my eye. Joe and Issie were standing there while people were in between us. I told Joe he had fucked up and was going to get it. The look in his eyes told me he knew it too. I saw the fear in them, but I guess he couldn't stand to see his cousin getting his ass whopped and had to jump in. Looking back on it, I don't blame him. He did what he was supposed to do. Somebody went and told my cousin Fats and Donnie I was up on Ashland fighting Joe and his cousin. Joe must have seen them coming. I just heard him tell Issie, "Let's go," and they ran off. By that time, my cousins Fats and Donnie had run up there, but Issie and Joe were gone.

I didn't feel too bad about my defeat because I knew one-on-one, I would have gotten out on Issie. Plus, what they had done looked worse than what it really was. Everybody in the neighborhood was talking about how I had beaten Issie's ass until Joe got in it. About a week later, I was with my boy named Chris Crawley, and we walked right up to Issie. He was standing in front of S&R game room on Eighty-Sixth and Ashland. I remember the look on his face when he saw me! He looked stuck, shocked, and scared! I could see the fear in his eyes. He couldn't run. Chris Crawley was a true gangbanger, and he wanted to fuck Issie up so bad. But since he was being humble, I left him with his dignity. Plus, I had already whooped his ass, so there wasn't any need to touch him. I wanted his cousin Joe for jumping in. I told Issie we were cool but that when I see his cousin, I was going to fuck him up! I didn't see Joe after that for a while. It was about a year after that when I saw Joe again. We talked, and he apologized and said he was wrong for getting in our fight. I let it go. I was over it. Time had healed my wounded pride, so there was no need for me to keep it going.

The craziest thing happened between me and Issie. We became the best of friends. We started hanging out. It was me who introduced him to this girl who lived on the same block as me. Her name was Wanda. He and Wanda would end up having twin daughters together. Issie turned out to be a real street dude. Just like me, he had cousins who lived in Englewood, on Sixty-Seventh around Damen, gang-affiliated to the letter! Why did they show this fool the ropes? He became all about it and learned fast. He started hustling, and in a lot of ways, he became more involved in the streets than I was. Issie was a couple of years older than me too. We remain friends until this day.

Chapter 8

1983 Bittersweet

The FALL OF 1983 was bittersweet for me. It was the beginning of my sophomore year at Calumet HS. My father had died that September at the start of the school year, and I was struggling trying to cope with his loss. That was the worst thing that could ever happen to me, but at the same time, something special also began! I remember having a double period of horticulture in Ms. Miles's class, my favorite teacher ever! I can't remember why, but I had missed the first day of school. So when I went the next day, I was looking forward to seeing Ms. Miles. When I walked into the classroom, I spoke to and hugged my favorite teacher, then she told me to find a seat. As I glanced over the lab-like classroom desks, it seemed like all the seats had been filled. I scanned over the classroom again, and I finally spotted an empty seat.

There were two seats for every lab station, so when I saw the one open seat, I naturally looked to see who was seating in the seat next to it. I couldn't believe my eyes. She was the prettiest girl in the classroom and, I would even go as far as to argue, maybe the prettiest girl in the whole school. As I approached the station, she had a look on her face as if to say, "Please don't come over here and bother me!" Guess what? I did just that! I asked her, "Is this seat taken?" Not waiting for her to answer, I took my seat next to her. I felt like I was the luckiest dude in the school! I asked her name. She said "Tamara!" after a moment of hesitation while never looking up at me. Although she seemed like she had this attitude, I felt like the luckiest dude in the school to be seating next to this freshman.

I started breaking down the walls that she seemed determined to hold up against me. I did it by being as charming as I could and as funny as I could and making her laugh often. Sometimes she would try to do everything in her power not to laugh at my silly jokes, but she couldn't resist me, and I would have her laughing and smiling from ear to ear all throughout our double period. I told her she was going to be my girlfriend early on. I really believed that. My confidence was high. I had an advantage over everybody who was trying to talk to her because I had a double period of horticulture sitting right next to her.

One day, I grabbed her notebook and looked in it. She had all these phone numbers written in it. Every dude in the school was trying to holler at her. Every dude I knew who went to the school, their names and phone numbers were written in her notebook. So what I did was write my name and number as big as possible on one piece of paper to fill the entire page and tore up the other page with all the other names and numbers on it without any resistance from her. I had to do something drastic because since the beginning of the start of that school year, the teachers were talking about going on strike. I didn't want to lose the momentum I had made with her, so if they went on strike, I knew the chances of me seeing her during a strike was slim to none. A month after school started, the teachers did go on strike. I knew she started liking me although she wasn't making it easy for me. That was why I wrote my number on the entire piece of paper after tearing up the piece of paper with everybody else's number on it.

The next day, school was closed due to the strike. That night, I was at home watching TV when the phone rang. When I answered, I heard on the other end a female voice asking to speak to me. After I said it was me, I asked who it was. It was Tamara's friend Carla. Tamara was too shy to call me herself, so she had Carla call me, but Carla immediately gave Tamara the phone. When I heard her voice,

I was so excited and glad she had decided to call me. My infatuation for this female was so strong it felt like I had lost my virginity all over again when I heard her say, "Hello!" I didn't think she was going to call because at school when I had asked for her phone number, she wouldn't give it to me. So while I had her on the phone, I instantly devised a plan to trick her into giving me her phone number. This was before cell phones and caller IDs.

I told her as soon as she got on the phone that I had something to do for my mother, so I asked if I could call her right back when I was finished. She agreed, and I asked her to give me her number. Without really putting much thought into it, she said okay and gave me her number. I wrote it down on a notepad my grandmother always kept next to the phone. As soon as she gave me the number, I hung up and called her immediately right back. When she answered, I was laughing and said, "I just tricked you. I didn't have nothing to do for my mother. I just wanted to get those digits, and finally, I got you to give them up." She laughed because she knew she'd been had.

We ended up talking on the phone for hours that night, and good thing we didn't have school the next day because I would have been very tired because we talked well past midnight. From that day on until the strike ended, we talked every day. After a few days into the strike, I really wanted to see her and asked if we could meet up. She agreed to let me see her. It was a typical fall October evening. The temperature was brisk and windy, and the sun had already started to set early. I was standing in the doorway of the church on the next block from where I lived on the corner of Eighty-Sixth and Bishop, waiting for her to walk by. This dude name TY walked up, and we started talking. A few moments later, Tamara and her friend Angie walked past us. She didn't see me as they went by, so I came up from behind and tapped her on the shoulder. She was slightly startled until she realized it was me. That began our romance, and from that day on, we became inseparable. We spent every free moment of every day after that together.

Maybe about four months into us seeing each other, I was over her house just hanging out. As the evening started making its way into the late night, it was my cue to head home. She, like always, didn't want me to leave. Tamara never wanted me to leave and always made it very hard for me to go. It was almost like a ritual we went through when it was time for us to leave each other. I had to get one more hug or a kiss or cater to her pampering whimper that protested to keep me there just a few minutes longer. The love was young and fresh! She didn't want me to leave, and honestly, neither did I, so our departure took at best an hour for me to finally get out the door and be on my way.

This one night as I made my way home, I walked maybe six blocks before I was stopped by the police. Unaware to me was that some guys had just been fighting on the block minutes before I walked up. The people involved in the brawl had all fled from the scene. I also learned later that the person who had called the police was an off-duty police officer who lived on the block after he came out to break up the disturbance. Totally oblivious to what just went down, I was stopped by the police, who happened to be a white police. I was slammed up against the wall and was asked "What the fuck are you doing out here?" as if I had no business minding my own business in my own neighborhood where I lived!

After being slapped up the side of the back of my head, a paddy wagon drove up. I told the police I was on my way home leaving my girlfriend's house. They couldn't care less where I was going or where I was coming from. Situations like this for black people in America can be one of the most frightening situations you can find your way in, being detained by the police at night and not knowing how the situation is going to turn out when you are being treated like you are guilty of a crime you didn't commit! I knew I was in trouble for something I had nothing to do with. I feared for my life because of the aggressive way they were treating me. They had already assaulted me, and I just braced myself for the inevitable ass-whopping I knew was coming next. I had no choice but to just deal with it. I was just praying they wouldn't kill me. No one was around except me and four white police officers, who had hurled also the *nigger* word in my face after slapping me up the side of the back of my head a few times.

They asked me if I was with those other niggers out there acting like fucking monkeys. I had no idea what the hell they were talking about. So the more I appeared to resist, the more I was slammed up the side of my head. I couldn't answer their questions, and because of the way I was feeling, I shut down completely! As I was being put in the back of the paddy wagon, I saw out of the corner of my eye this black dude walking up. I saw him show the white police his badge while announcing at the same time he was a police officer. He said that he lived on the block and was the one who called for the police. He told the police I wasn't one of the people who were out there fighting.

They closed the door of the paddy wagon, leaving me inside. It was pitch-black behind the closed doors. I was sitting in the back of this police vehicle, trying to sort out my confusion and not sure what the outcome was going to be. In the dark, under the custody of four racist paddy rollers, and being accused of doing something I knew I didn't do was not an ideal situation to be in. I was scared of going to jail for something I knew nothing about or, worse, being hurt physically further by these racist-ass police who seemed liked they were more intent on doing me harm than serving and protecting me. A few minutes later, the doors opened again, and one of the white police officers pointed his flashlight directly in my eyes, temporarily blinding me, and snatched me by the arm and told me I was free to go. The black guy told me, "Come on, lil brother!"

I didn't hesitate. I got out, and he grabbed me by the arm and walked me around the corner. He asked me where I lived. I told him. He said, "Listen. I'm going to take you home. It ain't safe out here. Get in the car." At this point, he was the only reason I started feeling halfway safe, so I got in the car, and he drove me to the crib. As he drove me home, he explained to me that I was lucky he was there because, in his words, "I don't know what them crackers was going to do to you, but it wasn't going to be nice. They wanted me to sign off on some bullshit so they could lock you up, and if it weren't for me, you were headed to the audie home tonight!" He called it sandbag! He said, "They wanted me to sandbag you!" He didn't go for it. He said he wasn't going to have a hand in setting me up to be locked up for nothing. I got a blessing that night. I forgot his name, but he took me home and came in and spoke with my mother and grandmother and told them about what had happened. Of course they were grateful for what he had done for me, and after thanking him, he left.

I called Tamara and told her what happened later that night. She was shaken by what I said but was glad that I was all right. During this time in my life, she was a distraction to the pain I was going through over the loss of my father. This was the first time I felt this type of love inside me, and I fell hard. I actually met Tamara three weeks before my father died, and our relationship kicked into full gear soon after that. In a lot of ways, she was the comfort to my grief. She was my first love. My mother and grandmother fell in love with her too. Her mother liked me a lot, but her father didn't. He never said more than two words to me. Tamara and I dated for almost a year but became friends for life.

Maybe about eight months into our relationship, we were on a fake break for about two weeks. She called herself trying to make me jealous, and it worked. I tried to not let it show, but I wasn't that good. Still, I was putting up a front and trying to be too cool by trying to act like I really didn't care. We weren't talking, and when we did, it turned into arguments. But one day, she forced my hand into showing how much I really cared. I was hanging out around Foster Park School on Eighty-Fifth and Woods. My friend JJ lived on that block. I saw Tamara and some of her friends with some guys I knew who I was cool with and went to school with. It was these dudes named Gerald, Rico, and Casey. Casey was JJ's brother. I was cool with all of them, but I noticed Gerald called himself trying to talk to Tamara as they were walking down the street. Suddenly, I started feeling like we weren't going to be that cool after that night, especially with Gerald!

From what I could see, Gerald was trying to push up on her hard; and when she saw me, she acted like she was liking the attention she was getting from him. I don't know, but maybe it was my fault due to the lack of attention I had been showing her during that time, but it didn't matter. Gerald was in violation for trying to talk to her, and I felt like she was too for using him to try and make me jealous. I had to address this situation, so I said in a commanding and demanding tone, "Tamara, come here!" I could feel the bass in my voice reverberating in my own head. When I saw her standing next to Gerald, my blood started to boil. I was about to make a scene if she didn't come to me. She was acting hesitant, and I could tell by the look in her eyes she knew I was serious, but she started walking toward me. I saw Gerald reach out to grab her arm, and I immediately started walking up to confront him when Rico stepped between us. Rico said, "Man, Billy, chill out, folks!" Gerald wasn't saying anything.

I knew my anger was misplaced and being directed toward Gerald as I started verbally challenging him. I didn't think he was scared. Gerald was just being quiet and just probably realized it wasn't worth accepting my challenge. It's hard to say if he had sensed he was being used as a pond by Tamara because we never talked about it, but Tamara admitted later that she did that to get my attention and to get under my skin. He knew how serious Tamara and I were and probably felt it was better to leave this bullshit alone. Gerald wasn't a punk, and honestly, I don't know how that would have ended up if it had come to blows, but I was ready to go there with him if necessary.

Rico was able to get me to calm down. Rico was a dude who used to come around and hang out with us. He was from around Eighty-Third Street, a dark-skinned brother who was cool as hell, bowlegged dude who always had a toothpick in his mouth. He kept a hat on his head and always cocked to the right, ace duce. Tamara walked over and grabbed me by the hand and led me off. I realized then how much I loved her. As we headed off, I felt the tears rolling down my face, each one representing how sincere my love for her was. Each tear that fell cleansed me from the fake facade of me portraying I didn't care that I had been projecting. My tears betrayed this phony image of the mask I had tried to cover my heart with up until that moment. My tears exposed me for the actor I was. Each tear testified against me and told the truth that convicted me to her. Seeing her with Gerald, I felt my heart breaking. All I wanted from her at that moment was for her to repair it.

We left everybody we were with behind. While I walked her home, I expressed how much I was sorry for acting the way I had been acting toward her. It was a happy moment for me. We were back to being happy. We had made up, and I promised no more games. When we got to her house, it was about 10:00 p.m. We both weren't ready for the night to end. She snuck me in the house through the basement and up to her room. Now I knew if her daddy caught me in his house, especially in her room, I was certain he would kill me. I could only assume that her father knew that his daughter had finally gotten to that age where she was getting attention from the opposite sex and possibly showing her interest in return, and that was something he was struggling to come to terms with. I don't think he was ready for that.

Our relationship was a serious one. She had lost her virginity to me, and we were in love with each other. He didn't like when I came around. But when I did, I was always very respectful. Tamara was the oldest of her five siblings. I would tell her younger sisters that I would buy them things like dolls if they didn't say I was over their house when I wasn't supposed to be there. So I knew getting caught wouldn't be good for me.

After she safely snuck me in her room while everyone else in the house slept, we started to make up! At some point during the night, we heard her mother go into the bathroom that was next to Tamara's room. Tamara rushed me into her closet, which locked from the outside, so I was stuck in there, and the only way out was if she let me out because I couldn't open the door from the inside of the closet. As I was in there contemplating my present predicament being trapped in her closet, I realized too much time had passed by, literally hours! I whispered Tamara's name so that she could come let me out of the closet. She didn't respond. It was dark and small, and with every minute, I was getting more and more nervous. I tried to keep my cool as I thought about my escape plan. I began to feel like claustrophobia was setting in. Tamara had forgotten I was in there and had fallen asleep on me.

My whispers became louder, and I started knocking on the door, hoping to only get her attention and wake her up. Suddenly, I heard the door to her room open, and the light in the hallway outside her room illuminated through the small crack to the door of the closet that concealed me behind it. Then I heard her mother opening her bedroom door and call out her name, flipping the light switch that brightened the whole room. "Tamara, wake up. Is somebody in the closet?" I heard her mother say. *Damn,* I thought, *what am I going to do when she opens this door?* I felt my own heart beating, and before I could answer my own question, the closet door opened.

The shock of seeing me turned into a look of fury, but instantly, she lowered her voice and said in a whisper, "If Kenny sees you, he's going to kill you!" I looked over at Tamara, who at this time was now sitting up in her bed, wiping away from her eyes the half sleep she had just been awakened from. Her mama now was forced to conspire to help me escape out of her house without her husband knowing I was ever there. As her mother distracted her husband, Tamara escorted me out of her room, through the dining room, and out of the front door. It was 5:30 a.m. Although I thought I had gotten away, I had another problem. I had to now sneak in my own house without waking up my mama and grandmother. But guess who was up waiting for me when I got home and when I walked through the door? My mother and grandmother. Tamara's mother had called them and told them what had happened. I got an earful and got Tamara grounded.

During the time Tamara and I were together, the one problem I had with Tamara was her friend Carla. It started seeming like every time I saw Tamara or when we were around, her friend Carla would be there. Carla just irritated me, and I got tired of seeing her. I asked this dude named TY to talk to Carla for me so she would have something to do instead of being around me and Tamara. I asked Tamara to stop bringing Carla around every time she came around. The reason why I didn't like Carla was because Carla didn't like me. Every chance she got, she talked shit about me, trying to get Tamara to stop dealing with me. It was my opinion that Carla was jealous of my and Tamara's relationship. She didn't have a boyfriend, and I never saw anybody trying to talk to her. That was why I asked this dude named TY to talk to her so she wouldn't be up under us all the time.

It worked, but only for a little while. Carla was the reason why we broke up. As I look back on this situation, I respect Tamara. She was loyal to Carla and wouldn't stop being her friend. But that was my reason for ending it with Tamara. I asked Tamara to stop brining

Carla over my house, but she wouldn't, and Carla wouldn't stop coming around either and continued to hate on me. I broke her heart but also broke mine too, and because of my pride, I didn't give in. I was being immature. This was one of the many stupid things I had done. It was the end of the summer of 1984 and the end of my relationship with Tamara. I can honestly say she was my first love.

Chapter 9

'84

As the summer of '84 was coming to an end and the fall approaching, I was getting ready for the start of the new school year, my junior year. This was around the same time when Tamara and I were going through our break up. A lot was going on in 1984 in Chicago and in the country. Prince's purple was raining on us all with his hit album and movie *Purple Rain*! Madonna was still a virgin. Michael Jordan had just been drafted and adopted as the first son of Chicago. Harold Washington had a year under his belt running shit from the fifth floor at City Hall as the first black mayor of Chicago. House music was the prevailing sound dominating the party scene in the city, and for the first time in Chicago's history, a young kid from the South Side had just been anointed the number one hooper in the nation, Benji Wilson, who many believed could have been the best basketball player to ever play the game! Oprah was hosting the number one talk show, and Jessie Jackson had run for president, the first black man to do it!

I felt so much a part of what Chicago's culture was. I was proud to be from the city of broad shoulders. There was something special about Chicago and the people from this city. Going to house parties and partying to house music was something most young people lived for. Stepping was Chicago's brand, and through that style of dance, our culture was defined as being the coolest shit ever to be seen! I remember the Sheba on Eighty-Seventh in between Ashland, and Justine had parties that the best steppers came to show off their classic moves! The Sheba is now the famous Mr. G's. Homecoming games at Gately and Stagg Stadiums were where most South Side public high schools played, and everybody showed up.

Just like stepping, skating in Chicago was another special thing to see. Chicago's style of skating was an art form that we put on display at places like the Rink, Stake City, the Loop, and Markhem and the Loop. This was when the Rink was on Eighty-Ninth and Ashland over the tracks. Wearing Lees and Levi's blue jeans with bucks and Frank Foti's on my feet was the status quo for the slick boys. Foti's was the best handcrafted Italian shoes ever made. If you didn't have a pair, you were a square! Reefer coats and pea coats were on my back too while being in the members only club at the same time. Polo's shirts and loafers defined the preppies. Butters was when you permed your hair, and Kangols was the hat of choice. Hats broke Ace-Deuce either way. To the right or the left defined what street organization you were affiliated with.

Watching girls in their Jordache and Sasson jeans was the pastime of every dude I knew. We had weekends trips to Evergreen Plaza shopping mall and spent most of that time in the basement arcade game room for most of South Side kids. I'm sure some of these things were present for young people in other urban cities across this country, but this was definitely Chicago during the eighties.

I started school that year with the hopes of it being a better year than the previous school year was for me. I wanted to make sure I went through that school year passing with flying colors. That was my goal because of the promise I had made to my father before he had died the year before. I wanted to graduate from high school on time. His death was still fresh in my heart. I knew the one thing I felt I needed to do to honor my father and his memory was to apply myself, pass my classes, and graduate high school on time. I was on a mission to achieve my goal. I don't think there is another time in my life when I was more serious about being focused on a goal and working to accomplish it.

School was a struggle for me because, honestly, I didn't like school. I never put my best foot forward. I didn't work as hard as I was capable. Several of my teachers had told me how intelligent I was but that I needed to work harder. My father would tell me all the time, "Man, you need to start applying yourself!" So that was what I had prepared myself to do: try hard and apply myself.

As a kid, every time I would go to visit Grandma Ola, my father's mother, my uncle Gary would always have me doing an assignment of some sort, whether it was math problems to work on or something to read. I had to complete my assignments before he would take me outside to play catch or go to the candy store. I felt like I was being tortured by my uncle. I told my Grandma Ola one day that Gary was bothering me, and she said, "Gary, leave Lil Billy alone." He said, "Ola, Billy needs to do his timetables." Grandma Ola said, "Oh, okay. In that case, keep bothering him." I was forced to apply myself because I wanted to go outside to the candy store. Looking back on those times, I hate that I had only done enough to get by and did not take the advice of my father and really apply myself like I was capable, but that was my plan for that school year.

When school finally started, I was really psyched about getting off to a good start. I was focused on achieving my goal of keeping my word to my father, but I was still excited about school starting back so I could see all the new females who would be coming in that year. Being a teenage male, most of my decisions were driven by the testosterone flowing through me. That was the one thing that was influencing most of my thoughts and actions. It had me operating in high gear for most of the time, although, inside, I secretly was missing Tamara. Every time I saw her, I wanted to make up, but then I also wanted to still prove to her I was serious about how I felt about Carla. I was being stupid! So at school, I did my best to try and avoid her. I allowed my pride to get in the way of how I dealt with the situation. I decided to act like she didn't mean anything to me, but this taught me a valuable lesson throughout my life. Every time I allowed my pride to influence my position and decisions, I usually ended up being humbled by regret and the mistakes that followed the stupidity of my pride. Humbleness is the antidote of pride, and I've been humbled a few timed by the mistakes I've made.

This was around the time I met Omar Dixon. He was this skinny dude who was a little taller than me with confidence out of the roof. He was a real cool guy. O seemed a lot older than his age. He was years beyond the fifteen of them he had lived. He was kind of quiet but aggressive at the same time. O was a quiet storm! He was a freshman when I met him. This kid had a lot of heart and wasn't scared of anything and would fight anybody on the drop of a dime. He was from the 9 (Seventy-Ninth Street), the neighborhood to the south that was next to the one I lived in. We both had mutual friends, which allowed us to hang out within the same circles, two of which we both knew were brothers, Leo and Puncho. Puncho was a year older than me, and Leo was a year younger than me. They were from the 9 too and were game for anything. They were cool, but Leo and I were closer than Puncho and I were. I consider them friends.

Two months after school started, the hawk, as we in Chicago describes the harsh winds, began to swoop upon the city with its cool, crisp lake-effect winds blowing in from Lake Michigan, gripping the shit out of our city with winter temperatures as an uninvited guest. The winter season in Chicago can be so brutal that even the born and bred of Chicago never gets used to it. With the summer long gone and seeming like it never happened, the winter months was a time when school and all its activities became the focus. This was when you spent time with other friends at school whom you haven't prob-ably seen on a daily basis over the summer. I found myself hanging out with O, Puncho, Leo, and other dudes now that school was back in session more than I would have if school was not in because they didn't live in my immediate area.

Everything was going as planned. I was working toward my goals and feeling pretty good about myself. I was glad to be back in school. I promised myself I wasn't going to let anything pull me off my square that school year. It was Monday, November 19, 1984, after school. My cousin Cindy came home clearly pissed off about an unfortunate incident that happened to her at school earlier that day. She was a sophomore at Simeon. She told me and her brother, Fats, that some guy decided to fuck with her while she was in Mr. Heads's store a block north of the school on Eighty-First and Vincennes.

She said she was playing on one of the arcade games when she felt someone go inside her purse. When she turned around to confront the guy, she told us she noticed he had ten dollars in his hand. Immediately, she looked in her purse and saw she had money missing from it. This dude had taken her money! She demanded he give her the money back! As if he hadn't been disrespectful enough by going in her purse and taking her money, she said he told her, "Bitch, if you want your money, come get it!" Then he proceeded to put the ten dollars down the front of his pants, turned around, and walked out of the store.

Cindy was furious. I told her I would come up there the next day and get her money back. I was upset knowing my cousin was disrespected in that manner. Hearing her describe how she was violated didn't sit well with me. I never understood how people make themselves welcome to things that belong to other people as if they had some type of entitlement to shit that don't belong to them. The nature of a thief is cold and without conscience!

I remember when I was about ten years old, my career as a thief began and ended all in one day! I was hanging out with my beloved auntie Carolyn, whom I love with my entire heart. She married my uncle Rico when I was around four years old and been in my life ever since. She was on her way grocery shopping one day, and I begged her to let me go with her. We went to Jewels on Eighty-First and Ashland. It's a CVS now. Just like most kids, I was touching shit I wasn't going to get, which really wasn't a problem until I saw this yoyo. Yoyos were popular back then, and I wanted to learn how to master them. Auntie had already set the ground rules before we entered the store like most black women did before going into a store with her kids or anybody's kids for that matter: "I'm not buying shit, so don't ask when we get in here!" There was no use in asking her to buy the yoyo for me. I knew what the answer would be. So I decided to do some stupid shit and without putting too much thought into it. I let my desire to have that yoyo overrule any sense of reason and rationale, and I stuffed it in my pocket as I stood in the aisle waiting with my auntie to pay for what she came to get.

After my auntie paid the cashier, we headed toward the door. This was my first caper, and I was feeling so nervous, hoping the stain I just busted wouldn't be detected. *Busting a stain* is a slang term for committing some type of criminal offense, usually involving stealing something. Only a few more steps and I would be out the door and free with my stain, but it wasn't to be. Right before I got to the door, the security guard walked right up to me and grabbed me by the arm and demanded I come with him. My auntie asked him what was wrong and why he was grabbing me. He told her she needed to follow him while he led me through the doors of a security office.

As my auntie asked again what was going on, ignoring her, the security guard reached into my pocket and pulled out the yoyo. It might as well have been my heart he snatched out of my pocket. I was caught! I looked at my auntie, speechless and unable to explain why the security guard had pulled that yoyo out of my pocket. Looking back at that moment, I know I must have embarrassed my auntie probably more than I was embarrassed. I can still remember the disappointment in her eyes as she looked at me. The only thing I could do was apologize to both of them. I was scared I was about to go straight to jail. My auntie went in on me like never before, and I deserved every bit of her wrath. The guard let me go with a warning, and my auntie told me that she was going to tell my mother on me when we got home. All I was thinking about was that ass-whooping I knew was waiting for me when I got home.

You can never prepare for getting your ass whooped! I apologized to my auntie again and promised I would never do anything like that ever. I can only assume that the ride home cooled my auntie's anger, and the fact that she knew I had thought about what I had done and what I had coming when I got home must have been enough for my auntie because when we got back home, she never told my mother. That was the only time in my life I attempted to steal something, and I got busted. Because of that, I was afraid from that moment on to ever steal again. That was my career as a thief.

I remember when Cindy was describing what happened to her, I felt like it was my duty to protect my cousin. I wanted to make sure she got her money back. I didn't know who this guy was, but I did know some people in that neighborhood. I knew the dude who pretty much had the juice around Simeon, Bobby Jo. My cousin Pook introduced me to Bobby Jo about a year before this, but I knew Bobby Jo by reputation, which was well-known and established before then. My plan was to go up to Simeon the next morning and talk with Bobby Jo to see if he knew who the guy was who took Cindy's money. If he knew who he was, I didn't anticipate a problem getting her money back with an apology. But if Bobby Jo didn't know who took the money, I realized that I would be dealing with a situation not knowing how it would end. So I wanted to make sure I got the money back with less chance of it getting out of hand.

I thought about the gun I saw under my auntie's mattress. I thought it would be a good way to intimidate and manipulate a bluff, which would probably help me get the money back without an incident. This was the mind of a sixteen-year-old trying to rationalize using a gun without using it! I was being naive, especially to think you couldn't bluff the average dude in the streets without thinking that if the bluff didn't work, what would plan B be. Never thinking he might get just as disrespectful with me as he did with my cousin Cindy, this was my best thinking; and as anyone could see, it was totally backward. Looking back on it this day, picking up that gun was never going to rectify that situation. Guns are never a good ploy or prop to be used to intimidate someone to try and make a point. The wisdom of a sixteen-year-old doesn't amount to sound judgment! What I've learned is that when an individual decides to carry a gun thinking it will resolve a problem, it is usually when you create the worst of problems. Guns don't solve problems. They bring them. Playing with guns, you find yourself bargaining for more than you expected and, quite frankly, can handle!

Bobby Jo was one of those dudes who was exceptional with his hands. He was a guy who was known to fight and beat up police and knock cats out with one punch. I've personally seen Bobby Jo act a fool in the streets. He had put in the type of work that would make you think either he was crazy as hell or he just wasn't scared of anything at all. For example, one night up at Gately Stadium, it was a crowd of us walking through the parking lot when a police on a horse got too close to Bobby Jo. The horse sneezed, and slob got in Bobby Jo's butter (his hair was permed). Bobby Jo turned around and straight punched the shit out of the horse! This caught everybody by surprise. It looked like a scene out of a movie! I couldn't believe what I had just seen. I just knew the police was going to kill him, but Bobby Jo wasn't going. He started fighting the police and gave them the business right there in Gately Stadium's parking lot.

Another time, I saw Bobby Jo in his IDGAF element. Omar and I were in court one day for a status hearing. I saw Bobby Jo sitting in the courtroom. He nodded at us in acknowledgment. Coincidently, he had a court date on the same day. When court was over and we were being escorted back to the bullpen in the basement of the courthouse, I saw Bobby Jo in the bullpen looking as if he had been in a tussle. I said, "Damn, folks, what the fuck happened?" He said, "Man G, I just got through fucking up the police in the courtroom!" True story, Bobby Jo had beaten three police up in the courtroom before he was subdued by them and the sheriff bailiffs. Bobby Jo was a goon for real!

The night before, Monday, November 19, I had gone over to my auntie Poo Poo's house. I knew she had a .22-caliber revolver under her mattress. She was at work when I got there. I went into her room to retrieve what I came for and concealed it into my waistband. The next morning, Tuesday, November 20, Fats and I went to school. When we got there, we saw Omar and Puncho. We told them what had happened to Cindy, and that was when we cut school to head up to Simeon. Omar and Puncho said they were coming with us. Puncho had gone to Simeon the year before but had gotten kicked out, so he wanted to go with us so he could see some people he was cool with when he was up there.

We jumped on the bus and made it up there at about 9:00 a.m. As we walked down Vincennes, I saw Daniel, (Macafee), and we talked for a minute, and then he headed toward the school. Puncho and Fats walked and went with Macafee. Omar and I walked one block east past Vincennes on Eighty-First Street where we went to meet up with Bobby Jo. We told him about what happened to Cindy. He said he knew the guy and that he would deal with it. He gave me twenty dollars out of his own pocket. I made sure I gave Cindy the money when I saw her later that morning. We pretty much hung out with Bobby Jo for a minute. I didn't want to try and go hang out inside the school like Fats and Puncho did because I had that gun on me.

I did walk down toward the front of the school. That was when I saw Erica. Erica was the sister of Karen, the wife of my cousin Pook. Erica was Macafee's ex-girlfriend. Erica was a very pretty female whom I knew for certain most guys I knew would want to date. We were cool, friends for about four years at that point. I told her she should hang out with us since we were up there and really had nothing to do. She told me to wait around until her lunch break.

When her lunch period started, she and this girl named Kim came outside and met up with me and Omar. Kim and my cousin Cindy were close friends just as she was with Erica. She also lived around Omar's house, so we all knew each other. Kim also had a crush on Omar. We started walking toward Simeon's school store named Mr. Heads. It happened to be the same store where my cousin Cindy had been accosted. As we made our way down Vincennes heading north, we eventually found ourselves standing in front of the store. Erica went in while Omar, Kim, and I stood outside waiting for her to come back out. While talking to Kim, who was standing to the right of me, Omar was standing a few feet in front of me to my left, standing in the grass.

There were not too many exceptional events in my life before this moment, maybe the only one being the passing of my father fourteen months before. My life was normal and basic, but everything—and I do mean everything—would change, and life as I knew it would never ever be the same after this moment. Other than the weather being true to its November season, brutally cold and windy, which we Chicagoans affectionately refer to as the hawk, it was slapping tears and snot from my face. The moment was normal, and like before most approaching storms, it was calm, nothing out of the ordinary as I was standing there talking to Kim, waiting for Erica to come back out of the store so we could head to where we were going to end up at, having no idea that seconds from that moment was the inevitable event that would change the trajectory of my life for the next twenty years and the city of Chicago's history and a dream that unfortunately would never be fulfilled.

I do remember feeling like I needed to move around instead of just standing in this one spot and not just because I was getting cold but also because of my uneasy feeling for cutting school, and in the back of my mind, I knew I had no business being at Simeon. Being under the attacking hawk, I started feeling the wind in my face again, wiping away the freezing tears that rolled down my face, each one making me interrogate my sanity of why I was standing out there feeling each subdegree of the falling Chicago temperature. I felt like I started to literally begin to freeze, then out of nowhere, boom, I got shoved so hard and with so much force from behind on my back's left side that had it not been for Kim standing next to me to break my fall, I would have hit the ground.

My first thought was, somebody must be running from somebody and accidently pushed me to get away, but the way I was shoved, it felt deliberate, intentional. It was a blatant violation of all my personal space! I immediately looked to hear an "Excuse me" to follow this brutal shoving. I never heard the courteous gesture of an apology. It never came! What came next was me forcing my mind to try to catch up with what was happening in the moment. I was trying to catch with the moment at hand and make sense of what was really going on! I couldn't understand why I had to be the subject of this assault! As I was falling into Kim, I was able to get a glimpse of this person who had pushed me out of his way. Only then did I start realizing what was really happening. I was getting treated by a giant, and he kept walking! I remember thinking, "Damn, he big!" I couldn't help but to hope this wouldn't go wrong. But everything indicated that it was about to go all wrong, and it did!

As he kept walking away, I felt belittled. For me, it went past him being rude. It was total disrespect. This was how I was left feeling. The adolescent male in me rose up to the surface, and ego took over! I was now forced to speak up for myself and not allow this guy to just push me and keep walking. Every step he took away from me made it clear that he had no intentions of apologizing and that it was no mistake. When I eventually gathered myself and got a good look at him from the back, he looked to be the tallest human being I had ever seen in my life! So not only was I staring down the barrel of my own pride but also I was now facing a potential conflict with the tallest person I had ever seen. He made me feel like I was nothing to him. I had to stand up for myself. I felt I had no choice but to do so. He left me no choice! As I stood there looking dumbfounded and thinking why he did what he did, still a little hope in me just knew he would turn and say, "Hey, man, excuse me!" But he kept walking as if he never touched me, so I said, "Man, ain't you going to say 'Excuse me?" He turned around and said, "Nigga, fuck you. I don't owe you an excuse. Now what?" I said, "Fuck you, nigga. You pushed me." He said, "And now what?" I said, "You needs to say 'Excuse me.'"

Now he was starting to pull away from the female with him. That was when I started unzipping my jacket thinking that if he saw this gun, it would make him back down, humble him, because the last thing I wanted to do was pull it out. I stood there feeling like David in the face of an angry giant who was getting overly aggressive by the second. The female with him became hysterical and said, "He got a gun. He got a gun, Ben!" This was when I heard his name for the first time. He said, "Ah, so you got a gun, huh? Whatchu going to do, shoot me now?" I said, "Man, don't walk up on me!" That was when he snatched away from his girlfriend and lunged toward me. I stepped back as I pulled the gun out and pulled the trigger twice! He was hit! This was my first and only encounter with Ben Wilson. The female turned out to be his girlfriend, the mother of his child.

I was baffled and in a state of shock. I was struggling to wrap my mind around everything that I had just done. It was hard to accept I had just pulled a trigger and shot a human being. "Why did he make me do it? Why didn't he walk away?" I kept asking myself. "Man, you fucked up big time. You just shot somebody!" There was nothing I could do to now change the reality of that moment! It had happened! Never before this moment in my life was I more in touch with my own humanity as I had been at that time, realizing that the most terrible possible outcome of my actions could result in the loss of someone's life. I had crossed a line I knew I could not go back to change. There was nothing I could do to fix it. Instantly, I was hoping for the best for him and his full recover. I prayed his condition wouldn't be too bad. I went from wanting to do to him what it seemed like he wanted to do to me to wanting and praying for nothing but the best for him. An instant and constant sense of anxiety gripped my heart. Despite the fact it was a crisp and cold November day, I felt my temperature had risen to almost a fever pitch with fear. I was scared and overcome by confusion and uncertainty. My thoughts stayed on him. He became the most important person to me. This unknown tall stranger by the name of Ben, who I left struggling for his life, I only wanted to see him make it through this!

I had heard the girl call out his name, Ben, but still had no idea who Ben Wilson was. The fear I now felt inside me was all for him. I feared for his life. I didn't want him to die. And for me, I didn't want that on my conscience. This stranger who had threatened my peace made me see the value of human life very clearly, and I immediately understood how precious it is. If I could, I would have given him a portion of my life to ensure the survival of his life. As I felt he forced me to use that gun, I was left without the power to control the outcome of my actions. As I fled the scene, Omar in tow, I felt like I was running for my life. I remember I saw one of the guys I was cool with named Dave standing on his porch. We ran to his house, and after I got on his porch, I noticed Puncho coming behind us. We didn't tell Dave what had just happened, but I was sure he knew something wasn't right by the way we were acting. We asked Dave for a ride to Puncho's house on Seventy-Seventh and Ada. When we got in Puncho's house, his mother asked us why we were out of school so early. We said that we had a half day!

I was in a state of shock and disbelief. I really didn't know what to do. I gave Omar the gun and asked him to take it to my cousin Fats house for me. I forgot Fats had come with us when I asked Omar to take the gun to his house. He nodded in agreement. I was waiting for Omar to say something, but there wasn't a word. The silence was loud, and the message was clear to the both of us that this was the worst situation I could be in! I was stunned. My anxiety elevated with every moment that passed by. I felt like I needed to stop moving to try and settle my thoughts, but at the same time, I had to keep moving because my mind wouldn't stop racing. So I left Omar at Puncho's house and headed down to my cousin Pook's crib. I walked east on Seventy-Seventh to Racine.

I tried to sit still at the bus stop and wait for a bus. It seemed like a bus was never going to come, so I started walking north on Racine, constantly looking back over my shoulder. I remember hearing the blaring sounds of sirens getting louder and louder, which only added to my fear of what the worst possible outcome would be. Those blaring sirens only intensified my anxiety, and I'm sure they had nothing to do with what I had done. Sirens are the hood's theme music, playing an ominous melody of traumatic crisis constantly unfolding.

The noise made me a nervous wreck. I couldn't focus on any one clear thought. My mind kept racing back to that moment of me pulling the trigger, replaying everything that led up to that and questioning what other possible actions I should have taken. I knew this was the worst mistake of my life. Nothing since or before would be greater. It was too late for that. I had shot him, and I couldn't take it back. I kept thinking, *Damn, why didn't he just walk away?* I guess he wasn't so much different than me and most young black males in the hood, trying to hold down the only thing we think we have: our pride!

Finally, a bus came. I didn't realize I had walked as far as I did until I looked at the bus stop sign. I had walked all the way to Seventy-First and Racine. I jumped on the bus, and as it rode off, I kept thinking the police was going to come and catch up with me and pull the bus over and snatch me off it at any moment. I had never faced this kind of trouble. I couldn't come up with the right thoughts to settle my mind to better handle the moment. Finally, the bus was at Sixty-Third and Racine. I decided to get off the bus and walk the rest of the way. I couldn't continue to sit still on that bus.

I had no one around me, no one who could possibly understand what I was going through. I was trapped! Inside my head, I felt tortured by every thought popping up. I didn't know what to do or what was going to happen and what the final outcome was going to be. My mind kept racing back to that final moment, the moment that was never going to ever change for Benji or for me. Part of my fear came from the uncertainty of not knowing Benji's condition. I was too unsettled and couldn't relax. Never being able to calm my nerves, I felt walking in the brisk, cold wind would help, but there was nothing that could have eased my mind from all the uncertainty of everything that happened. I had just shot someone in broad daylight. I believed my actions were not too far from catching up to me, and I was not sure how that was going to play out. All this added to my anxiety.

I reached Pook's house on Fifty-Ninth and Loomis. When he came to the door, as he stepped aside, I could see on the TV a breaking news flash. Nothing was going to let me escape from my transgressions! Everywhere I went was reminding me of the worst mistake of my life. It was breaking news now, breaking news about what I had just done. The report was, "Benji Wilson, Simeon star basketball player, was shot by two gang members in an apparent attempted robbery." While I was watching this, I looked over at my cousin to see his reaction. Pook went to Simeon and was familiar with who Benji was and said, "Damn, shit finally caught up with him!" I was stunned. I didn't know what to expect, but I definitely didn't expect to be seeing this on the news. Now that I had found out who he was, I knew just how much I had really messed up. I had to talk to somebody, and my cousin was probably the best person at the moment I could to talk to. I knew no one could help, but I had to get this off my chest. I told Pook, "Man, Cuz, I shot him!" He said in disbelief, "Get the fuck out of here!" "Naw, Cuz, I shot him, but I wasn't robbing him." I explained what happened. "He started it by shoving me from behind and started talking crazy, and one thing led to another, and when he tried to walk up on me, I pulled out the gun and shot him twice!" The conversation became unclear between me and Pook because my attention kept getting drawn to what was on the TV. All normal programing had been interrupted with the news of Benji.

Literally every moment became worse than the next. I didn't know what to do with myself. While we sat there watching what everybody in the world was watching, which was my most fucked mistake ever being reported on, the front door opened. It was Erica! Immediately, when she saw me, I could see the look on her face was that of confusion and distress. She asked me did I realize who I had shot. I couldn't say a word. Once again, I couldn't sit still. I had to move around. So I left. I knew no one could help me. I felt the weight of the world on top of me, and it felt like it was about to come crashing down on my head. It was like I was in a nightmare fully awake. I could see the look of hopelessness in Pook and Erica's eyes as they watched me leave their house for the last time in my life.

I remember watching old Western cowboy movies and seeing how the villains would be wanted dead or alive. I never imagined I was going to be a wanted individual like the villains in those movies by the police, especially at sixteen years old, but that was the reality, and it was the worst indescribable feeling ever. And just like in the movies when the villain sometimes ended up dead, I would be lying if I didn't think this was how this was going to end for me. I thought every corner I approached or walked around, the police was going to jump out and arrest me or, worse, kill me! I really believed I might not live through this. The way the news was reporting on this, I had never in my young life seen something attract so much attention the way this was being reported on. I knew my actions had all of law enforcement efforts focusing on apprehending me. To say it was overwhelming is an understatement. I had few to no options. I didn't feel like going home was the best decision, but I knew I had to talk to the one person who could probably help bring me some amount of comfort and help me to think clear: my mother! I had to tell her that her son was being searched for by every police in the city and that he didn't know what to do!

I decided to take the bus to my auntie's house, my mother's youngest sister, Valerie. Valerie and husband, Curtis, lived on Seventy-Second and Morgan in the big yellow house on the corner. I was hoping she was at home because I didn't think I had anywhere else to go. If she were at home, I would call my mother from her house. I found myself back on the bus, riding to Valerie's house, mind racing and all over the place.

Once again, it seemed like forever because of the cloud my thoughts were trapped in—confusion, uncertainty, anxiety, self-condemnation, and fear. I was at my auntie's door. When she opened the door, the first thing that greeted me again just as it had happened at Pook's house as I walked through the door was the breaking news on her TV reporting on Benji's condition. He was still alive! That news brought about a small amount of relief to my tormented conscious, but what I heard next erased that immediately when the reporter said that the police had two in custody and looking for a third. Damn!

It was like my brain instantly exploded inside my head with fear. I couldn't hold it in, and I said to Valerie, "They are looking for me!" She apparently was not clear by what I had just said. She wasn't putting it together what was being reported on TV about this young man who was shot at Simeon and me telling her the police was looking for me for shooting him! I said, "Valerie, I shot him. They are talking about it on the news right now." I'm not clear how she responded, but I said, "I need to call my mama."

The house was quiet as I dialed my mother's number. I remember my uncle Curtis walking in the room as I waited for my mother to answer my call. The look in my auntie's eyes told Curtis something was terribly wrong. I heard him ask, "What's wrong, baby?" She didn't respond. My mother answered, and when she heard me on the other end, I said, "Hey, Ma!" She said, "Hey, boy, what's going on?" I said, "I have to tell you something. I'm in trouble. Have you seen the news? The boy that was shot up at Simeon?" She said, "Yes!" I said, "I did it, and the police are looking for me." She immediately said, "Where you at? I'm coming to get you!" I told her I was at Valerie's house. I could hear her on the other end starting to cry. She said, "Billy, what happened?" I began to tell her, and she just started uncontrollably crying. My grandmother took the phone from her and asked what was going on. I said, "Granny, the police are looking for me because I shot that boy at Simeon." It was hard for everybody to process.

I told my Granny to tell my mama not to come get me from Valerie's house because I didn't know if the police were waiting for me to come home, and I just wasn't ready for that. I hung up. Curtis asked me what happened, and I told him. Valerie called my granny back, and my granny told her the police was at the house and that she would call her back. It had to be a few hours later when my granny eventually called back, but it seemed like it took her forever to do so. I was so nervous, and my anxiety level was on ten. Now that I knew the police had been at my house, I figured it was only a matter of time before they came and arrested me at my auntie's house. I knew the police was closing in on me. I had this oxymoronic feeling of having some sort of relief from my anxiety when I got caught but on the other hand sheer fear of the unknown of what was going to or could happen to me if I was caught in the streets or while in custody. My granny said that Russ Ewing had come to the house and told them if they talked to me that I should turn myself in. He ensured that he would escort me into the police station and guarantee my safety so that the police wouldn't have to catch me in the streets and it all goes wrong.

Russ Ewing was a newsman who gained notoriety for helping people turn themselves to the police. People who ended up in serious trouble with the law would go to Russ Ewing before they got arrested so that he could ensure their safety by helping them to turn themselves into the police. He would escort them into custody, literally walk people into the police station and safely hand them over to the law. Some people suspected of high-profile crimes or just people wanted by the police sought out Russ Ewing's help, or he would offer his assistance. Russ Ewing made sure black men especially would make it alive and safe into police custody.

Now that my family knew what the situation was, they were as much in a state of panic and confusion as I was. When the police came to my house, they were so hyper to apprehend me. My granny had to tell them to get out of her house because the police from the Gresham Sixth District located on 85th and Green at the time got into an argument with the police from 111th 5th district over who had jurisdiction to arrest me. My family and I had decided to take up Russ Ewing's offer to let him help me and us turn myself in with him.

At that point, that was the best thing I could do; but at around midnight, there was that unmistakable knock on my auntie's door, loud and authoritative! *Knock, knock, knock*! My auntie said, "Who is it?" "Police!" Curtis opened the door. "We have a search warrant for Billy Moore!" They stepped in, looked at me, and asked me my name, and I told them, "Billy Moore!" I saw one police officer speak through a radio and say, "Subject has been identified!" Then he put me in handcuffs and told my auntie Valerie what police station they were taking me to. He then led me out by the arm into the back of an unmarked police car. Once inside, an officer said, "Billy, we been looking for you all day. You better hope that boy don't die, 'cause if he does, you're fucked, son!" They called me by my name as if they had known me all my life. Whether he died or not, I was thinking I was fucked anyway. I was hoping and praying he wouldn't die because I knew that was going to be a heavy weight to carry on my conscience that I didn't know if I could bear.

It was a long ride to the police station cuffed in the back seat between two police officers who seemed overjoyed to have me in their custody. Finally, we made it to 111th and the police station. They drove in through a back entrance indoor garage. Once I was led inside the station and paraded in front of everyone, all the police and people I was forced to walk past, it seemed like everybody stopped doing whatever they were doing to look at me as if I was some sort of circus attraction. People were saying things like, "You little fucker. You shot that boy for nothing!" One ugly-ass white police officer belched in my face, and that shit smelled as bad as he looked. I felt like I was on display in a freak show. Everybody wanted the one who had the city in a buzz that whole day.

I was put in a room and handcuffed to the wall. A short time later, the interrogation began. The same police who arrested me were the ones who questioned me. They asked me why I was up there. Was I looking to rob somebody? Where did I get the gun from? Did I know the victim, etc.? I asked more than once if I could see my mother, and they told me yes every time. But it was hours later until

I got to see her, and it was only for about five minutes. They kept asking me if Omar went into Benji's pockets, and I said no, he didn't. I said he was just standing in the grass and didn't have anything to do with it. All their questioning kept insinuating that Omar went into Benji's pockets. I kept telling them that that wasn't true and that it was Benji who started it when he pushed me from behind out of his way and wouldn't walk away but started punking me.

For me, the questioning wasn't going anywhere because the police weren't trying to hear me, so I asked for a lawyer. I thought that was the right thing to ask for. The idea popped into my head from watching TV and seeing people questioned by police asking for a lawyer. That was when the police questioning me left the room, and a few minutes later, in walks this white guy who introduced himself as assistant state's attorney James Brady. He came in to talk with me with a prepared statement in his hand. At sixteen years old, I was totally ignorant to the fact of what a state's attorney role was as it related to me and my situation but realized quickly he was not there to advocate on my behalf. I could now see he was there to help put me in prison and not the lawyer I asked for. What I got was a prosecutor with a statement already written out.

He read from the statement and asked me if it was true. I told him it wasn't. He kept going over the statement and asking me what was true in it. I told him a thousand times what happened, and he started telling me he had been told that Omar attempted to go into Benji's pockets and that when Benji resisted, Omar said, "Shot this punk," and that was when I pulled the trigger twice. This back and forth went on until about four in the morning. Eventually, I was told the only way I was going to be allowed to see and to talk to my mother was if I signed the statement they prepared. I signed it, but I was not allowed to see her at that time. In fact, when she arrived at the police station, she demanded to see me and not only was she not allowed to see me but also she was arrested for disorderly conduct.

Keep in mind that once I asked to speak with a lawyer, all questioning from the police and state's attorney was to cease. It didn't. It continued without me having representation, and then as a juvenile, I should have not been questioned without a lawyer and a parent present. That was not the case. The system took total advantage of the situation. They let my mother out of lockup, and only then did I get to see her. I was moved and placed into a holding cell around 7:00 a.m. Right in front of the holding cell was a TV attached to the wall. The TV was on, and once again, I caught the breaking news: "Ben Wilson, Simeon prep star, has died at seventeen!" My heart dropped into the pit of my stomach. Hearing that news made time stand still for me. What I had just heard was not what I wanted to hear. I felt an instant rush of grief inside me.

Honestly, the grief that overcame me for Benji's death, I felt it strongly. I don't want to be disrespectful to anyone who felt the grief of his loss, but I felt it too! It was one of the worst days of my life. It was hard to reconcile within me that now I was responsible for the death of another human being! I didn't look at this situation as me being responsible for a dream unfilled. I simply felt responsible for the loss of a human life. What came over me was an unsettled feeling. Fear and anxiety had overtaken me. The mental anguish that I felt wasn't enough of a price to pay that I cost a human life!

I thought that my life was over. I knew life was never going to be the same again for me. Benji's death affected me deeply in more than one way. The fact that he had died was a tough pill to swallow! I knew I was going to pay for this fully. The same creator, Yahweh, who created and put the spirit of life in me, I ended in another human. It was hard to embrace that. I felt worse than I did fourteen months earlier when my own father had died.

I can't recall how long I sat in that holding cell, but eventually, I was taken out and handcuffed. I looked up and saw Omar as he was being led in handcuffs walking toward me. We were still in the room where the TV was at. We stood in front of this door. When the police opened it, it led to a long hallway; and at the end of it, all I could see was a large group of people standing there with cameras and flashing lights, and I heard them saying, "There they are!" I remember thinking, *Damn. All the news people are here!* Usually, when you see something like this in the news, the accused is almost always covering up or holding their head down. I get it. This had be to the most shameful, embarrassing moment of someone's life, but

I said to myself, "Nope, don't hide. Keep your head up, and own up to what you did!"

The first person I recognized was this news reporter by the name of Chuck Goudie with ABC News. I remember him asking me and Omar, "Did you know Ben Wilson? Did you know him?" Of course he couldn't really expect me to stop and answer his question! This was not the time for Q&A. I was totally fucked up in the head, and now I knew the world had seen my worst mistake. The police were leading us away, and the reporters were running around, sticking mics in our faces and trying to keep up with us. The police opened this door that led to outside where there was another large group of reporters waiting with cameras on us to be brought out. As we stepped through the door outside in the back of the police station, there was a curb there that a camera man tripped over and fell to the ground. I mean a total wipeout. He went one way, and his camera went everywhere. All the other reporters and cameramen just stepped over this dude without offering a hand to help him up.

After being put inside the paddy wagon, we took that long ride from the police station to the Cook County Criminal Courts building where my fate would be decided. Judgment beat me there. My fate had already been decided before I stepped one foot in a courtroom. Once Chicago was able to see my face as the person responsible for shooting Benji, I knew the court of public opinion had placed me on trial, convicted and condemned me before I reached Twenty-Sixth and California, the courthouse.

This was a quiet trip. I remember I felt every bump on the road and bouncing around in that steel box paddy wagon I was cuffed and bolted to inside. Despite the ride being a quiet one, I had so many chaotic thoughts running through my mind that it was hard turning down the volume on them in my head. There was no one thing for me to focus on to calm me down in this time of uncertainty. Not knowing what the outcome of this was going to be, it took my mind to a level of consciousness that I didn't know the mind could sink to.

Eventually, we made it to the courthouse. We were ushered through an underground tunnel, walked into an elevator, got off, and were placed inside a bullpen in the back of a courtroom. Once again, everyone wanted to see the villains responsible for this tragedy. Lawyers, sheriff bailiffs, and whoever had access came to the bullpen back there to look at us. We were eventually brought in front of the judge for a bail hearing where, of course, bail was denied. After being taken from the bail hearing, Omar and I were about to be put into a room when I heard a little old lady, who was also a sheriff bailiff, say, "You killed that boy? I hope they give y'all ass the death penalty, and they let me pull the switch on you motherfuckers!" She pretty much summed up the attitude and feelings toward us that everybody we encountered had showed us.

Chapter 10

The Auddie Home

WE WERE TRANSFERRED from the courthouse on Twenty-Sixth and California to Eleventh and Hamilton, the Cook County Juvenile Detention Center. The auddie home is what it was called in the streets. This place was filled with a bunch of young knuckleheads just like me. The auddie home is a place where the ages range from thirteen to sixteen years old. Everyone there was within the same peer group. There was no one detained there who was more than a three- to two-year age difference. Everyone there was caught in the same cycle of ignorance. There was a lot of pain in that place with very little self-regulation.

We were all lost in our adolescence and thinking we had found ourselves in our manhood. Every day and all day, it was about posturing to impress one another without knowing any better. Except for staff, there was no mature men around for these young lion cubs to look up to for any real examples of how to carry themselves and deal with those circumstances, no real leadership and anyone who had real-life experience to share with these young men. It was always a benefit to young guys to have older guys around. The benefit of their mentorship is valuable. Old lions hold credibility for young lions to listen to. Every young dude felt they needed to prove how tough they were, ready to prove themselves at the drop of a dime. In many situations, this was all an act.

The combination of unregulated emotions, impulsiveness, and youthful testosterone didn't make for the best environment to try and promote and correct positive behavior. Over time and only with time do we learn how to develop the skill to not rely on the weakest trait we have: our feelings/emotions. And without anyone who has grown to that level in life around them every day, we can't expect young men / teenagers grouped together of making good decisions.

While Omar and I were getting processed in the center, I knew for a fact we were going to have to box when we got in there. We felt the hate instantly from the beginning as soon as we stepped foot in there. After we were processed in the juvenile detention center, because we were being charged as adults, we were placed on the county jail section, which was on the fourth floor. We were separated and placed on two different decks. I was placed on 4-D, and Omar was placed on 4-B. I was held in confinement behind a steel door on the deck. There were two cells with steel doors for disciplinary, and eighteen other cells with Plexiglas doors. I was told I would be in there for evaluation for my own safety. For me, I just felt like it was a way to punish me. It was also a way of getting me to understand what being locked up was all about. I was now fresh off the bricks and locked in the box! I spent the next twelve days behind the steel door.

That first night, I got a visit to my cell from a juvenile attendant, a correctional officer. His name was Sorrell. He woke me up in the middle of the night after he banged on the steel door. I looked up and saw him looking at me through the narrow glass window. I thought, *Who the fuck is this, and what do he want?* He said, "I bet you won't be hiding in somebody's closest at five in the morning no more for a while!" Immediately, his statement brought me back to the night Tamara's mother caught me in her house hiding in the closest. I realized he looked familiar. A few days after that incident happened, Tamara's mother asked Sorrell, who was a friend of the family, to come up to the school to speak to me about getting caught in her house. He was cool but warned me not to do that again. If I didn't feel ashamed at this moment, I would be lying because I didn't feel good about being seen in this situation by someone who knew me.

After he broke the ice with what he said, we talked a little bit about how I ended up in there. He said to me, "Man, how did you end up in this shit?" I had no answer for him. He said to keep my head up and stay out of trouble and that he will be back to check up on me. I appreciated that. I knew he didn't feel good about seeing me in there and facing what I was facing. Under those circumstances, seeing a familiar face brought a sense of comfort despite the initial embarrassment I felt when I realized who he was.

I was next door to a brother from the Greens, Cabrini-Green Projects, who was also behind the other steel door. His name was Stanley Bills but better known by Swan. Swan was a real dude and a genuine brother. He was well-respected from where he was from and by everyone who knew him. Swan was maybe about three inches taller than me at the time, a dark-complexioned brother with a serious look and just as serious of a disposition. We would talk through the door at night when everybody was locked up and during the day when they were out of their cells. When he was let out of confinement and I was still locked up, he would come and hold conversations with me. Shortly after I got there, Swan got transferred to IYC (Illinois Youth Center) Little Joliet about three weeks later. I never saw Swan again. Sad to say, years later, after Swan got out of prison and while I was still locked up, I got word that that brother got killed. He was a soldier who kept a solid name in his community and in the city. I felt his loss.

I was finally let out of confinement and moved from behind the steel door to a regular room with a glass door. A couple of days later, I got a visit from my mother and grandmother. I wasn't allowed to have any other visitors but them. One good thing about getting visits at the juvenile detention center was, they allowed your family to bring you food. Since the auddie home was located on Roosevelt and Hamilton, I asked them to bring me a Maxwell Street, aka Jew Town, polish sausage. At the time, when I still ate red meat, I looked forward to getting one of those polish sausages every time they came to see me.

That first visit wasn't easy. When we sat down and started talking, I could see the worry in their eyes. This was an overwhelming experience we were going through, and I couldn't imagine the stress they had to be feeling to see me in the situation I was in and knowing there was very little they could do to help me. I knew they felt beyond helpless and hopeless. I knew there was nothing I could do to help ease their anxiety, so I just told them that I was going to be as strong as I needed to be to get through this and that if anything happened to me, they could rest assured that it wouldn't be by my own hand.

I told them to not let anyone tell them I did anything to harm myself, and if something happened to me, just know it was by someone else's hand. I told my mother and granny I was standing strong. I told them I was in it for the long haul, however long that might be. I wasn't going to hurt myself. That would never be an option for me. I told them both that I knew how much they were going to be worried for me, and I promised them that day that I wasn't going to do anything to add to their worry.

My mother told me that someone reached out to them about a lawyer they should talk to. His name was Skip Gant, a protégé of Judge Eugen Pincham. So after they spoke to him, he told my mother he wanted to come and meet me and had planned to come see within a couple of days. The look in my mother's eyes that day spoke directly to my soul and told me of all the pain she was feeling, but there was no way I could fully understand what my mother was feeling and going through. So I had to speak to her soul and make her believe I was going to make it through this, and that was when I looked directly into her eyes and told her I was going to be all right.

I knew I was the only thing she had, and I knew she felt she had lost me to the system, so how could I possibly bring comfort to her from this feeling but by doing everything I could to not put myself into more fucked up shit while I was locked up. I had to make sure I wasn't going to be making decisions that would continue to cost me again and have my mother be forced to pay with her worry and stress for something stupid I did. The visit came to an end. We hugged, and my mother committed to me that she would handle the outside and told me to handle the inside. That was the pact we made that day, and we both lived up both ends of our bargain.

A few days later, I got another visit. It was Isiah "Skip" Gant, the lawyer that my mother got me. Skip was one of the top lawyers in Chicago, and he was an African American. I remember him being well-dressed. He was impressively dapper, wearing an expensive pin-striped suit with a red rose pinned on his lapel. He also wore wire-framed glasses as if to emphasize his intelligence. He was a brother with a presence he presented with full confidence in his ability, and when he spoke, it came through. When we talked, he was straight-forward and direct with me. He didn't sugarcoat anything. He was as real as a person could be.

He told me this case was going to be very hard to beat but that he was going to give me the best representation that he could. That was the only promise he was going to make to me. He told me not to lie to him and asked me to tell him everything that happened, and that was what I did. I told him the entire story. He explained to me that he had taken on tough cases before. One in particular was the Pontiac Seventeen brothers. They were the original Brothers of the Struggle, a case he helped to beat. He was part of that major trial that took place a few years earlier that involved some prominent leaders of multiple Chicago street organizations that had been accused of causing a riot in Pontiac prison where three white guards had been killed. There were seventeen young black men charged and tried, and all had been acquitted. One of the young men who had been placed on trial and who Skip had represented was Larry Hoover! Skip had a lot of respect for Mr. Hoover and was proud of the fact that he helped to get him acquitted in that case. So I felt good about my representation. I still believed I wasn't going to get a fair shake in court during this process.

A few weeks later, Omar and I had a court date. Word had been circulating around the county section leading up to the day we were going to court that some guys who had court on the same day and who had affiliations with those who considered us opps was going to push on me and Omar. For those who don't know what opps means, it means oppositions, being in a different organization that opposes the organization you are a part of. That day we went to court, there were ten of us—eight guys and me and Omar. I asked Omar if he had heard the rumor of these dudes planning on jumping on us. He said yeah, he had heard. There was no way I was going to let anybody jump on us.

As soon as we were loaded into the van to be transported to court, they started talking shit in a roundabout way, not direct but saying shit like, "They like Dunkin' Donuts!" That was what BlackStone's called Disciples—donuts! Omar and I clearly understood their message. Once we got in the bullpen, I knew I had to minimize the threat of them trying to fuck us up, so I figured I would play on their toughness and really see how tough these niggas were. I told Omar I was going to call them out on a one-on-one challenge. I could take four, and Omar could take the other four, one-on-one. He was down for it, so I told everybody in the bullpen we heard about what they were supposed to do to us, but I asked them if they were willing to give me and Omar a fair fight and each one of them fight me and Omar one at a time. It was still an unfair fight, but at least they agreed to it. We even let them pick which one they wanted to fight.

I told them everybody would get two minutes apiece. I would go first, and Omar would go second. I went 4-0, and Omar went 4-0 decisively! We were 8-0! Omar and I beat them niggas' asses in that bullpen and earned their respect from that day forward. We took care of our business and boxed our way to another level of respect. We had a few minor bumps and bruises, but we finished on top that day.

The next fight I had in the auddie home came about a week later. It was just another normal day in the center. I was in the day-room playing cards and watching TV. Things like this always happened in jail. One minute, everything is cool and calm; and then the next thing you know, bullshit comes out of nowhere. This day was no different. This dude from the West Side who was new on the deck wanted to play cards. He was a classic loudmouth. He got into the card game and immediately started talking shit. We were playing Cutthroat. It was like playing Spades but without a partner, every man for himself.

While playing cards with me and a couple of other guys, JC and ToTo, West Side started getting loud with his shit-talking. Although it was annoying, we paid him no attention. For some reason, dudes from the West Side would call guys Charlie regardless of what their name was. So while we played cards, he started calling me Charlie and getting louder and more hyper. Now his antics were beyond annoying. They were becoming disrespectful. He had to be winning because he wouldn't stop talking. I didn't have a problem with him talking shit. I just didn't like him calling me Charlie, and when I became one too many Charlies, I started getting aggravated by the minute and asked him to stop calling me that.

I started feeling like he was zeroing in on me for some reason, so I started preparing myself for a fight. I knew in these surroundings, fights jumped off so spontaneously, and things like this were usually the indicators of how they start. I was ready although I wasn't look-ing for trouble, but trust me, I wasn't avoiding it either. In the aud-die home, you couldn't afford to not fight or not accept a challenge that could come your way because everybody in there wanted to be known as a tough guy.

After asking him to stop calling me Charlie, he said okay, and then called me a vic! That was short for victim and therefore was considered disrespectful. I told him, "Okay. Meet me in the back." In the adrenaline, I told Dude to come meet me in the bathroom. A few minutes later, I saw him ask Q if he could go to the bathroom, and he said, "I'm going to show you who a vic is!" In order to go to the bathroom during dayroom time, you had to ask for permission, then you were allowed to walk to the back to the bathroom. One day, the attendant working the deck was an old man named Q. All Q used to do was signify, whistle, and fall asleep. I asked Q when I caught him nodding if I could go to the bathroom. He said to go ahead and went to catch up on his nod.

I walked to the back where the toilets were and prepared myself for what would come next if he came back there. I was a little ner-vous, but it was only nervous energy of adrenaline. I watched him from the back and heard him ask Q if he could go to the bathroom. Q had forgotten he said I could go to use the bathroom just minutes earlier. When he came back there, he walked up on me. This fool was still talking when I punched him straight in the mouth so hard all I saw was his lip busting wide open. It only amounted to a split lip, but the blood that came from it made it look worse. He fell back into the wall behind him, and I snatched him and started punching him repeatedly. By this time, everybody on the deck had run back there, becoming spectators. He was trying to cover up and turned his back to me, so I pushed his head into the sink and started punching him again in the back of his head.

Q ran back there and pulled me off him, and I remember seeing a couple of his teeth mixed with the thick blood he spit inside the sink. Q apparently called for assistance because, all of a sudden, about five or six more attendants stormed the deck, pushing people back while trying to figure out what was going on. West Side was dazed and bleeding bad from his mouth and nose! I was hyped along with everybody else. The attendants grabbed me and walked me straight into the first room behind the steel door. I was pumped and filled with confidence. I had whipped his ass. It was timely because everybody who saw it knew that I would fight.

For the next few weeks I was there, I didn't have any more fights or anyone trying to challenge me. They brought West Side back to the deck after getting a few stitches in his lip. He was placed in the room next to me behind the other steel door. We were locked down for a week. During the first few days, West Side was talking shit again, saying how he was going to get me back, which I wasn't listening to. A couple of days before we came from the steel door, he apologized to me for calling me out of my mind. I accepted his apology, and when we were let out, we didn't have a problem with each other.

Chapter 11

Eye to Eye with the Devil

I STAYED AT the auddie home for a total of forty-one days. On January 2, 1985, the forty-second day was also the day after my seventeenth birthday. I was transferred to the Cook County Jail. The intake process at Cook County Jail lasted all day and all night. We left the auddie home early that morning, and I didn't make it to the school wing I was placed on in Division 6 until around 2:00 a.m. the following morning. This was an exhausting experience and one of the worst of my life.

Cook County Jail was literally hell on earth! From the time anyone set a foot in there, Cook County sheriff's staff became so disrespectful. They talked so much shit. They were bullies with badges and became instant tough guys when they came to work. Every chance they got, they used their power to intimidate everyone being detained there. For example, if they told you to get in a single-file line, they would follow up that command with something like this: "If one of you stupid motherfuckers step out of line, we are going to fuck your bitch ass up!" This was the attitude they brought to their job and how they welcomed people being detained there. This was the welcome party into the jail.

Some of these sheriffs acted like they were the little peons who got bullied in grammar school, and now that they had a job working in the jail, they took full advantage of the power that came with their badge and authority. The power of the badge and the influence that came with it got out of control. I saw so many people get jumped on by Cook County sheriffs during my time in the jail. They should have been charged with war crimes!

It didn't take much for them to get physical. One guy in line, clearly dope sick and complaining and not moving fast enough, aggravated this one CO (correctional officer / sheriff deputy). This CO kicked the guy in his ass so hard that he kicked him off his feet. You could hear the pain scream out in the loud sound it made. The guy lay there throwing up all over the floor, groaning in discomfort and pain from withdrawal and that swift kick to his ass.

Being processed in was exhausting and very discomforting. At one point during the processing, you had to see the dick doctor! Yep, I said it, the dick doctor. Some dude wearing a white doctor's coat would have you drop your underwear and stick this long-ass Q-tip-like object in the urethra of your penis. I still cringe at the thought of that experience! Throughout this process, I was moved in and out of about ten bullpens. Finally, I made it to Division 6 School Wing 1B.

Little did I know I would be getting a personal invite by the welcome party sooner than later! The next day after the early morning count was taken after shift changed, it took about an hour for the count to check. As soon as the count cleared, the CO unlocked the doors to the cells on the wing, and most of the guys started coming out of them. I looked around to see if I recognized anyone. I didn't. As guys started congregating in the dayroom, talking to one another, I could tell almost everybody recognized me.

Jail culture is unique. The first thing people want to know if they don't already is what your affiliation is. If it was not known, somebody would approach you. This was how it usually sounded, something like this: "What's up, you Folks?" or "All's Well!" or "What up, Lord, Solid World!" Whatever your response was, that was who you associated with from that point on.

I quickly picked up on the vibe that everybody recognized who I was. This short, stocky dude who was about 5'7" and at least a solid 200 lbs. approached me, and he said, "What's up, Folks?" As he extended his hand to shake mine, we shook hands the way the Folks do. "My name is Tattoo. You got that Ben Wilson case, right?" he said in a voice just as rough as he looked. Tattoo had the right name because it looked like he had a million jailhouse tattoos. He looked like a battleship ready to sail into battle. He looked tough! I nodded my head in acknowledgment. "What they call you?" he asked. "Call me Billy or Lil Moe!" I said. He said, "Okay. Let me introduce you to the rest of the guys." We walked around the wing, and I was introduced to all the Folks on the deck.

Now because my case was so high profile, everybody wanted to talk to me about my case and know what had happened. The one thing Skip emphasized to me the most from the first day I met him was to not talk about my case to anybody! So whenever anyone asked me what happened, I simply said, "I don't talk about my case!" They understood. In this situation, some people are looking for a way out, so you never want to start running your mouth off about what you are accused of and have somebody listening. You give them the wrong information they don't need to know and they run to the state's attorney to try and cut a deal by telling them you made a jailhouse confession. So I wasn't talking.

There were a lot of dudes on the wing from everywhere in the city and county. One guy I met was this brother named RoRo. RoRo was a tall, skinny dude about the same complexion as I was who wore his hair in loose jailhouse braids. He turned out to be a funny dude, joking all the time. As we talked about where we were from, I told him I had some cousins who lived in his neighborhood, and not only did he know my cousins but also they were friends. As it turned out, his sister was my cousin Donna's best friend. RoRo and I ended up becoming friends until this day.

As my first day in Division 6 went by, I learned that in jail, there's never a moment when you can just totally relax, so it was a challenge trying to get used to this county jail life. I knew it wasn't going to be easy. I felt more isolated and unsure with every moment that passed by even in spite of me being taken around and introduced to the guys on the wing. To make matters worse, I noticed every so often, COs would walk up to the wing in the interlock just to get a look at me. Once again, everybody wanted to see me, even the staff at the jail. I felt like Tupac back then, "All Eyez on Me!"

I picked up on how popular I was becoming. The guys started trying to school me on the politics and the basics of jail life. I was wearing a pair of white Converse All Star gym shoes with blue and white shoelaces. RoRo and Tattoo told me I should take those blue shoestrings out because it was gang colors, so I took their advice and started removing the blue strings. I had already seen how super hyped those bullies could be *sheriff* bullies. *Sheriff* could be they seemed like they were constantly looking for reasons to whop somebody's ass, so I didn't want any unwanted attention, especially since I had started getting all the attention.

I literally had one shoe in my hand, removing the lace out of it, when I saw in the hallway about six or seven COs walking up to the wing again and walking into the interlock. Immediately, I sensed some bullshit. I knew something wasn't right with this picture. They weren't there just to get a look. Intuition told me the welcome party had finally showed up! I immediately asked the guys playing dominoes if I could use the pen they were using to keep score with and a piece of paper. After they gave it to me, I wrote my mother's number down, gave it to Tattoo, and asked him to call her if the COs pulled me off the wing.

Within seconds, I heard my name being called over the intercom: "Moore, report to the interlock!" Yeah, I knew this wasn't going to be good! The only thing I hoped was that Tattoo would do what I asked him to do and call my mother and, even more important, that she would answer! The interlock was like this outer station where the CO could monitor the wing from. It was enclosed by glass and a steel door that led to both the wing and the hallway. It was not separate from the wing, but it separated the CO from us on the wing. It was also the control center that electronically controlled all the cell doors on the wing.

When I heard my name ring out through the speakers, instantly, I felt a rush of nervous adrenaline overtake me. My whole body prepared itself as my mind started thinking the worst was about to happen but at the same time not knowing how this was going to turn out. I was fully aware that people had lost their lives while being detained in this jail, so I just prayed that I wasn't going to end up becoming a victim of some mysterious incident resulting in my life being taken the day after my seventeenth birthday!

As I approached the steel door to the interlock, I realized once again I was caught in another situation I had no control over. There was no way I could get around it. I was at the mercy of the moment, and it didn't appear at the moment that mercy was what I was about to get, so I was going to have to face the music! I could feel my heartbeat. It was louder than the click I heard when the CO pressed the button to unlock that steel door! It was a white sergeant named Zurick. He was a short, pudgy guy with stringy, dirty-looking blond hair and with an evil demeanor. Because of his rank as sergeant, he wore a white shirt, but with the vibe and aura he was giving off, he should have worn a white hood! He was with his minion, this little skinny white CO named Bosco. They were inside the interlock when I walked inside it.

Zurick motioned for me to step into the hallway. This had bullshit written all over it. Bosco walked up and grabbed me by the arm and forced me to stand against the wall once we were in the hallway. He started barking out orders for me to stand up against it. Bosco now was standing directly in front of me. It was something inside me that wouldn't allow me to turn away when he locked eyes with me. I sensed he was becoming uncomfortable, and his insecurity made him look away. He said to Zurick, "He thinks he's tough, Sarge!" Then with the weakest feather fist punch that I had ever been hit with, he threw to my gut. Then he shouted, "Don't look at me!" I thought, *He not for real. He trying to impress his racist sergeant.* If this was the worst of it, I could handle this shit with no problem, but it wasn't—well, at least not Zurick. Bosco was just going along for the ride with Zurick. He really wasn't intimidating and clearly not a tough guy.

After a few minutes of Bosco's fake tough guy impersonation, Zurick started interrogating me. Zurick attempted to try and slap me but missed. When he swung at me, my reflexes and instinct took over without me putting any thought into it. I was able to lean back enough to the side and avoid being slapped. My skills as a slapboxer instinctively took over, and he missed terribly. The momentum of his body caused him to damn near fall on his face. This infuriated him. When he gathered himself, he was so mad he spit in my face and told me, "Stand still, motherfucker!" He was so close to my face I could smell his nasty-ass breath.

Now it was me and Zurick in a direct staredown. It was like staring down the devil! His eyes invited me to take a look into hell, and all I saw was bigotry and hate. That was what was in his soul. As a seventeen-year-old kid, I felt like I was standing face-to-face with Satan; and honestly, I felt fear inside me. But for some reason, I couldn't pull myself away from breaking my stare with the devil. At this point, I was thinking, *Don't show fear, and don't give this racist motherfucker the satisfaction.* He might win this war, but I won't let him win this battle! I had come face-to-face and eye to eye with the devil in the form of a short, pudgy white Cook County jail guard sergeant named Zurick. I'm sure if you ever have to have an eye to eye staredown with the devil, it probably means you wouldn't live to talk about it.

I felt like this could be my last day alive, and it was going to end in Division 6 of Cook County Jail! Damn! I was trapped with no way out of this situation. All I could do was hope and pray that Tattoo would make that call and that my mama would answer it! Zurick threw a hard uppercut, and he wasn't faking it like his soft-ass comrade Bosco. This punch buckled me over and left me gasping for air. It sent pain throughout my entire body. Then came a slap. The only difference from this slap and the first one was that this one landed square on the left side of my face and ear. It was so hard it left my ear ringing for several days after it happened.

Feeling shook up and disoriented, Zurick snatched me by my collar and started laughing. I wanted to fight back, but I knew I couldn't win this fight. I heard him say, "This motherfucker ain't tough. He's a pussy!" As he said that, he forcefully turned me around and handcuffed me. He intentionally put the cuffs on extra tight to the point that they left swelling and deep impressions on my skin. They both grabbed me by both of my arms, one on each side of me, and led me down the hallway so forcefully that it turned into them dragging me. They led me to this office. At this point, I could tell this wasn't just about belittling me. There was more to it than that. They took me to the captain's office, and a black guy by the name of Dunnigan was in the office. He was the captain of Division 6.

Captain Dunnigan was a middle-aged black guy and tall, maybe six feet tall, and somewhat slim. He wore a short dark brown afro. You could tell he was a seasoned veteran and commanded respect. When they dragged me into his office, he was sitting behind a desk and asked Zurick, "Who is this motherfucker?" "This is the piece of shit who killed the basketball player, Captain!" Zurick said. Dunnigan said, "Why is his ass standing in my office?" "He thinks he's tough, Captain!" Zurick said. Dunnigan stood up from his desk, walked around from behind it, and now was standing directly in front of me and asked me, "You think you tough, motherfucker?" Instantly, I knew this dude was serious!

He then asked me, "What gang you in?" My answer clearly was an uninformed one to his question. I had no idea and didn't know any better that my answer was going to be the wrong answer when I opened my mouth to respond to his question. I'm sure some people would agree with the treatment I was being subjected to, but the way I saw it, these were professionals dealing with me in the worst way on a personal level that went beyond any grief they may have felt for Benji. These men were being criminal through their lawful positions, and the way they ran the jail back then was definitely criminal.

My response to Dunnigan's question was, "I'm a GD." Dunnigan said, "What did this motherfucker just say?" Zurick said, "You heard him, Captain. He said he's a GD!" Dunnigan quickly walked back around to the desk so fast I knew that what I had just said just got me in trouble. He moved like he had food burning on a stove. "Sit down, motherfucker," Dunnigan said. But before I had the chance to comply, Bosco pulled a chair that was in the corner of the office; and at the same time, Zurick snatched me by the handcuffs and force-fully shoved me into the chair. Dunnigan asked Bosco who was my celly. *Celly* is another word for *cellmate*. He told Zurick who then told Bosco to find out. While Bosco went to go get my celly, whom I don't remember the name of, Dunnigan went into this tirade about how there were no gangs in his jail, that there were only inmates, and that I was going to learn today the difference.

A short time later, in came Bosco with my celly. My celly walked in with a look of terror on his face! Dunnigan shouted out in a command to my celly, "What gang are you in?" My celly said in a timid voice, "I'm not in a gang. I am an inmate, Captain Dunnigan!" "So why didn't your stupid ass tell your celly ain't no gangs in my jail?" Dunnigan said. He went on to say, "Since you know that then, I should whoop your ass, motherfucker!" Dunnigan told Bosco to take my celly back to the wing. Dunnigan then pulled out a night stick that was in his desk and walked up to me while I was seated and swung it. It landed square in the middle of my chest. Dunnigan then asked me, "What gang are you in?" I said, "I'm an inmate!" He said, "That's all that's in my jail. I run this shit!" I understood this was a messed up situation, and still not knowing what the outcome was going to be, in my mind, I kept thinking the worst.

Chapter 12

The Boiler Room / Belly of the Beast

WHILE I WAS still trying to recover from Dunnigan's night stick attack, Bosco walked back into the office. Dunningan walked back behind his desk, sat down, and told Zurick, "Get this stupid motherfucker out of my office!" Zurick asked Dunningan, "What should I do with him, Captain?" Dunnigan said, "I don't give a fuck what you do with him!" With that, Zurick snatched me up and barked, "C'mon!"

As they led me down the hallway, I still didn't know the worst was yet to come. I kept hoping Tattoo had called my mother and that she was on her way to save me. Seventeen years old and in jail for murder and I was hoping Mama was coming to save me! I was clearly in need of a savior because I didn't know then that Dunnigan's last words to Zurick were giving him a license to take the liberty of doing something real stupid.

As we walked past the hallway that led toward the wing I was assigned to, I realized we were taking a detour and that they had some more bullshit up their sleeve. We walked up to an elevator, and when the door opened, I was shoved inside. The elevator descended to the boiler room. The door opened, and it was obvious we had gone to the basement. My mind sunk to a desperate level of desperation. I was in the basement of Division 6, and I knew I had no real business to be down there. It felt like I was in the belly of the beast! I wasn't given a chance to step out of the elevator because without any warning, Zurick pushed me out of the elevator; and because I was handcuffed, I almost lost my balance.

Zurick grabbed me by the arm and walked me a short distance away to a room that Zurick had keys to. When he opened the door, I could see that the room was dimly lit. With dark-gray-painted walls. Everything about this picture looked sinister. I knew I was all alone with two racist COs who had been given the green light on my life by an Uncle Tom captain. The only thing in the room were a couple of chairs and a table in the middle of the room. Above on the ceiling were these big exhaust pipes crisscrossed. There was a constant annoying humming sound coming from above that became very irritating and was not helping and only elevating my stress levels. All my senses were in hype overdrive. I could hear, see, and smell everything, and it all stood out. I was in high alert!

This shit was all wrong. I stiffened up and initially refused to move. My legs locked on me, and that was when Bosco kicked me. The force of the kick forced me across the threshold. I could see the intent in their eyes. With every minute, I was feeling condemned. Somehow, I found the strength to speak and said, "Man, what's up?" Bosco told me, "Shut the fuck up!" Zurick said in a calm voice, "Sit down!" He walked toward the back of the boiler room and faded into the darkness of the corner. When Zurick reemerged, I could see he was carrying something in both hands. In one hand, he was carrying a gallon plastic jug; and in the other hand, he had a wire hanger, a piece of paper, and a pen. I could see the jug read "FLAMMABLE" in bold letters on it. He put everything on the table in front of me.

At this point, I knew without a doubt what their intent was and why they brought me down into the basement of Division 6's boiler room. It was to take my life, to kill me! Through their actions, they had pronounced me guilty and condemned me to death. They were going to be my executioner by forcing me, under duress, to cover up their crime by an alleged suicide letter by my own hands. Zurick sat down across the table from me while Bosco stood behind me by the door. "This is how this is going to go," Zurick said. "You're going to write a letter to your mother telling her you can't cope!" Clearly, that was their plan, but my plan was to stay alive! I thought, *No matter what happens, do not writer that letter. Be strong, Billy. Be strong!* If I refused to write this letter, then they were just going to have to kill me by their own hands; but I knew if I broke down and wrote that letter, I knew without a doubt they were going to kill me by my hands.

I wasn't ready to die, and I wasn't going to allow fear to take my life! I realized in spite of how it looked, I still had a little control over how I could respond. It was a life and death situation, so I wasn't going to let them force me to do anything. I wasn't going to give them my life. They were going to have to take it. Apparently, their plan was the opposite of mine. For them, they wanted to instill so much fear in me that I would give in and let the worst thing happen to me. I'm not going to lie. I prayed to Yahweh to give me the strength that I needed to conquer my fear at that moment. I prayed for the strength of life to overcome the fear of death, and he granted me the strength I needed!

Zurick actually told me I wasn't walking out of that room alive and that I had no choice but to write that letter. I shut down. I didn't say a word. At one point, Bosco came up from behind me and put me in a choke hold. He seemed to be serious now as if his hate influenced his actions as the situation continued to play out. He became motivated by his hate for me. I questioned why they were so adamant about the way they were dealing with me. They didn't know me, and it was safe to assume they didn't know Benji. I could only come up with one thing: They had hate in their hearts for black men, and this sellout captain gave them an avenue to express it.

I couldn't do anything to resist putting up a struggle because I was handcuffed with my hands behind me, and I was seated, so the only thing I could do to protect myself against the hold he had around my neck was to try and press my chin down against his forearm so that I wouldn't get choked out. This lasted for a few minutes until Zurick told him to let me go. "Now you ready to write the letter?" I think I was in shock because I couldn't respond either way. My mind and body had locked up on me. Zurick told me that he was going to take the cuffs off me so I could start writing. I remember when he stood up, I heard a phone ring. The sound came from behind me. I saw Zurick nod to give his approval for Bosco to answer the phone. I could hear Bosco picking the phone up. This was a welcome relief. I had a minute to try and gather myself, if only for a moment. Every second was important to my life.

I looked up at Zurick as he walked past me to get the phone from Bosco. I heard him say, "Yeah, okay!" And then he hung up the phone. This was when he called me a nigga for the first time. "You're a lucky nigger!" he said. He went on to tell me that if I told anybody what had happened, he was going to make sure he finished what he started. After saying that, he snatched me up, and we walked out of the boiler room. Yahweh had answered my prayers! He helped me weather the storm, and contrary to what Zurick had promised me, I did walk out of that room alive!

As it turned out, Tattoo called my mother, and she answered! He had told my mother that the COs pulled me off the wing and that it didn't look good. He told them they should come to the jail immediately. They did, but before they left to come to the jail, they called my uncles Ralph and Lawrence because both of them worked in the county jail as COs, and they called a guy by the name of Reverend MacAfee. MacAfee was a special kind of guy. When Omar and I were arrested, the media posted our photos in the news and in the papers. That wasn't supposed to happen due to the fact that we were juveniles. Our addresses were also printed in the papers, and people took the liberty to start mailing letters to the house. A lot of them were death threats, but there were also letters of support and visits by people who wanted to help my family during that bad time. One of those people who came by the house to offer support was Reverend MacAfee.

From what my mother and granny told me about MacAfee, he was a guy who had come up hustling in the streets, a life that led him in and out of jail and prison for most of his life and then eventually found God and turned his life around and started living a life of service and advocacy. Due to his life experience in and out of the system, MacAfee knew people who were high ranking in the jail. So when my mother received that call from Tattoo, she immediately reached out to all of them. My uncle Lawrence was the same uncle who played in the Negro league, the Kansas City Monarchs. She told them what Tattoo told her over the phone. Apparently, my uncle and MacAfee reached out to someone at the jail, then my uncle rushed to work. The superintendent of the jail got involved. My uncle and MacAfee got the ball rolling over the phone, and my mother and granny, when they arrived at the jail, demanded to see me.

According to my mother, they were told that because it was not my visiting day, they couldn't see me but was ensured that I was all right. The superintendent came and met with my mother and granny and told them that MacAfee had called him and that whatever happened he would get to the bottom of it and make sure that nothing would happen like that again. I was told that my uncle wasn't allowed to see me either when he had gotten to work. I was taken to segregation and placed in a cell by myself. Clearly, I had no idea what was going on. I had no idea that my mother and granny were out there raising hell. I was unaware that my uncle, after being told he couldn't see me, went to go look for Zurick and that when he found him, Lawrence beat his ass right there where he found him in the jail! Of course my uncle was suspended for this.

After I was put in segregation and finally by myself, admittedly, I was shaking from everything that had just occurred. I was thinking how these people just tried to kill me! I didn't know what to expect next. I still didn't feel safe, and because I was in their jail, I felt like I had no way out. My mind just went blank while I got lost just staring at a spot on the wall inside this dark, gloomy cell with dull-painted cinder block walls coated with dirty tan paint with graffiti and gang signs etched all over them. The floor was concrete and cold. I tuned out the faint sounds of voices in the background coming from outside the cell from other people locked up in the hole. Suddenly, I heard a loud click of the cell door that grabbed my attention. The door came open, and immediately, my anxiety reemerged. I immediately jumped up, and without thinking, purely out of instinct, with my back against the back wall of that cell, I squared up in a defensive posture, ready to defend myself. I was in a hypervigilant state of mind.

It was Captain Dunnigan. He acted surprised when he saw me, so with both of his hands, he held them up in front of him as if to reassure me that I was safe. He said, "Young man, calm down. I want to apologize for how me and my officers treated you!" I was in disbelief and stunned at his demeanor and what he had just said. It was the opposite of how he had treated me earlier. At first, I thought it was a trick. I was looking around him for the cavalry to come rushing in behind him, but that wasn't the case. What he said next made me believe he still needed to save face in light of what he allowed to happen with a degree of arrogance that you only see in law enforcement: "Young man, you have to learn the rules, and when you break them, there's consequences!" He also added, "We may have overreacted, but there's only inmates in my jail, and when you are given a direct order, you have to comply!"

All this caught me off guard. I could see he was serious. "We may have overreacted"? They were all ready to kill me. That was more than overreacting! I did start to feel a small amount of relief. He told me that my mother and grandmother came out there, but because it wasn't my visiting day, they weren't allowed to see me. He said he told them to call out to the jail when they got home, and he promised he would let me call them back. About an hour later, the cell door was opened, and the officer in the interlock told me to come out. He walked me to the captain's office. At this point, this was not somewhere I felt safe going, but I had no choice, so I went without any hesitation uncuffed. Dunningan told me I could call home. He gave me five minutes.

I picked up the phone and dialed my mother's number. Dunnigan looked at me, and without saying it, his eyes told me I better not say shit about what they had done. I heard my mother's voice say, "Hello!" I said, "Hey, Ma. It's me." She started crying when she heard my voice. "Are you okay, baby?" she said. "Yes, Ma, I'm okay." She couldn't stop crying. I told her, "Ma, stop crying. I'm okay!" She told me she was coming to see me on my visiting day and that she loved me and to keep my head up. That was the extent of my conversation with my mother.

When I hung up the phone, Captain Dunnigan told me that he knew my uncle Lawrence and that because he worked in Division 6, I couldn't stay there and was going to be transferred to Division 1. He said that the captain in Division 1 was a guy named Sipes. I never saw my uncle while I was in Division 6, neither he nor my other uncle Ralph, who worked in Division 1 on the night shift. The next day, I was transferred to Division 1. When I got over there, I was taken straight to Captain Sipes's office. He told me I didn't have to worry about what happened to me in Division 6 happening in Division 1. He said, "Stay out of trouble. You're in enough trouble already!" Division 1 was a better place to be in if you had to be in the jail. It was considered the old jail because it was the oldest division of the jail. There were wings with young guys, but most of Division 1 housed older guys. From that day forward, I spent my entire time fighting my case in Division 1. I had a smoother bit, but I did have a couple of incidents in Division 1.

Chapter 13

Gladiator School

THE FIRST INCIDENT I had happened about four months after I got there to Division 1. It started over some stolen magazine that belonged to me. I got cool with this guy from the West Side named Goon Squad. Goon Squad stood around six feet, one inch. He had a big mouth and tried to act like he was a bully, but somehow, we got cool. We used to play this card game Casino every day. The way we got cool was, one day, he called himself trying to impress me by showing me a letter he got in the mail from some woman who had written to him. He didn't just show me the letter. He wanted me to read it. When I started reading it to myself, he asked me to read it out loud. I read the first few sentences out loud and then asked him what she was talking about in the letter. He asked me to keep reading it, and this was when I realized Goon Squad couldn't read!

At first, I let him act like he just wanted me to see what she wrote. I didn't want to embarrass him. After him doing this a few more times, without doing it in an embarrassing way, I asked Goon Squad if he wanted me to help him learn how to read! At first, he tried to front like he could read and didn't need my help, but I told him he didn't have to front, that I would help him. His reading was very sketchy, and I told him all he had to do was start reading more and more, and I would help him learn to pronounce the words by reading with him. I was seventeen years old. I didn't have the skills to teach anybody how to read, but I did remember how I was taught. So I told him the first book we were going to read was *The Autobiography of Malcolm X* by Alex Haley, the first real book I had read in jail that wasn't a Donald Goines or an Iceberg Slim book.

Malcolm's story personally touched me—his upbringing as a kid and the trauma of being harassed by the KKK and his father being killed by them, his attraction to hustling and street life and his transformation from it, his intelligence and love for his people, his dedication to his religion and his spiritual growth and, eventually, acceptance of all mankind, his unswerving loyalty and integrity in the face of betrayal. I was inspired by Malcolm's life. So if I was going to help to elevate someone and educate them, what could be better than to use *The Autobiography of Malcolm X*? I was just going to teach him to read and let Malcolm education him! Looking back, I now understand the reason why Goon Squad was a bully. It was because he couldn't read. It was his way of intimidation to overcompensate for his illiteracy. But I knew his secret, so he couldn't use it on me. Plus, I was not going for being bullied anyway!

We were about three chapters into *Malcom X*. I had a collection of *Jet* magazines, and I would set them in the bars that were in the back of my cell. I looked and realized some of my *Jet* magazines were missing. Stealing in jail was a big no-no! That could cause a major problem on the wing. Whoever got caught stealing was going to get hurt no questions asked. I made an announcement that I had some missing magazines, so basically, it was time for a shakedown but not by the COs, who were not told what was happening. Goon Squad was playing the role like if whoever was caught with my magazines was going to get fucked up. He had his bully suit on. After looking in everybody's cell, this dude named Boo came in my cell where Goon Squad and I were at. Boo told Goon Squad, "Nigga, you the thief!" Boo took the magazines out of his back pocket and threw them in Goon Squad's face! I blanked out. I jumped up and immediately started punching him in the face until he fell on the bunk. I was on top of him, still punching him, and now he was yelling out. Boo grabbed me off him and then started kicking Goon Squad.

Because he was making so much noise yelling and screaming, I heard the CO open the bars to the catwalk and started walking toward the cells. I grabbed Boo, and we walked out of my cell and went to the dayroom and sat down. Goon Squad came out bleeding from his face and yelling to the CO that we, all the GDs, had just jumped him. I immediately stepped up and said that wasn't true. I didn't give up Boo, but I said it was just me and that honestly by the time Boo got in, I had beaten Goon Squad up. Boo just wanted to get in on it. I didn't want anybody else getting in trouble. They were my magazines. Goon Squad had stolen from me.

More COs ran up on the wing, and Goon Squad kept saying we had jumped him. I told them it was only me and that if they didn't believe it, they could let us go in the pump room—this was a room on the main floor—and I would whoop his ass again! Of course they weren't going to allow that. After they handcuffed everybody, Goon Squad ended up telling on me and Boo. I was put in seg for fifteen days. Although Division 1 wasn't as hostile as Division 6, this was still jail, and there was constant tension. It was a hostile and volatile environment, and at any moment, something like this could happen. Everybody in there was under extreme amounts of stress. Everybody in there was fighting for their freedom or hoping not to lose too much time out of their lives. There were a lot of hair-trigger attitudes in there walking around ready to let loose on somebody at any moment.

One of the outlets we used to unpack some of the stress that came with being incarcerated was going to gladiator school. This was something younger guys participated in. It was a way of looking to prove their heart in front of one another by challenging one other in a friendly bout of body punching. It came from the same spirit of bravado that motivated slapboxing matches. Those matches would never get carried away or turn serious because usually it was among guys who were cool with one another and who would spare in these matches.

Maybe eight months into my time in the jail, I started to notice this CO named Officer Bills, who occasionally worked on the wing I was on and who watched me every time he came to work the wing.

I could be watching TV or playing cards, and I would turn around and notice Bills watching me.

This one particular day when Bills was working on the wing, he decided to speak to me for the first time. He called me to the front of the wing where he was standing on the other side of the bars in the officer station. The bars separated the staff from the men on the wing. He said, "Mr. Moore, how are you handling this shit?" I can't remember how I responded, but what he said next really didn't surprise me, but it was still unexpected. He said, "Man, I know you've noticed me watching you!" He went on to say, "Honestly, I don't see the person the media is making you out to be!" He also said, "But I knew Benji, and unfortunately, I wasn't surprised when this happened!" He told me he was an assistant football coach at Simeon. He said, "We all tried to talk to that kid, but he didn't listen!" He said he hated to see me caught up in this situation and really hated to see what happened to Benji! He wished me luck. It was more of a rhetorical statement because we both knew I didn't have a chance in hell, but in the spirit of just being positive, he wished me luck. After that, every time Bills saw me, he would speak to me and ask how I was doing.

After that situation with Goon Squad, I managed to not get into more trouble, so I asked the sergeant if I could have an assignment so I could move around and have a little freedom in the jail. I was given a job to clean the well. The well was the stairwell that led to all the wings in the division. I was on F4. Each well had four wings, and in Division 1 I believed there were eight wells—A well, B well, C well, D well, E well, F well, G well, and H well. F well had F1, F2, F3, and F4. I would sweep and mop the well every day, and because of my movement, I was able to communicate with everybody in F well. It gave me some jail freedom. I didn't cause a lot of problems in the jail, and the attitudes of most of the COs I encountered who got to know me, they started treating me differently like CO Bills and like they did when I first got in there.

One day, I had court. When I got to the courthouse, I saw the bailiff, the little old lady whom I saw when Omar and I were first arrested, the same bailiff who told us she hoped I got the death penalty and that she would be the one to pull the switch. Because of that, I wasn't looking forward to seeing her and tried to do everything I could not to be seen by her. I wasn't in the mood to hear her judge me and condemn me again, but as much as I tried to not be noticed by her, I wasn't successful, and she saw me. I just braced myself for her to say something negative or, at best, look at me crazy. Well, she threw me a curveball I wasn't expecting because I didn't expect anything less from her than what she showed me the first time I saw her. Her energy was different toward me. It was positive and pleasant.

I admit, she messed me up in the head when she said, "Hey, baby, how are you doing?" Still, in spite of her politeness, I questioned if she was really talking to me, and I paused to respond to her, and I guess I had that look on my face as if to say, "You talking to me?" She said "How are you doing today?" with a smile on her face. I said, "I'm all right!" She returned with, "Okay, baby. Good luck today in court!" Wow, I didn't see that coming, but I received it in the spirit in which she gave it to me. It's funny, but I walked away feeling her grandmother's vibe, not a correctional officer. My experience in the jail was still a major adjustment, but as time went on, it wasn't made worse by the staff. I didn't have any more conflicts. I kept my nose clean and stayed out of trouble.

Chapter 14

My Day in Court

MY TRIAL WENT fast. It only lasted four days after my jury was picked. I remember my twelve peers being middle-aged and border-line elderly people—oh, and mostly white. I believe there was one black man and an alternate black woman. There was no talk of any plea deal, and after an hour of deliberation, at the end of the four-day trail, we were found guilty. I had already known a conviction was inevitable. Every day, I had a court appearance leading up to the trial, and the news reported on it. I knew that I had to pay the price for what I did. I knew a whole lot of people would say that Benji wasn't given due process the way he died if I made the case that my due process was violated, but the way the legal system was set up, there was no equity in how justice was applied to black and brown people coming from underserved and neglected communities.

The system cared for Benji just as much as they showed how they cared for me and Omar. Benji was shot at 12:37 p.m. He didn't make it to the hospital until 1:20 p.m. and didn't go into surgery until 3:14 p.m. It appeared there was no urgency to save his life. On top of the fact it took him so long to get to a hospital and into surgery, he was sent to St. Bernard Hospital. St. Bernard's was not a trauma center and, thus, didn't have a trauma surgeon on staff. They had to wait for one. Benji lost a lot of blood waiting. So the point

I'm making is that however we end up in the system or find ourselves depending on it, there's not much value put on our lives.

The first day of court after the jury was picked, when I got back to the wing, the TV in the dayroom was on one of the news channels. I heard some reporter summing up my day in court and said, "If Billy Moore and Omar Dixon are convicted, they could both be sentenced up to seventy years in prison!" Everybody in the dayroom who heard what the reporter had said got quiet. I could feel my heartbeat speeding up after hearing that. I almost lost it. I felt a panic attack about to take over me, and I struggled to keep it together, but I would be lying if I didn't say I saw my life flash before me. I had to talk to somebody, but not just anybody. I had to hear my mother's voice.

I looked at the phone. Somebody was on it. I walked up to the guy on the phone and asked if anybody was next. As I waited for my time to get on the phone, I kept hearing the words of that reporter in my head, and they wouldn't let my mind settle down. I started thinking I was never going to get out. I believed I was going to spend the rest of my life in prison. Finally, it was my turn for the phone. I called my mother. She answered and accepted the call. I would try my best to not let my mother know when we talked that I wasn't in the right state of mind, but on that call, I knew she could hear the panic in my voice. I had lost control over how to pronounce my words clearly without speaking with a slight stutter of panic in my voice. I needed to hear her voice to calm me down.

I told her what I had just heard. She saw the news too and had the same reaction, but she told me not to worry because I wasn't going to get seventy years. She said she had called Skip Gant, my lawyer, and told him what she saw. Skip explained to her that if I were convicted of all counts, murder carried the maximum of forty years, which was a class M. The attempted arm robbery, which was a class X, carried the maximum of thirty years. If I got the maximum time on both counts, forty and thirty, then technically it was seventy years; but since I couldn't be sentenced consecutively, the thirty years would concurrently go into the forty years and not be added on or stacked on top of it. But this was just another example of how the media sensationalized the story. So the most I could get was the forty years, and that was how much I would eventually be sentenced to. Hearing my mother explain to me what Skip had explained to her helped me get past the panic I had felt from hearing what was said on the news.

I think it was the second day of trial. I remember looking into the crowd of the packed courtroom. I could see Ben Wilson Sr. actually sitting next to my mother and grandmother. Later that evening, when I called home, my mother told me that the arrogant Christopher Darden-type (the black prosecutor of O.J. Simpson) assistant state's attorney Art Hill, the token black prosecutor, tried to coax Mr. Wilson to sit on the other side of the courtroom far away from my family. My mother said he refused to move. Even despite Hill's repeated insistence, he didn't! She said he told Hill that he was fine where he was sitting at. I couldn't really explain it, and despite why we were there, my heart went out to Mr. Wilson. I couldn't help but to feel sorry and bad for the crime I had committed against him and his family. For him to refuse to leave my family's side made my mother and grandmother feel even more sympathy for him and his family.

October 10, 1985, almost eleven months after the confrontation between me and Benji, was the day the jury went into deliberation. I knew in my heart going into the trial that I wasn't going to be convicted and possibly sentenced to the maximum amount of time. The jury didn't need to hear Sean Bayless's lie about what he claimed he saw from inside the store. I did feel like during the cross-examination of Benji's girlfriend that it came out that Benji provoked the incident, but that wasn't going to make a difference. My only witness, Kim Smith, got amnesia and didn't tell the whole story of what she told my lawyer when he first spoke to her. I came to later find out that her mother was dating a Chicago police officer, and he didn't want her speaking in our behalf. With all that was said or not said, I knew I still had to pay for Benji's death. The one thing that I felt real bad about in the end, besides Benji's death, was that Omar got caught up in this.

Like I said, it only took the jury about an hour to find us guilty. Honestly, after the verdict was given, I felt a sense of relief. Up until then, everything was so undecided and chaotic for me, but now I knew that it was over, and I was ready to leave the county jail. When the jury's verdict was read, I looked over and saw Omar put his head down. I reached over to tap him on his arm, and I whispered, "Hold your head up, O!" I knew no matter what, we had to be strong and face this situation head-on. So he did. Shortly after that, we were led out of the courtroom and put in two separate bullpens next to each other in the back of the courtroom. Those bullpens behind the courtrooms always reminded me of zoo cages—dark brown and dimly lit, steel walls with bars in the front with a narrow walkway on the other side and maybe the size of two bathrooms combined.

Omar was still coming to court from the juvenile detention center because he was only sixteen at this time. There were no conversations, nothing to talk about. The reality was that our young lives seemed to be over. I don't think I fully understood the entirety and scope of my current situation. I think I had made up my mind that my life was not meant to ever be an easy one. I just lay back on the cold, hard steel bench and just kept hearing the word *guilty* repeatedly in my head.

The silence was broken when people came to transport Omar back to the auddie home. I listened to the steel chains and handcuffs being used to restrain my brother, and when he walked past, we looked at each other in the eyes and just nodded. What we were feeling was understood among ourselves, but it didn't need to be explained. It was a loss for everyone involved—me, Omar, and more importantly, Benji!

After the guilty verdict, we returned to court about a month later for sentencing. We were brought back in front of Judge Bailey. For the first time in ten months, Judge Bailey looked at me and Omar and asked if we had anything to say before he pronounced his sentence. I said, "Yes!" I turned to face the Wilson family and said, "I want to apologize for what I had done. This was not my intention!" After that, Judge Bailey said to me and Omar, "No matter how much time I sentence you two individuals, you both will still be young men when you get out!" He went on to say, "I have no sympathy for you! William Moore, I sentence you to forty years for first-degree murder and ten years for attempted arm robbery in the Illinois Department of Correction with three years of mandatory supervisor release. Both sentences to run concurrent!" He sentenced Omar to thirty years for murder and ten years for attempted arm robbery to run concurrently. Bailey sentenced me to the maximum amount of time I could receive under the law.

When I heard him say it, it was hard to conceptualize the end zone of a twenty-year sentence as a seventeen-year-old kid. People that age didn't look past their tomorrows, and there I was trying to see twenty years down the road! So many young people that age unfortunately are living without hope of the future. They don't think they will live past twenty-one, so twenty years seems impossible to do. The sentencing guidelines at the time in Illinois was determined sentencing, which meant that the time someone would be sentenced didn't provide an early release or parole before the sentence was completed. Whatever time you received, you did it day for day, which also meant that for every day served in prison, one day was taken off your time. So basically, 50 percent of the time was done if you didn't mess up and lose any time. So basically, I had to do twenty years in the joint!

Twenty years still made me think I was going to get out during a Buck Rogers era. I literally thought there would be flying cars and "Beam me up, Scotty" devices people would be operating when I came home after doing twenty years. I knew the world would advance without me. The other thought that was in the back of my mind was if I was even going to live through it to make it. Also, I was hoping the people I loved the most would still be around if I made it.

Chapter 15

This House Is Not My Home

A FEW WEEKS later, I was transferred to Joliet, the penitentiary. Joliet was where you were sent to be classified and determined what security level you would have and also what prison you would be sent to because Joliet was basically a holding, classification, and transfer prison. You would spend around four weeks in Joliet before it was determined to what prison you would be sent to do your time. Once again, this, too, was a long process, an all day long tedious one. By the time I ended up getting to the cell, it had to be at least eight hours later. It really didn't feel no different for me than the process I went through in the county jail.

There were three prisons I was classified for—Stateville, Pontiac, and Menard. All three were the maximum prisons in Illinois. Depending on who you asked, each one of them was considered the most dangerous prison in Illinois! I was hoping to be sent to Stateville because it was also by Joliet and, out of the three, was the closest to Chicago. Mostly, all the real leadership of street organizations was there. It was a better place to do time if time had to be done. The one prison I didn't want to be transferred to was Menard. This prison was the farthest from Chicago, about seven hours away, and the most overtly racist prison in Illinois, both from staff and prisoners. The North Siders had a prominent presence there. They were a racist white gang.

To digress here, the time I was being processed in through the Illinois penal system was the same time the Chicago Bears was having its best season ever, the '85 Bears! While in the county jail, I watched every game the Bears played. The one game I missed was when I was transferred to Joliet and was there that Monday night game against the Miami Dolphins. Because I didn't have access to watch a TV, I missed the only game that resulted in the defeat the Bears suffered that year. I was able to watch them win the Super Bowl.

After being in Joliet for about a month, I was wakened up at about 4:00 a.m. one morning by a CO shouting out, "Moore, you going to Pontiac. Get ready!" I didn't want to go to Pontiac either, but I preferred Pontiac over Menard. Pontiac had a reputation of being a prison where staff was regularly known for being assaulted. COs were getting stabbed and jumped all the time down there. Depending on who was there doing time, the politics of prison and the power struggles were always being manipulated. That was what made Pontiac one of the most dangerous prisons in the country at the time.

Pontiac had a violent legacy. This was the same prison in 1978 where a riot happened where three white prison guards were killed. Seventeen young black men who were considered all high-ranking gang chiefs who were from various organizations were placed on trial for the murder of these prison guards. I've met a few of these brothers, for whom I have a tremendous amount of respect: Benny Lee, Omega Jackson, and Larry Hoover. The seventeen came to be known as the Pontiac Seventeen, but they called themselves the original Brothers of the Struggle. These men went to trial and were eventually acquitted on all charges. Some of these brothers had passed on. Those who were alive, most of them were now free, except for Mr. Larry Hoover, whom I would eventually meet when I was eighteen years old.

Pontiac-bound, I was nervous as hell and, to be totally honest, scared! I believe everyone who has ever been to prison for the first time is lying if they tell you they were not scared! This is true for the bravest, hardest, and toughest cat! The fear is in the unknown. *Fear* and *the unknown* are usually synonymous with each other. It's a natural feeling. What separates people is how well they can manage their fear and overcome it, or not!

Riding shackled on that bus to Pontiac was very uncomfortable, both physically and mentally, but as uncomfortable as that ride was, I didn't want it to end. I was not in a rush to get to the destination. I didn't want to see it. If I could, I would have done the next twenty years of my life on that bus ride rather than a Pontiac prison cell that I knew I would soon be occupying. What was strange to me was, Pontiac wasn't in some desolate and isolated cornfield or situated in no-man's-land. It was in the middle of a neighborhood, suburban white USA. I saw houses, parks, and American flags proudly waving in the wind. I got the feeling as we made our way through the town that the only place for black people here was where I was headed, the local prison. Of course we were not allowed to come out and mingle. I don't know what slavery was like, but the feeling I felt had to be comparable to that of a slave on his way to the plantation!

Pulling up to the sally port and looking at the back wall of this place, everything about this prison looked old and dim. I instantly started feeling a heightened state of depression. The energy of this prison was ominous! I felt the depressed souls speaking to my spirits that seemed to escape when those large gates rode back to welcome me into the residence hell the state of Illinois was landlord over! The energy of the depressed spirits entrapped by this old prison welcomed us to join them and take our place among the company of the misery. It wasn't lost on me that Pontiac prison wasn't completely surrounded by a wall, but nevertheless, the security was of maximum proportion.

Once on the other side of the gates, I listened to the eerie sound of them closing behind the bus, which sounded like a vault locking me in on the other side of freedom. We were immediately taken off the bus and led to the B of I, Burial of Identification. I had my picture taken for a prison ID I was always ordered to wear. In every prison, the process of entering the system is a long one. Next, we were taken to the clothing room and given that state blue uniform, were issued a pair of hard-ass state boots, freshly washed but used sheets, and a pillowcase. But you were lucky if a pillow was in the cell you went in.

The receiving unit was in the captain's office at this time in Pontiac. That was where the fish line (the fish line refers to the people coming in on the new) were taken before being assigned to what cell house they were going to go to. This was December 1985. Pontiac was on lockdown when I got there. The reason for the lockdown was because a guard was stabbed numerous times in the west house.

In receiving, I was put in a cell right next door to this dude named Brian Dugan. He was this white dude who had raped and killed several women in the Western suburbs and would eventually confess to raping and killing Jeanine Nicarico, a young girl that the state of Illinois had convicted initially Rolando Cruz and two other men who were charged and sentenced to death for.

I stayed in receiving for two weeks before being released to general population. I was sent to the upper south house eight gallery, the school gallery. When I walked through the doors of the south house, I said to myself, "Nigga, you made it to the Big House. Not good!" Fuck! The joint was still on lockdown. The inside was painted battleship gray as if I needed anything else to add to my depressive state of mind. This damn place looked miserable! When I was told I was going on eight gallery, cell 845, the CO said the cell assignment was temporary. When I got up to eight gallery and looked down the gallery, it looked like a city-long block. Once again, the familiar sounds of an incarcerated environment. I could hear music blaring, the sounds of TVs in the background, indistinct conversations, and toilets flushing. Then as we entered and made our way down the gallery, people started yelling out, "On the new! The fish line on the gallery!"

Now at this point, you are on display because everybody in the cells are standing at their bars looking to see who's coming through; and at the same time, you are looking too to see who you might know. "What's up, shawty? All's Well!" came from the dude in the first cell we walked past, and standing next to him was his celly, who hit his chest with a clenched fist, which clearly communicated to me

they were BlackStones. I responded by saying, "What's up, but naw!"
"Oh, okay. My bad, shawty!" he said.

As we covered particularly the whole gallery, every cell we walked past, everyone in there was at the bars on point, wanting to see who was on the new. Eventually, I walked past a cell when a dude by the name of Rick Dog said, "You Folks, lil bruh?" I said, "Yeah!" He said, "GD?" I said yes with all the confidence in the world even though I was still feeling this nervous energy inside me. He said, "Aight! Hey, Sarchet, what cell are you putting him in?" Rick Dog asked the CO. "845!" Officer Sarchet said. He said I was only going to be in there while the joint was still on lockdown, and once we came off, I would be moved in a cell according to my affiliation.

That became a mute issue because the dude who was already in 845 was Folks. He was a brother who was no more than a year or two older than me, and his name was Mike. Mike was an SD (Satan Disciple), which was a branch of the Folks that was predominately Hispanic, and although Mike was a black dude, he was affiliated with SD's organization because of where he grew up at around Hispanics on the West Side of Chicago by Douglas Park. Mike was a quiet dude but real cool. As it turned out, I knew his cousin from the county jail, a dude I was on the wing in Division 1 with. His name was Whimp. He was an SD too. Whimp and I became cool, and unlike quiet Mike, Whimp was outspoken and funny! All he did was joke on people.

When I walked into the cell, I noticed Mike didn't have shit, no TV or a radio. He was in the dark, so I knew it was going to be a long lockdown staring at the walls. I had a few books that I had brought with me from the county jail, so I started reading one. It was some bullshit urban novel, but it helped me focus on something besides the long hours of nothingness I had to contend with. Two weeks later, the cell doors rolled one morning, and the lockdown was over. After a prison comes off lockdown, there were always new faces that popped up and some that disappeared. This was my introduction to Pontiac Correctional Center on December 1985!

One thing for certain in prison, you are going to know some-body there. As people started recirculating and moving around after a long lockdown, I started seeing people I knew from the streets and people I had met in the auddie home and the county jail. I was only a few cells down from my boy who became a lifelong friend, Shorty G, who was Rick Dog's celly, and three cells down from them, a dude I knew and is still cool with until this day by the of name Zoe. The way the gallery was situated, everyone according to their affiliation was in cells within proximity of one another, so I would say we had about the last third of the cells going to the end of the gallery.

Although Pontiac was a blur for me because I was only there for about eight months, there were a few eventful things that I remember happening during my time in Pontiac. One was the '85 Bears winning the Super Bowl, undoubtedly the greatest defensive team I'd ever seen play. January '86 and two days later, the space shuttle Challenger exploded soon after takeoff. The day this happened, I was standing with my back against the railing on eight gallery talking to Rick Dog and Shorty G in front of their cell. The bars in front of the cell was open, and I could see the TV in the back of the cell. I wasn't really paying attention, but the TV caught my eye. The TV happened to be on the channel that was broadcasting the takeoff. All of a sudden, I saw the flicker of fire under the rocket booster, then before my eyes, I just saw the shuttle explode. I couldn't believe my eyes! It took me a minute to realize what I had just witnessed. As the boosters spiraled out of control and the plume and fire engulfed that doomed vessel with human lives aboard turned into a smoke ball, it left me in a stunned state of mind after witnessing this tragedy.

Besides that, Pontiac was nothing special. I did meet some good brothers in the Yack, the nickname for Pontiac, who had become lifelong friends, brothers like Big T, Blood, T Bone, Cat Daddy, Ace, Zoe, Cocaine, Spade, Shorty Ruff, Forty-Third, Jodie Mack, Red Cloud, Cap, T21, G Brown, and at least a dozen others dudes whom I became cool with.

In the spring of 1986, this black guy by the name of R. Taylor came to Pontiac as the superintendent of the upper south house. Although he worked in the system, he seemed like a fair man. One day, he came to the yard to speak to the guys about their concerns as it related to the conditions of the prison and how the treatment of the mostly white staff was playing out. I didn't believe anything was going to change. I questioned his leadership as a black man working with a predominately white and prejudiced staff. That was one of the reasons why I wanted to leave Pontiac and didn't think anything would change when he came on the yard to talk with the guys.

I did get a chance to speak with him. I asked him if he could help me get a transfer to Stateville. He told me if I didn't catch any tickets in three months to come see if he would keep his word but that first, I had to keep, and he would put me in for a transfer with his recommendation. I wanted to see if he was a man of his word because despite my doubts in believing nothing was going to change mine, he seemed sincere. All I had to do now was not catch any tickets. Three months went by, and I didn't catch a ticket. I went and asked Taylor if he can now put in for my transfer. He told me to submit it. I did, and within weeks, I heard back from Springfield, Illinois, the capital, that my transfer had been approved. I was just waiting on bed space.

Chapter 16

The Castle

I WAS EIGHTEEN years old. It was July 8, 1986, and I had been transferred to Stateville, the Castle, a nickname given because of the leadership that was there from various street organizations that were doing time. The cell houses at Stateville were unique by design. It was the only prison of its kind in the country that had round houses. By the time I had gotten there, there were only two round houses still standing, E House and F House; but originally, there were four, C House and D House, which had been demolished by the time I had gotten there.

Stateville was far more stable because there wasn't much prison politics being played out because of the individuals who were doing time. Real leadership! So it was a better place to do time. Don't get me wrong, it was still a prison with a dangerous environment and with deadly consequences. For example, within the six years while I was there, fifteen people got killed, and three of them were staff. As stable as Stateville was, it could turn deadly without notice in a second.

I stayed in receiving for about a week before I was sent to F House, three gallery, cell 353. When I walked through the tunnel that led to F House, it was a strangely quiet place. The light in the tunnel came from the sunlight shining through the brick glass that lined the tunnel walls. As I stepped inside F House, the only way I could describe it was that this shit really looked like the Big House—these circular galleries stacked on top of one another, four high with protected railing that was only about four feet high with four rails each. The cell house had a very high ceiling arching toward the center. I noticed that the ceiling was riddled with dents and chipped paint from years of warning shots being fired into it as if the ceiling was used for target practice. In the middle of the flag, the main floor of the cell house was a gun tower with a 360-degree panoramic view with no obstructions that was about thirty foot high with an armed CO constantly prowling within with a watchful eye.

Most of the recognized leaders were in E House and probably the heavy of the heavies. One man in particular, Mr. Larry Hoover, the Chairman, was in E House. Honestly, I was anxious to meet him because up until this point, he was only a name to me, and his name made him more like a folklore rather than an actual person, especially since I had never met him in person. I know for young black men growing up in the streets of Chicago, if you had the oxymoronic fortune of meeting Larry, it most likely came by the unfortunate circumstances of your incarceration. I can honestly say, after getting to know Larry, from what I came to know of him, it didn't please him to see so many young black men come to prison that he ended up meeting and becoming a mentor to.

As I mentioned earlier, my lawyer Skip Gant had represented Larry on the Pontiac Seventeen trial; and when I came to Stateville, Skip reached out to Larry about me. So within days of me going to general population, someone came to F House and told one of the guys to go get me. I wasn't expecting to be sent for, so I didn't know why somebody was asking me to come to the door of the cell house. I didn't know what to think, but I was curious to know who it was and what they wanted. I came to the front door of F House and saw a guy about six feet tall and muscular and who looked tough. He spoke with a Chicago tone and said, "You Lil Moe?" I said, "Yeah!" He looked at the CO working the F House door and said, "Chief wanna see him!" When the CO opened the door without any questions asked and followed his orders, there was hesitation and a surprised look on my face. The CO immediately picked up on it, and he nodded at me to let me know it was okay to go. I knew the influence was real, so after I saw the CO wasn't refusing his orders, the brother waiting for me looked at me and said, "C'mon." So just like the CO, I did what I was told and followed behind him.

As we walked toward E House, he said, "Lil bruh, chief want to see you! Damn, lil bruh, you got that case on old boy, huh?" I said, "Yeah, man!" He said with a handshake, "My name is T Vski! You gon be good." T Vski turned out to be a guy who became a lifelong friend of mine. Just as the CO working the door in F House followed orders to let me leave the cell house, so did the CO working on the door in E House when T Vski told him, "Let me in. Chief want to see him!" Once again, without any question, he pulled out those big-ass prison keys and unlocked the door to the Castle.

When I stepped foot inside E House, I saw that it looked ancient and outdated. Unlike F House that had apparently been renovated, E House was old and decayed. It looked condemned. It looked as if it hadn't been touched since the day it was built. The paint was gray, spotted, peeling, and patchy. The cell house looked like an abandon building with people living in it. The railing around the galleries was only three rails high unlike the rails in F House that was four rails high on each gallery. In E House, if someone wanted to toss somebody over the gallery, it was easier to do so since the gallery railing wasn't as high as it was in F House; but in all the years I was there, that never happened, but I'm sure during the history of Stateville, it had happened more than once.

As I walked around one gallery, the environment was as normal as any prison environment could be; and just like every other prison or cell house I had been in, there were the same familiar sounds of music, background chatter, cell doors opening and closing, and the occasional yelling of people trying to get other people's attention. It was a little overwhelming, which had me in a slight state of awe because of the decrypted ascetics of this legendary ancient cell house, the Castle, E House!

Among the annals of prison cell houses, E House had its own reputation throughout the prison world in the state of Illinois. It was never lost on me that I was in E House to meet and check in with the one person whose name was just as renowned in the streets of Chicago as that of Harold Washington, Al Capone, or even Oprah. My awe was only usurped when, unexpectedly, I looked up and saw Larry standing right in front of cell 128, which was maybe about a hundred feet away, talking to two other dudes.

As I approached Larry, wondering what I would say, the picture contradicted this image I had always had in my head of him holding court in some way or another. All he was doing was just standing there engaged in a casual conversation like a regular dude.

T Vski said, "What's up, Chief? This shorty!" Larry said in his Southern country accent, "They call you Lil Moe, right?" I said, "Yeah, Chief, or Billy Moe!" He said, "Listen, you gon be all right. Keep your head up, and don't get caught up fucking around with knuckleheads!" He asked me, "How old are you?" I said, "Eighteen!" He said, "Okay. You going to school!" He looked at T Vski and said, "Make sure he gets in school!" I was thinking, *Damn. I'm just meeting him, and within five minutes, Larry Hoover is giving me orders!* He said, "I don't care what you did to get here, but while you here, I need you to be doing something positive. You young niggas ain't gon be wasting time doing nothing counterproductive. It's enough dumbass niggas around here. You ain't gon be one of them. You gon go to school and get your GED!" I said, "Okay, Chief!" He asked me, "You need anything?" I said, "Naw, I'm cool, Chief!" He said, "Okay, cool!"

He stuck his hand out, and we shook hands. He nodded toward T Vski and told him he could take me back to F House. This honestly was a surreal moment. There're people out there who will say things about Larry that may be very negative, and there are a lot of people who will express nothing but love for him. I have nothing but love for that brother. But one thing everyone will agree on about this man is, he is a true leader. I took my marching orders seriously when he told me to be positive, go to school, get my GED, and to not be a dumbass nigga. That was what I did.

Eventually, I got a job with the help of a guy named Fletcher. Fletcher and I got cool when I first got to Stateville. Fletcher was in

F House with me. He was on the paint crew and got me a job painting with him. With this ability, I had the chance to move around the prison. I really didn't want to paint, so I asked Captain Morgan to help me get a job. Captain Morgan was actually Tamara's stepfather, my high school sweetheart. When I got to Stateville, Captain Morgan saw me and called me out of the line. He said, "Billy, damn, man. I hate to see you in here. I would rather see you out there with Tamara than with the guy she's with now!" He also said, "If you need anything, just let me know, within reason, son!" Morgan in that one conversation said more to me than he had ever said to me when he used to see me almost every day when I was coming to his house to see his daughter. He showed me nothing but love and respect while I was there and made sure things like my visits were never interrupted. I'd seen Morgan since being in Stateville, and even those times, he referred to me as his son.

When I got tired of being a painter, I asked Captain Morgan if he could help me get a job working outside the cell house. He was with this lieutenant named Rodriguez. He asked Lieutenant Rodriguez if he had something I could do. Lieutenant Rodriguez ran the tunnel crew on the first shift, so he put me on the tunnel crew. Rodriguez was a shit-talking jokester, so he was easygoing. I liked working for Rodriguez. If you did your job and joked with him, he didn't fuck with you.

I didn't forget what Larry told me I needed to do, so one day, I was talking to one of the guys named Starsky about getting my GED and told him I was going to put a request in to go take the test. He said, "If you go, I'mma go too!" At that time in prison, if you wanted to get your GED, you could go take the pretest; and if you scored high enough, you could take the GED test without enrolling in the GED class. But if your scores were too low, then you would be put in school until your scores came up.

I had the pretest workbook, and I remember studying it over a lockdown. When we came off lockdown, Starsky and I put our request slips in to go take the test. We were called over to the school building, took the pretest, and scored high enough for us not to have to be placed in school. We had a year to take the GED after scoring the necessary score on the pretest. We went the following week to take the test. We both passed. One of the greatest feelings I'd ever felt was when I passed my GED test. All I had to do next was take the Constitution test, both the state and federal. I messed around for almost a year for various reasons—lockdowns, procrastinations, and idle monotony—before I went and eventually took the Constitution tests. Within weeks, my diploma was mailed to me. I made a copy of it and sent it home to my mother. This was the first real accomplishment in my life academically.

When I was in grammar school, for whatever reason, I didn't apply myself. When it was time for me to graduate from eighth grade, I hadn't done well enough to do so. I was held back when all my other eight grade classmates had transitioned on to high school. This was an embarrassing time of my life. When school started the next year, my supposed freshman year, I was back at Foster Park grammar school. I was still in the eighth grade, feeling embarrassed and depressed. Maybe two weeks into the new school year, the principle came to my classroom and called me out. I was told that Hubbard High School had accepted me and that I was being passed on. It made me feel good that I was a high school student. I promised myself that I was going to do the best I could in high school. I knew I wasn't stupid or dumb. I knew I was intelligent. I just needed to apply myself. I spent only half of the year at Hubbard before I convinced my mother and grandmother to transfer me to Calumet High School because I had friends and family going there.

Larry made sure that if anybody got diplomas, whether it was a GED or a college degree or any vocational certificate, he would look out for them. When Starsky and I got our GED, we got certificates of recognition for our accomplishment. I got some money but not sure what Starsky got. I was given the equivalent of a hundred dollars and an Outstanding Membership certificate signed by Larry. I was beaming with joy and confidence! I was so proud of myself because I had an equivalent of a high school diploma. I have always felt that anyone who spent enough time in prison, if they didn't have a high school diploma when they came to prison had to get at least a GED before they were released! No one should never finish doing theirs without getting at least that! If not, that was wasted time! So after I had my GED, I decided to take a few college courses and earned some college credits, but I wasn't able to sustain any momentum due to the prison always going on lockdown. But I did earn some credits, and I promised myself that whenever I got transferred to a medium-security prison, I would go to school until I graduated with a college degree. That was actually what I did, but that wouldn't happen until almost six years later. As I was doing my time in Stateville, I started adjusting to doing time every day.

Chapter 17

The Sweet Science

I WANTED TO take advantage of any perks that was available there. Because I was very young and athletic, I tried out for the traveling twelve-inch softball team and the boxing team. I made both. This was how I made the boxing team. In prison, boxing was a sport that was very popular. One of the brothers I looked up to at the time was a dude named Boston. He had just come back to Stateville after spending a year on the circuit in segregation. The circuit was a way to punish people through intense isolation for disciplinary reasons by sending individuals to multiple prison segregations units. IDOC's administration would place individuals on the circuit if they considered them extremely hostile, dangerous, and influential. Anyone on the circuit would be transferred every thirty to sixty days to different prisons, one after another, for at least a year. Doing all that time in segregation, it was a severe form of punishment.

Boston was just coming off the circuit. He was one of the state's best welterweights. So when he was let out of seg, he was sent back to F House and got his job back keeping the tunnels clean. During the day, he would work out to get back in shape in F House's basement. I asked Boston if I could work out with him because I wanted to learn how to box. I wanted to learn the sweet science of it. He told me he would but only if what I had learned would be used for self-discipline, take it seriously, and come work out every day. I said I would, and I did.

I worked out with Boston every day in F House. This was in 1987 through 1989. I had learned the basics and gotten pretty good. In the sport of boxing, experience is the greatest teacher, and there's only one way to get that experience: getting in them gloves. There was a lot to learn before getting in them gloves, though. I even started sparring with different dudes who knew how to box. I got to the point where I would spar with Boston every day, and although he wouldn't go all out, as I began to learn more and started getting better, he would press me and every day turn it up a notch. I started sparring with this Vice Lord brother, who became a lifelong friend of mine, also named Rice. Boston wanted me to learn from Rice because he was left-handed, a soft paw, and a good boxer. Boston wanted me to learn how to face a mirror fighter because a lefty stance when you faced off will mirror your stance. So it was important to keep your lead foot, which was your left foot, for a right-hand fighter positioned on the outside of his right foot, which would be his lead foot. The objective was to move toward your left when jabbing to be better able to score and set up your right hand.

I learned what I needed to know and what I wanted to know and even tried out for the boxing team and made it, but honestly, I didn't like getting hit, and I stopped taking it seriously and eventually stopped. My real passion was playing baseball, but since you couldn't play league ball, the next best thing was twelve-inch softball. We played every day during the summer, and because I was pretty good, I was invited to try out for the traveling team, and I made it. Back then, different prisons had teams that could travel and compete against one another. There were softball, basketball, and boxing traveling teams that would travel all over the state. Also, we had intramural teams in the prison where cell house teams played against one another. I spent a lot my time playing ball. I even started playing basketball every day, but twelve-inch softball was my passion.

Chapter 18

So Close yet So Far Away

IF THERE WAS any benefit of being in Stateville, it was its proximity to Chicago. It was closer to home. But despite Stateville being so close, it still felt so far away. That's how prison is. No matter where you're doing time, you will feel like you are on a faraway, isolated island and that the whole around you is revolving; but for you, time is standing still even though you are doing time!

I was able to get visits almost every weekend. Of course my mother and grandmother visited frequently, but I was also able to see my little sister and cousins, and occasionally, some of my friends would visit. I remember my mother told me over the phone one day that this young lady who worked with her would like to come visit and meet me. Her name was Juanita. Her interest in me was sparked by the long conversations she had with my mother while they rode together from work. My mother would often give her a ride home from work. Of course, being my mother's son, she talked about me like I was the greatest son a mother could have even while I was serving time in prison. After weekend visits, my mother would let Juanita see the pictures we would take in the visiting room. So I put Juanita's name on my visiting list.

Before our first visit, I think we spoke over the phone a couple of times and had some good conversations. Eventually, the day came when she visited me with my mother. I was impressed. Juanita was an attractive woman with a vibrant personality. She wasn't wearing tight or revealing clothes, so I couldn't really see how she was shaped, but I could tell she was put together. Overall, though, the visit went good; but because my mother was right there, it made the visit a little awkward, so I couldn't really talk to her the way I wanted to. I wanted to get to know her better. Overall, we had a good visit, and she agreed to come back and see me. I got her to promise that the next time she came to visit me, she would come by herself.

I learned through writing letters back and forth with Juanita that she didn't have any kids and lived with her mother. She shared with me that her first cousin had been killed a few years earlier around Brainerd Park where I had played Little League Baseball. As it turned out, I knew the guy who was convicted for it. He was in Stateville at the time, serving his sentence for the death of Juanita's cousin. I never told her that. I knew the guy and was familiar with Juanita's cousin. I didn't want to further add to her pain for the loss of her cousin, whom I knew through our conversations was very close to her, so I never mentioned I knew anything about her cousin.

Juanita had a lot going on in her life. She was going to school and working full-time, not to mention she was five years older than me. This was 1989. I was twenty-one, and she was twenty-six years old. Because we had talked several times after she came to see me with my mother, the conversation went good and easy, and we both looked forward to seeing each other again. We started writing, and eventually, she started coming by herself regularly to visit me. I started looking forward to those visits with Juanita, but despite our attraction for each other, there was not a real romantic connection. The reality of my circumstance made it hard to pursue anything serious, which was understandable.

I was on a visit with Juanita one day during the spring of 1989. It was still early on, maybe a few months after she started coming to see me. I saw Cheryl, my cousin Cindy's friend who we went to Foster Park grammar school with us, come into the visiting room. She didn't see me at first. Cheryl was slim, always was, with a pretty face highlighted by her dimples. I didn't want to be disrespectful to Juanita by saying something to Cheryl, so I knew approaching Cheryl was out of the question. Plus, I had no idea who the guy was that she was visiting. During the visit, I glanced over at her at one point hoping to catch her attention. I was sure Juanita picked up on my wandering eye. I didn't want to make her feel disrespected, but I did want to make the connection. Eventually, we did lock eyes; and when Cheryl noticed me, I remembered how deep her dimples sunk in when she smiled. Her smile seemed to catch her own self off guard because the guy she was visiting immediately turned around and looked in my direction. As I smiled back, she blushed, and I saw him ask her as he turned back around, "You know him?" From that moment on, as discreetly as we could, we seemed like we couldn't stop looking at each other.

For the first time since Juanita started coming to see me, I couldn't wait for the visit to come to an end. I figured that when it was time for the visit to be over, I would walk her up to the front of the visiting room and see her out without the usual lingering to keep her with me as long as I could. This day was different. I needed to steal a moment with Cheryl before she left, but I didn't know how I was going to pull that off since I had to try and do it without the guy knowing about it. It seemed like mission impossible! But as I watched them, I figured it wasn't anything romantic between them, so I decided to make a bold move.

After Juanita walked up the stairs to leave the visiting room, Cheryl and the dude she was visiting walked up on her way to leave out. I was standing there on the side where the visitors were walking up the steps, and as Cheryl started walking up the stairs, the guy she was visiting stood off to the side. I literally put my finger in Cheryl's belt loop and gently pulled her back to get her attention. When she turned around, I said, "Man, Cheryl, how you going to leave without speaking to me?" All I saw was teeth and dimples as she smiled and blushed. Then a voice snapped me out of the moment when I heard dude say with what I detected was a slight agitation in his voice, "You know her, playboy?" I turned to him with a smile on my face and said, "She didn't tell you? We go a long way back!" Cheryl said, "Yes, we went to school together, and his cousin is my friend!" I told

Cheryl to stop by over my grandmother's house later if she could because I was going to call later. I had set a pick, and she rolled with it.

I forgot the guy's name, but apparently, Cheryl had been to see him a couple of times. He tried striking up this generic conversation with me after Cheryl left the visiting room and told me this elaborate lie about his involvement with Cheryl. I could only assume that he was telling me this to try and discourage me from pursuing her. What he said was that he and Cheryl had just gotten married and that she didn't want her mother to know about it! I was thinking, *This shit sounds made up.* From how it looked to me, after I just sat there for a few hours observing them on that visit, I saw absolutely no indication of a romantic connection, let alone any indication of them being married! Cheryl couldn't stop looking at me to the extent he even noticed it. If they were actually married, the constant eye contact would have been disrespectful; but because they weren't and there was no romantic connection, there was no disrespect on her part. And by that standard, I can admit it was disrespectful on my part toward Juanita; but as I listened to him, he sounded like a clown when he told me that. I found out he had actually told a few of the guys working in the visiting room and some of his guys after she came to visit him the first time that Cheryl was his wife after they saw she came to see him that first time.

Cheryl revealed the truth of why she was coming to visit this guy when I talked to her later that day on the phone over my grandmother's. She told me that she had been to see him only one other time before that as a favor to her brother after he asked her to go see him. Her brother was locked up in another prison at the time, Menard prison. He was doing some legal work for her brother, and he didn't have any other way to communicate with him, so she was just helping her brother when he asked her to go visit him. Cheryl was serving only as a go-between, nothing else. She told me she had no interest in him whatsoever. She never came back to see him again.

Needless to say, word went around Stateville that I had stolen this guy's make-believe wife. We talked on the phone, and she promised she would write and visit me. I submitted a request to have her put on my visiting list, and when she was approved, she started coming to see me at least twice a month. She wrote me so much, and I couldn't respond fast enough to every letter. Sometimes, I would get two and three letters at the same time in the mail almost daily. Within a short period of time, our relationship evolved fast.

At the time, Cheryl was working and going to school while also still living at home with her mother. Cheryl and my mother became close. Her relationship with my mother also grew fast. My mother became a mentor to Cheryl. My mother motivated her as she took on the challenge of going to school and working at the same time. I offered up as much support and motivation as I possibly could from where I was. Because of this, our bond grew stronger through every letter, phone call, and visit. I became the person she confided in about things she dealt on a daily basis. Every encounter we shared seemed to deepen the bond between us in spite of my circumstances. She offered a degree of dedication that was usual for the situation.

As our relationship grew, honestly, I looked for the bottom to fall out at any moment because prison romances tended to last as fast as they started. But that wasn't the case. I couldn't believe how consistently supportive she was of me. She stuck around for a solid five years. Fully aware when it started between us, I literally had fifteen years left to do in prison. She gave me a small amount of normalcy in an abnormal time in my life, which meant at the same time she sacrificed a normal life for herself to be fully committed to an abnormal situation. She was my ray hope during the most depressive time of my life.

Chapter 19

Immaculate Conception

WITH MY ENCOURAGEMENT, we took advantage of how the system was loosely ran and exploited the gaps when we could. The visiting room in Stateville provided much discretion for those looking to have relations with their women. There were side rooms that were separated from the regular visiting area that provided a large amount of privacy. Of course being incarcerated, one lost the privilege of having the ability to be with women the way men loved; but in Stateville and the way the system was then, we had privileges that allowed for men to fully enjoy their time on a visit with the women who came to see them. It was no different with us.

I got my chance to enjoy my visit with Cheryl when I could. I was twenty-two years old and in my prime, and just sharing a hug with her wasn't enough for me. So yes, we shared some intimate time together; and as a result, she got pregnant. I found out in early August of 1990. I went to the yard one day and got on the phone and called her as I normally did. When she accepted the call, I could tell from the tone in her voice that something was wrong. I immediately asked her what was wrong. She started saying repeatedly, "You going to get me in trouble with my mother!" I didn't understand what she was getting at, and I started to get frustrated because she just kept saying it. After what seemed like a hundred times of me asking her what she was talking about, she finally told me I had gotten her pregnant!

I didn't realize at the time that this wasn't probably the best thing to happen for everyone involved, but as a twenty-two-year-old kid locked up with pretty much a dormant future for at least the next fourteen years, I didn't process this news the way I should have. I was pretty much thinking as a self-centered, selfish person. Joy took over me and an extreme amount of pride. This was no immaculate conception as impossible as it could have seemed. It was as real as it could get. I was in no capacity of being someone's father. I never fully considered the total ramifications of how this was going to affect Cheryl's life, the embarrassment of having to explain this to her family of how having a baby with a dude who had fourteen years left to do in prison.

What type of life was I setting our child up for? He would be starting out without the odds in his favor, and I was fully responsible for that. The reality is that black children in America need every advantage they can have in order to reduce the odds, and whether or not anyone wants to believe it, being born black still puts the odds against you in life. The odds increase with an absentee father who's in prison. Black kids far too often are born into circumstances with more than one disadvantage against them that creates great odds against their success. As I looked back at the thin margins my son would be born into, I felt deep inside myself that I robbed him of the most important thing a black boy can have: his father! But at the same time, I realized what was meant to be would be and that it was meant for my son to be. So on Monday, April 1, 1991, at 11:17 a.m., my son was born, six pounds, seven ounces, and twenty-three inches long. I regretted so much that I was not there to witness his arrival into the world—not only did he need me to welcome him into the world but also from day one to be there to guide him through it.

My son was ten days old when I laid eyes on him and able to hold him for the first time. This was the most surreal moment of my life. I realized that he was the purest form of who I was. If there was any form of perfection in me, I saw it in him that day. I could not stop looking at him. I remember praying that he would remain sanitized from the grit and grim of this world. I wanted him to stay perfect. I felt compelled to thank Cheryl for giving me a son in spite my present situation. That visit seemed like the quickest visit I ever had. It seemed to end as soon as it began. I was riding a huge high and looking forward to the next time I would see my son. It was the type of visit that you have that as soon as you see the people coming to visit you, you start missing them even while they are still there because you know the visit will soon be over and because you are already looking forward the next time you see them.

That day, I didn't think anything could get in the way of my happiness or disrupt and destroy my mood. My spirit was dancing out of my body right in front of me. I kept replaying in my head the very first moment I laid my eyes on my son. I didn't want to let the moment go, but eventually, it was gone, and I had to watch my newborn son leave the visiting room as I went back to my life behind the walls of Stateville!

Since I was in the visiting room during the time lunch was served in the prison, I wasn't able to eat, but the prison ran miss out chow for anyone who missed out because of visits or being at health care or for any other valid reason that caused someone to miss out. When I left the visiting room, I went straight to miss out. The only thing I got was a sandwich and a Styrofoam cup of water. My adrenaline was so elevated that I really wasn't hungry, so after taking a few bites of the sandwich, I ended up tossing away the portion I didn't eat. I kept my water as I headed for G Dorm, which was the unit I was assigned to at the time. G Dorm was located all the way in the back of the prison. As I walked out this door from the tunnel that led to the outside, I had to walk past B West cell house and B West yard, which were maybe a hundred feet in front of me. This happened to be the same time some guys were coming off the yard as I was walking toward them.

As I got closer to the yard, these two Hispanic dudes were walking directly toward me. I recognized one of them. His name was Smokey. At the time, there was some tension in the prison with this particular group of guys, so there were some people walking around with some short fuses! As Smokey and the other dude walked past me, the guy I didn't know intentionally bumped into me with his shoulder hard enough that it knocked the cup of water out of my hand. Next thing I knew, I was drenched! Water was all over me! So now I was wiping water out of my eyes and off my face, and they kept walking. I became pissed off because I knew he did it on purpose. I said to him, "Hey, man, look at what you did!" When he turned around, instantly, my mind went back to that day with Benji, but this wasn't a do-over moment. The difference between the two incidents is that I believe Benji just expected me to stand down, but this dude expected me to stand up! He wanted a fight! I honestly don't think Benji was trying to start a fight. He just expected me to stand down and to acknowledge his presence. This was not that, and this was prison, different politics.

It turned out the tough guy's name was CJ. When he heard what I said, he turned and started walking toward me. CJ asked me if I had a problem with him. I pointed out the fact that I was soaking wet by looking at my clothes. As he got closer, I could see he was drunk, apparently, off hooch, jailhouse liquor, which was made from fermented fruit and yeast. I told Smokey, "Hey, Smokey, you need to get yo boy!" Smokey replied by saying, "He a man. He don't need me to get him!" At this moment, CJ asked me again if I had a problem; but only this time, he poked me in the chest with his index finger! As soon as he poked me, out of reflex, before I knew it, I had hit CJ so hard on his chin. I saw his eyes go blank as his head sharply snapped to the side, and then his eyes went to the back of his eyelids where all I could see was the white of them.

The punch was so effective that the torque it caused made his head snap so quickly. He was separated from senses and instantly went unconsciousness before he hit the ground. There was no need to count to ten! He was out cold! He hit the ground so hard the back of his head hit the pavement, which also caused him to bust his head. That was when I heard Smokey say in a panicked voice, "Man, bro, what the fuck? Why you do him like that?" I said, "He a man, remember? I told you to get your boy. You want some?" I looked up, and all his guys were coming off the yard toward me. The CO who was running the yard line ran over there, and I saw him get on the radio and call a "10! 10! B West yard! 10! 10! B West yard!" That was the code for an emergency.

I turned around and saw one of my guys named Dollar Bill run up from behind me and asked Smokey, "What's up, nigga? Back up!" He pushed Smokey on his chest so hard Smokey damn near fell on his ass. Within seconds, there were just as many of my guys on my side who came from the tunnel and the yard as there were of CJ's guys. This white lady who was a lieutenant named Bagley came on the scene. I knew Bagley when she was a sergeant in F House. She was cool and got along with everyone. I looked at CJ, and he was still out with one of his arms sticking up, looking freakishly stiff, and the rest of his body strangely contorted and convulsing. Now I was getting a little worried because now I was thinking about the possibility of him dying. His head did hit the pavement pretty hard. I didn't want that to happen.

Lieutenant Bagley told me I had to cuff up, which was the normal procedure, but I refused because there were too many of CJ's guys out there, and I wasn't going to leave myself vulnerable in handcuffs. She understood and didn't push the issue. She told me she had to take me to seg, the hole. I knew that was going to happen because it was a physical altercation. Lieutenant Bagley came to seg the next day and told me CJ didn't come to until they got him in the hospital. She said he asked what had happened. When the CO brought me the write-up, they wrote me up for an assault. That was serious because it carried a year across the board. What that meant was a year lost of good time, a year lost of commissary, and a year of C grade, which meant I would lose more privileges because of being in C grade and a year in the hole.

When I went to the adjustment committee to hear the ticket, I refuted the assault and told the committee that he put his hands on me and that I had a witness, this CO name Kennedy. He was the CO who was running the yard line and saw CJ put his hands on me. Kennedy verified what I had said, and the adjustment committee reduced ticket to just a fight, and I got thirty days across the board. I only did twelve days in seg. The following weekend, Cheryl brought my son to see me, but I was in seg handcuffed. I was let out of the hole early. I only did twelve days. When I got out of the hole, everybody in the joint was talking about how I had knocked out CJ. I don't know what happened to him, but I never saw CJ again after that incident.

My time in Stateville was pretty much a smooth bit. When I was transferred out of F House to G Dorm, it was December 1989. I met one of the realest dudes in my life, my brother Chuckaluck. This brother was from the Wild 100s in Chicago. All this dude did was read books; he was an investigator of things, very knowledgeable and wasn't scared of shit. Of course I must talk about the guys I came to know as I was growing up in prison. A lot of these dudes became my brothers for life: Omar, Big T, Lil John, JR, T Bone, Blood, Tvski, Boston, Lil C, Rice, Shorty G (Freddie), Shorty G (Xavier), Low Down, Jimmy Fletcher, Red Dog, Baby G (RIP), Besko, Billco (RIP), Killer Joe, Red Cloud, Tim Hinkle, Low Key, Meechie, Danny Lee, Insane (Kenny), Smokey (RIP), Colonel Bill, Hishamadeen, Peanut, Ace Dog (RIP), Starsky, Coffee Bell, my homie Tony Davis (RIP), Flip Toney, Kangol, Cash, Rico Mack, Cap, Zoe, Jodie Mack, Cocaine, Barksdale Bey, Lil Ride (Head, RIP), Biggie (RIP), and definitely Mr. Hoover. Of course there were so many more good brothers over my twenty years in prison whom I had met. I did a few months shy of six years in Stateville, five years and eight months there.

Chapter 20

Danville / Illinois River

I WAS TRANSFERRED to Danville Correctional Center in March of 1992. I was only there for eighteen months. While I was there, I got a job working in the gym and enrolled in college. Maybe after being there for about six months, I saw this new CO who had just started there who looked very familiar. He had to be at least six feet six inches tall. When I noticed him, I was coming out of the chow hall, and he was about fifty yards away, walking by the gym. Something clicked in my head. He looked like Erving Smalls! Erving Smalls was Benji's teammate on their '83–'84 state championship team at Simeon. He went on to play for the University of Illinois and was on that team that made it to the 1989 final four. That was a great team. I rooted for them to beat Glenn Rice and Michigan. Anyway, I was confident that was him although I had never met him. He turned around when I yelled out, "Smalls!" It was Erving Smalls, now a correctional officer at Danville.

I didn't know what was going to become of this situation since one of Benji's teammates was now working as a prison guard in the prison where I was doing time at, but I wasn't worried by it. I was interested in how it was going to be when eventually we saw each other face-to-face. It didn't take long for that question to be answered. The very next day, I went to the gym where I worked. I walked through the doors to the gym, and sitting in a chair fifty feet in front of me was Erving Smalls by the basketball court. I walked up to him and said "What's up, Smalls!" as if I had known him my whole life. I could tell he recognized who I was. I'm sure I was the last person in the world he was expecting to see, though.

He had a look on his face as if he had seen a ghost, maybe because he was caught off guard, but he recovered quick and appeared to be cool under pressure. He said, "What's up, B-bill?" It was in a tone as if he was waiting for me to confirm that he was right to assume it was, in fact, me. I finished his sentence. "Yeah, man, Billy. I'm Billy Moore!" I will not repeat exactly what we talked about word for word, but he did tell me how he spent the whole summer with Benji before he died and that he had been concerned for his friend. I could tell he was still very much affected by Benji's loss. Overall, I will say the conversation was a positive one, and I'm sure he would agree. We shook hands, and whenever he saw me after that, we would speak to each other.

I was only in Danville for eighteen months. During that time, I basically went to school and worked in the gym. I had a set routine. The prison didn't have a hostile environment, so I was cool being in Danville. Once a week, the transfer list came out, and I found out that I was on the transfer list in September of 1993. I found out the reason I was being transferred. It was because someone who had just come to the prison claimed me as an enemy. I had no enemies, but as it turned out, it was someone who—I won't mention his name—testified against me and Omar during the trial. I guess he was worried now and didn't want to be in the same prison I was in.

This was in September 1993. I had been transferred to Illinois River Correctional Center in Canton, Illinois, which was the next county over from Peoria. When I got there, I was almost at the halfway mark of my time. The summer of '93, the Mississippi River flooded real bad and devastated the region. I remember while I was on the bus ride from Danville to Illinois River I saw water everywhere. When I got to the River—that was what we called the prison, short for Illinois River—the mosquitos were terrible and big as hell! As soon as I got situated, I was able to get my first job as a TA (teacher's assistant) in the school building, working with guys in school for their GED. I also submitted a request by getting on the waiting list to work in the prison industry. The industry in the River was a bakery that made all the bakery goods for every prison and some state agencies in Illinois. In prison, the industry jobs are the best-paying jobs.

Maybe about six or seven months later, I finally got hired in the industry. When I started working in the bakery, I told my mother that she didn't have to send me any money and that if she wanted to, she could just make sure my son was going to be looked after. I worked in the bakery until the time I went home, mostly on third shift. I had the longest tenure in the bakery of any inmate at the time. I worked there for ten years. Half of my time in prison I spent working there, and more than half of that time, I worked as a production and tool room clerk.

Around this time in my prison bit was when I started seeing less of Cheryl and my son. The relationship with my mother and grandmother started to diminish with Cheryl. I felt depressed often at first. I knew I was going to experience this moment, and in spite of me knowing this time would eventually come, when it did, I wasn't ready for it. My resolve was tested, and I had to find the strength within me to overcome those moments that challenged my will. I knew I would get past it. I just kept as busy as I possibly could. I had consistently gone to school, and I was getting close to graduating, and that became my focus. It felt so good when I finished school. The day I told my mother I was graduating from college was one of the proudest moments of my life. The sense of accomplishment was an understatement. Once again, I had done something positive to show I was truly working on being a positive individual. My mother and grandmother were so proud of me. I knew that I had been doing the right thing with how I had done my time. I had established positive adjustment record in prison. I felt good about knowing I hadn't wasted my time in prison. Right after that, I signed up for the bachelor's program; but as soon as I was about to get started, the administration got rid of the program.

I got into working out consistently, just another way to get my mind off Cheryl breaking bad on me. My biggest goal was to do a hundred push-ups straight. The reason why was, when I was about eleven, I was at my father's house. At the time, he was living on Eighty-First and Evans in the Chatham neighborhood. He told me to count off the push-ups he was going to do. So as he got into a push-up position, he asked me if I was ready, and he started doing push-ups. I counted every one he did. I counted off a hundred straight push-ups. I thought this dude was Superman! To me, he had just done the impossible. So when I started working out in the joint, I was determined to be as strong as my father was when I counted off that hundred push-ups.

I started conditioning my body by doing push-ups in sets of twenty-five. I was also lifting and doing dips. As I got stronger, eventually, the twenty-five sets became sets of fifty. About four, maybe five months of going hard, I was in my cell, and I believed in my mind I was ready to complete the mission I had in my mind since I was eleven years old. I got into a push-up position. "1," I started counting, and I didn't stop until I said, "100!" One hundred straight! I really felt like my father's son, another accomplishment that meant something to me. I felt privileged to be his son.

Chapter 21

Seven Years of Winter

IT HAD TO be the winter of '97 when my mother basically told me on a visit that she was tired of seeing me in prison, that it was becoming unbearable. I didn't think I was never going to see my mother again. She never told me she was going to stop visiting me. She just stopped coming. I totally understood and held no resentment for the choice my mother made. I just looked forward to the next time she felt up to coming to see me, and I figured that was when I would see her again. We talked almost every other day, so we maintained our closeness just from a distance. As time went on, I stayed focused and out of trouble. I believe I only caught three minor tickets over an eleven-year time frame while I was in the River. I was now downhill on my time. I had finally gotten over the hump and was now within single digits to my out date.

It was in September of 2000 when one day I received a letter from my cousin Big. He wrote, "Cuz, you need to call home. Nettie is sick, and she ain't doing good. I'm pissed off that everybody is keeping this a secret and not telling you your mother is sick. You deserve to know what's going on with your mother!" My cousin didn't tell me what sick really meant, but I knew it had to be serious. I didn't want to assume anything, but in the back of my mind, I was thinking it was cancer. I kept thinking my worst fears were about to be realized, and the one thing I hoped the most wouldn't happen, was it going to happen?

While I was reading the letter, I was locked in the cell because it was count time. I needed to get on the phone. I couldn't wait for the count to clear. I just kept thinking, when the count cleared, I got to get on the phone and call home. This was turning out to be one of the worst days of my life, just thinking that my mother could be sick enough to be taken away from me permanently. Eventually, the count checked, and the cell doors were unlocked. I walked to the phone booth and called home.

My grandmother answered and accepted the call. She was like, "Hey, Bill, what's up?" I said, "Granny, where is my mama?" She said, "She's asleep!" Since I was kept in the dark, I didn't know that my mother had to stop working because of her illness! As often as we talked, I had no idea my mother was sick, and my family hid this fact from me for six months. I asked my granny what was going on with my mother and if she was sick. When I asked my granny that, at first, she didn't respond. I said, "Granny, please don't tell me my mama is sick!" Instantly, she got upset and asked me who told me that. "They had no right to tell you that!" I wasn't in the mood to be answering questions. I needed questions answered and ignored her and said, "So it's true? Is my mother sick?" Immediately, she started crying, and so did I.

She calmed down and confirmed to me that, in fact, my mother was sick, and it was cancer! She said she had a doctor's appointment coming up within a couple of weeks and that at that doctor's visit, she would find out if her condition was terminal or not. My grandmother said my mother told her that based on what the prognosis was going to be, she would decide if she needed to tell me anything. My grandmother told me my mother made her swear to her that she would not say anything to me until she found out, so my grandmother wanted me to wait until her next doctor's visit. We agreed that I wouldn't say anything to my mother until she said something to me. I prayed that after that doctor's visit, there would be no need for a conversation to be had.

After I talked to my granny that day, I talked to my mother over the phone multiple times leading up to that appointment, and I kept my word and didn't say a thing about what I knew, and my mother gave me no indication that she was sick at all. Every time we talked on the phone, I didn't detect any change in her voice or her disposition. I did brace myself for the conversation if she brought it up, but she didn't. She always sounded strong, both physically and mentally. Every day since that phone call with my grandmother, the only thing I kept thinking was, "Damn, my mother has cancer!" This was not good, and I couldn't help but think about the worst possible outcome. Worse was the fact that I could not be there for her and help comfort her through this time I was sure she needed me to be there the most. This was the worst feeling ever. As my heart was beating, it was breaking at the same time. The revelation of what I had just found out could also possibly mean my worst fear could happen, me losing my mother and while I was in prison!

When the day came for that appointment, I purposely didn't call home for a few days afterward. I didn't know what her state of mind would be. If it was not the news I was hoping for, I didn't know how I was going to handle myself if I heard my mother tell me there was nothing that could be done to change her situation for the better. When I eventually decided to call home, my mother answered the phone. She told me she had something she needed to talk to me. When she said that, I knew in my heart it wasn't the news I wanted to hear. My heartbeat sped up, and I got nervous and scared all of a sudden. She said, "Billy, for the last six months, I've been sick, and I have cancer!" Hearing her tell me that was like me hearing it for the first time all over again, and instantly, tears started falling from my eyes. She said, "I need you to be as strong as I know you can be and make sure you continue to take care the inside so you can get up out of that place!" She also said, "Billy, I may not be here when you come home!" Through my tears, I asked her, "Ma, is it terminal?" Void of any emotions, she said, "Yes!" I had to confess to her. I said, "Ma, I already know. I been knowing for weeks, but I'm still trying to build up the strength to deal with this!" She was being far stronger than I was at that moment. In this calm voice, she said it again: "You need to continue to be as strong as you need to be and focus on getting out of there!" She told me, "I'm so proud of you and proud of the man you have become. You are the King's kid. Remember that!" She had been calling me the King's kid since I got in trouble.

From the time I became aware of my mother's sickness, her condition only got worse. My uncle Garry knew the warden there and reached out to him to inform him of how sick my mother was. The warden had my assigned counselor call my grandmother and tell her that they had granted me approval to let me come see my mother the next time she went into the hospital. When my granny told my mother this, my mother made my granny promise her she would not call out to the prison because she didn't want me to see her in that condition. She didn't want me to have my last impression of her being sick. I didn't find this out until my mother went into the hospital for the last time on Monday, February 19, 2001. When I called home and found out she was back in the hospital, I asked my granny if she was going to call my counselor so I could come see her. She told me, "No, your mama don't want you to see her like that, and I'm going to respect her wishes!"

I was mad at my mama at first for not wanting me to see her, but then I had to realize that my mama was trying to look out for my interest. She didn't want me to see what cancer had done to her. In her weakest condition, she was being strong for me. She knew in her heart it would have killed me to see her almost at the point of death, so I respected what she wanted. She was right! Cancer was a thief. It robbed you of everything. It was not a behind-your-back thief. It was bold and in-your-face. It took all your strength until, eventually, it took your life! So I couldn't be selfish. It wasn't about me. It was what she wanted, and as I thought about it, I agreed with my mother. I accepted her position. I was told that Wednesday, the twenty-first of February, my mama went into a coma. Two days later, that Friday, February 23, around 11:00 p.m., she died.

The next morning, before count was taken, a CO came to my cell as soon as the shift changed at 7:00 a.m. and told me to get ready because I had a visit. This was usual. Visits were never called during this time of the shift. I had no idea what had happened the night before, totally unaware that my mother was no longer living. We were on lockdown. When my mother died, my granny had called my uncle Garry to tell him what happened and asked if he could go visit me since he lived in Peoria, the next county over from the prison, which was only a forty-five-minute drive. She wanted it to come from him and not someone at the prison, so Garry came early to tell me. Within minutes, the CO came back to my cell, unlocked it, and told me to come with him. This was still before the prison count started, and there was absolutely no movement allowed at this time. I didn't know what was going on and never imagined it had something to do with my mother.

When I finally reached the visiting room area, the CO told me to go into a side room that was not used for visits. So at this point, I was in an utter state of confusion. When I opened the door, Garry was standing there. I started smiling and said, "Hey, Garry. For a minute, I thought something was wrong!" Garry had this total look of sadness on his face. It was hard not to see it. He responded by saying, "It is, Billy. Vennetta died last night!" I noticed he had tears in his eyes after he spoke those words to me. Everything went blank after that. I can't remember what I said to my uncle. I just remember feeling this tremendous rush of emotional hurt overtaking me. This was the most painful shit I've had to endure. Thinking to myself I had never known what life was like without this woman in my life, I had to reconcile inside my mind that I would have to learn to live without having my mother in my life. I would never see her ever again. The last time I saw her was three and a half years before that, not knowing then that that would be the last time I would see her. The one consolation I had at that moment was that she was free from any more suffering and pain. I consoled myself with this thought.

When I got back to the cell house, it seemed like every CO knew that my mother had passed, and everyone I saw expressed their condolences. I'm not going to lie, that was by far the worst moment of my lift, but there was nothing I could do about it. She was gone! The best way for me to honor her was to do what she told me to do: "Be strong, stay focused, and come home," so that was what I did.

When it was time for her funeral, I had been approved to go. The day before the service, my counselor came up to my cell. I was sitting on my bunk when he walked in with the papers for me to sign so that I could go to the funeral. He didn't say a word. He just stuck out the paper in my direction. I told him, "I'm good. I don't need to sign it, and I'm not going!" He said, "You sure?" "Yep!" I said. I felt the same way my mother had felt when she didn't want me to see her like that. So my last impression was not going to be of my mother in a casket. I couldn't take that vision back with me. It was three and a half years before I would be released when this happened. So my last seven years was the winter of my discontent in prison. I knew she wasn't going to be there upon my release. The last time I had seen my mother before she passed was three and a half years earlier, healthy and full of life. This was how I wanted to remember her. When I had gotten released, seven years had passed since the last time I had seen my mother. In addition to the cancer, I also believed my mother died of a broken heart.

My last three years went by fast, but it was the last six months that felt like forever to go by. Within this time, I also started to feel some anxiety. My last six months couldn't go by fast enough. I couldn't help but to start looking ahead to when I would be eventually released. All this added to my anxiety, wondering if I would have to struggle or what challenges I would have to face as I start the journey of my reintegration back into society, not knowing if it was going to be easy or hard. I became preoccupied with the thought of thinking if people would be willing to give me a chance despite my background. Would they remember me for what I did and show only hate for me? I was very much aware of the double standard that society imposed on a returning citizen. It's expected that you do not reoffend by committing another crime or by living a criminal-free lifestyle once back out on the streets, but on the other hand, society has made it a crime to have a criminal background, legally denying you access to things necessary for survival, such as employment, housing, education, and even in some states, the right to vote. These things and more have been used to legally discriminate against people with a criminal record.

That so-called debt that's paid by serving the time the judge hands out supposedly is paid upon completion of the sentence. Anyone who has served time can attest that the debt comes with a high-ass interest rate that even after being released, it's never paid off! The debt needs to be spelled out in writing exactly what it is! What does it really mean, and when is the debt paid in full? This is the American way, keep you in debt one way or another until death! In this case, a life sentence with a criminal record. For people who have been convicted, there are very limited resources and unforgiving institutions unwilling to help make the transition back into society be as successful as it should and could be. So the challenge is to successfully navigate around these barriers without doing something that will land you back into prison again.

My anxiety was often reinforced by witnessing so many men come back after they went home. I didn't want to fall into that category. I needed a real plan on what I would do for that not to become my fate! Every night, when I went to work, I would read the newspaper. Daily, there would be multiple pages of ads looking for CDL (commercial driver license) drivers. I thought this could be a career that I could do with less resistance to my background. So I decided to get the rules of the road manuals for both regular and CDL. I studied them until I memorized both. My plan was to get my CDL when I got out and drive trucks. Every night, I studied those pamphlets until I knew them almost by heart.

Chapter 22

The Prodigal Son

THURSDAY, AUGUST 19, 2004, was the period punctuating the last full day of two decades of time I had served in prison. All I had left was a wake-up, one more day to do. That morning, when count checked, I was called to the interlock and was told to bring all my property with me. I couldn't believe it. I had done it almost! I was feeling elated. All kinds of thoughts were running through my head. My adrenaline was high, and it became hard for me to focus on just one thought, but the one I kept thinking about was that I was going home in the morning! Everybody I was on the deck with seemed glad for me. Everyone was wishing me well as I walked to the front of the deck with my property. I put my belongings on the cart and was escorted by a CO to Personal Property. I turned in my property after I packed up everything I was taking home with me.

After leaving Personal Property, I was taken to the B of I (Bureau of Identification) to be fingerprinted and have my picture taken. Then I was taken to the receiving unit, which was also the deck where everybody going home was put the day before being released. After getting on the deck, the daily routine was basically the same. Of course it was a different vibe for the guys going home, and it was also different for the guys just getting there to the prison. But for everyone there, it was still a day in prison.

That night, it took me forever to fall asleep because my adrenaline was still sky-high. It was about 2:00 a.m. before I finally went to sleep, but I was awaken around 6:00 a.m. before the shift changed when a CO opened my cell door and told me, "Time to go home, Mr. Moore!" There were six people who were going home that day. The CO took us to the chow hall for breakfast, then to Personal Property to get the property we were taking with us. We then headed for the administration building. I had this thought in the back of my mind that somebody was going to say it was a mistake and that I wasn't going to be allowed to leave prison, but as I was allowed to go through those doors to the administration building and no one never said it was a mistake, I was overjoyed!

Since I was being picked up by my son's mother, I had to wait after the guys who were taking the bus home were processed out first. They loaded them up in a van and took them to the bus station. Finally, I was called up the double doors. Before the first door was opened, the CO working it asked me my name and my IDOC number. I responded, "Moore, N54255!" As I spoke, he held up a picture of me to make sure I was the right person they were letting go. I heard that loud click of the first door being unlocked. I was urged by the CO on the other side of the door to come through. As it closed behind me, the next and last door leading to the lobby was opened after the first one closed. I went through it. I noticed Cheryl in the lobby, my son's mother waiting for me to take me home.

For the first time, I found myself standing in a space in this prison where I didn't have to wait for permission to go through the next door. The next door led to my freedom and the parking lot. Before I left, the finance office wasn't able to cut me a check of the money I had saved while working in the bakery. So I was sent to the local bank to get my money. I had to go to the town of Canton, Illinois. This is an example of how people who commit crime in our community are sent to prisons in rural and depressed white communities where prisons are built, and then the financial stability is surrounding the prison in multiples ways. One is only allowing our money to be put in their local banks.

See, the way it's set up in prison, if you want to open up a checking or savings account, the account has to be opened in the local bank where the prison is at. It used to be different. The system used to allow anyone to open up accounts in whatever bank an individual wanted to open one up in. They stopped that. Now any money that a prisoner wants to save has to be saved in their bank. Not only would they have your body but they also had your money too. I'm sure that money was used to give loans, home mortgages, loans for pickup trucks, or whatever else it was used to benefit those communities that were already benefiting from the plight of urban communities that sent thousands of black and brown men to their prisons. So I was excited that my money was no longer going to be kept in that bank. My money was out of their bank, and I was out of there prison!

Yeah, most prisons in Illinois are built in economically depressed and rural communities that are predominately white. In order for them to qualify for certain federal funding and support, the community needs to have a certain percentage of minorities as a population, so for these communities with prisons, when the census is taken, the prison population is counted, which counts for the quota of its minority populations, thus qualifying that community for the federal financial support. Crime is exploited, and money is made, and generally, crime pays.

When I stepped into that parking lot, the same parking lot I looked at from an incarcerated view from the cell I spent several years in, watching people come and go, in and out, vehicles driving back and forth, finally, the day had come when I finally got to see it by standing on the other side. It was no longer from the disadvantage of my former captive view that years I watched from that corner prison cell. The day came that I had the advantage of looking at it for the first time from standing in that parking lot. As I looked back up at that window to the cell I was in only a day earlier, wondering if the new occupant who replaced me was looking down at me filled with the same wishful thinking that occupied my mind for many years watching freedom pass me by from that prison window, it looked different from my new point of view, not like I thought it would. The freedom side looked far better! This wasn't a sentimental moment. I realized I had survived an ordeal of tremendous odds. It was the time of my liberation! I reflected back to that day in the boiler in the basement of Division 6 with Zurick telling me I wasn't going to walk out of that room alive. Now here I was, walking out of prison alive twenty years later!

We got in the car and left for the bank. Once I got my money and left the bank, the ride home was a long four-hour ride. I reflected on the time I was away and had a tremendous sense of gratitude because I knew over those years I could have easily got caught up and not made it to see this day—got more time, lost my mind, or worse, lost my life. But due to the blessing of the Most High, He helped me through that ordeal, and I walked up out of there alive and well.

By the time we got well into the ride home, the sun came out and started shining bright. The day started out cloudy. It had rained the night before. But as we were moving down the highway, the weather became perfect! The day turned out to be a beautiful one. When we finally made it to Chicago, the first place we went to was the house of Cheryl's mother. She wanted to pick up some food for the welcome home backyard party that was planned for me for the next day, which was Saturday. Cheryl's mother stayed on the next block from the grammar school I had gone to as a kid, so it was good to see the neighborhood I had grown up in after being away for twenty years. It still looked the same. The neighborhood was as beautiful and clean as I remembered it.

I started thinking about all the fun I had at that school, and for some reason, I thought about this girl named Vicki who lived on the next block. She was the first girl I had ever kissed. Thoughts were firing off in my head like crazy. I was all over the place once again. I wanted to leave because I knew my son was at home waiting to see me. As a little guy from the time he first started talking, the question he would always ask me was, "When are you coming home?" And at some point, he started to say after he would ask me that, "And don't say soon!" This day, his question was going to be answered with "Today!" and in person. I couldn't wait to see him. He was now thirteen years old. The first thirteen years of our relationship were long-distance. At times, it became very sporadic. We missed a lot, but I was so hopeful for our future. I didn't want to wait another minute, and although I wanted to nudge Cheryl so we could leave, the one thing I learned from my twenty years away was patience! So I just waited for Cheryl, and eventually, we left.

I have to go back about nine months before this time to November 2003. I received a letter from Cheryl asking me to call her. I hadn't talked or heard from her at all up until then. No accepted phone calls, no letters, and no visits leading up to that day I received a letter from her that November day. It wasn't a long letter and didn't say that much. She just asked me to call her because she wanted to talk to me about something important. So I called her, curious to know what she wanted to talk to me about that was so important. She basically asked me what my plans were when I got out. I told her that I was going to parole to Peoria, Illinois, to my uncle Garry and his wife, Denise, who were going to let me run a bookstore they owned in Bloomington, Illinois. But in my heart, I didn't want to go live in Peoria. Chicago was my home. Although I had something waiting for me in Peoria and my grandmother wanted me to go there, my heart wasn't into going to Peoria.

After being away for twenty years from the city I loved, all I wanted to do was go home. So when Cheryl asked me to come parole to her house to be with my son, it was the perfect excuse for me to change my parole plans, which had already been approved for Peoria. When she first mentioned it, I didn't instantly agree to move in with her when she offered me to come for a couple of reasons. One reason was because I had some resentment toward Cheryl for things that had taken place over the years that are not necessary for me to speak about now. A lot of shit left me heartbroken, and I know it didn't just affect me. It had an effect on my relationship with my son as well. Two, I wasn't in love with Cheryl anymore. I really didn't see me being with her in a real committed relationship. I was looking for something new as far as what I wanted in a woman. I was excited about getting out and whatever possibilities that would come my way, and I knew I didn't want to be tied down. I told her at first I didn't think it was a good idea if I just moved right in with her. I told her, "Let's get to know one another from the point of view of me being a free man, and let's see what happens. We don't have to rush into it." She was against that and said, "Your son is twelve years old, and he needs you now! You have been away out of his life too long already!" That statement changed my mind, and I decided to go live with them. I still didn't feel comfortable with paroling to Cheryl's house, but because I really needed to be with my son and was hoping I still had a chance to help mold him, I agreed to get my parole plans changed from Peoria to Chicago.

Nine months later, I was riding in a car with Cheryl, Chicago-bound, headed to her house where my son and grandmother were waiting for me. For my son, this was going to be the first time in his life outside a prison he was going to see me and for the first time in almost twenty years for my granny. I had giant butterflies in my stomach. I looked forward to seeing my grandmother because she had been there for me throughout this entire ordeal. My paternal grandmother was also still alive. I really wanted to see her and soon because she had been there for me during all that time as well. I was so grateful that both were still alive when I got out. My mother's mother was seventy-one years old, and my father's mother was eighty-eight years old when I was released. Honestly, I worried a little throughout my time in prison that they, too, like my mother, may not be there when the day came for me to come out. So I couldn't wait to see them both, and the first chance I got, I had planned to go to Peoria to go see my grandma Ola.

Finally, Cheryl pulled up in front of the house. The house looked so much better in person than I remembered how it looked on pictures I had seen that Cheryl had sent me over the years. We got out of the car and walked toward the back of the house. When I walked through the door behind Cheryl into the kitchen, my son, granny, and Cheryl's daughter, Chela, were waiting for us there. As soon as Billy saw me, he started smiling, and all I could see was his dimples. It could not be mistaken how happy he was to finally see me standing in front of him as a free man! For the first time in his life, I had come to see him! He walked up to me and hugged me tightly. I looked at my granny, and she started crying. Her tears were absolutely tears of joy, and I knew she was glad that she had lived to see this day. This moment was a surreal one. It was overwhelming for me. I was thinking about my mother and wishing she were with us. I know she wanted to see this moment.

Just as I had done in prison by living my life doing everything the right way by not adding extra stress on my mother, I decided to live my life as a free man by making decisions that would make her proud of me. I hadn't had the experience of living my life as a grown man without being under some form of control custody. I was fully aware that the challenges I was going to face were going to be living life on life's terms without much experience of doing that as an adult, but I was going to be man enough to overcome whatever challenges came my way. I was not unique in the sense of having spent significant amount of time incarcerated before the age of twenty-one, the age of legal adulthood. But unlike most people my age who haven't lived one day in prison, their transition into adulthood was usually a natural progression. There's really no way of measuring the learning curve for something like that. I had to jump right into my life as an adult and be prepared to meet my challenges and overcome them to be successful in my transition.

One successful ingredient for anyone's successful reentry from prison is having a strong support system. Without it, the odds become that much higher for failure. Success becomes a team sport. I knew I would need help. In addition to the help my loving family and friends who were there would give me every step of the way, I would seek it out too. I was so determined to prove to myself that I could take on the challenges of life and do good, but I won't lie, I was nervous just like I was when I first stepped foot into prison. I didn't know then what life was like in prison and how to do time. I had to learn, which I did. But first, just like in prison, I would take it one day at a time.

My first day out and getting past the moment I hugged my son and granny was special. My adrenaline was pumping high. I remember Cheryl asking me if I was hungry. I was, but I couldn't eat. It was excitement that fed my hunger, not food! I was feeding on each moment of my new freedom. When my cousins got wind that I had made it to Cheryl's house, I looked up, and there were about fifty people who had shown up. The welcome home party was supposed to be the next day, that Saturday, but it started early. Omar came over, and at that time, he had been out three years. He told me to follow him to his truck. We sat in the truck, and he pulled out a pocket full of money and counted off five hundred dollars and handed it to me and said, "Welcome home, Rappy!" We went back to the backyard. Everybody started coming over. We partied all that day, all the next day, and all day Sunday. My uncle Curtis hired a live band that played that Saturday.

I had met family members who had been born while I was away who immediately embraced me as Uncle Billy! And most of them were just my cousins. I finally met my brother-in-law Chuck, good dude whom I was glad that my sister had found happiness with, and I was just as happy for her. That weekend made me feel loved, missed, and special. The energy and vibe were festival. I realized that my family sincerely loved me and was glad to have me back in the family fold. We partied well into the morning my first night home. After everybody left the first night, Cheryl had another welcome home party for me. By the time I was able to settle down a little bit, in addition to all the day's activity, I was exhausted; but for some reason, I couldn't sleep. I was too wired up. So after Cheryl went to sleep, after a moment of just lying there and thinking that I was actually free, my mind automatically reversed to thinking about what was happening in the prison at that moment.

I decided to get up and exercise my new freedom and go sit on the front porch. In the joint, there was no way you could just get up in the middle of the night and go outside just to get some fresh air. So it made me feel good I was now able to get up and go outside whenever I wanted to even if it was four o'clock in the morning. Sitting on that porch, I also had thought about Benji. I don't think too many days had passed me by that I didn't think about him at least once. At this time in the morning, breakfast was being served in prison. I actually sat on the porch until the sun came up feeling grateful I was finally out with every intent of enjoying life. That weekend seemed like it went by nonstop from Friday through Sunday night. It took me about a week before I finally got a quality night of sleep. It was also the same with my appetite. I didn't finish a whole meal for about a week also.

The day I left prison, I was told I had twenty-four hours to call the parole office and to not go anywhere until my parole officer came to see me, so I did just as I was told. The whole weekend went by without me hearing from any parole agent. That Monday morning, right after Cheryl went to work, I got a call. It was the parole agent. He said, "Mr. Moore, I'm just getting back to work, and I see you came home Friday and been gone for a minute. I probably won't get to see you today, but I'll see you definitely before Wednesday, so I'm going to grant you some movement, okay? Twenty years is a long time. Welcome home. Keep your release papers on you until you get some ID!" I said, "Thank you!" He hung up.

So finally, I had an opportunity to move about and go some places instead of being confined to the house, but everybody I knew was at work, including Cheryl, except for my childhood friend Boogalou. Boogalou was one of the people in my life who made sure throughout my time in the joint, he stayed in touch. He would send me money, and I could always call him no matter what. So I called Boogalou and asked him to come get me. I had him take me first to Eighty-Fifth and Bishop. He still lived on the block in his grandmother's house, who was still alive. I wanted to see the house I was raised in. My cousin Cindy and her husband at the time had bought the house from my granny, and my granny had moved into the building my uncle had purchased while I was away in Englewood.

When I first saw the house I grew up in, now Cindy's house, it looked smaller than I had remembered. The block looked the same but felt totally different. For some reason, I didn't feel connected to it anymore. Time had separated me for far too long, and mostly everyone had moved away. It wasn't just the block that time had disconnected my connection to. It was the neighborhood too! I felt like anything but the prodigal son returning home. In spite of the familiar structures that were the same, I felt like a stranger in a foreign place.

We drove past Eighty-Sixth and Ashland, and the building that I had beaten up Issy in front of had been gone. Boogalou said it was demolished a few years before. So I just resigned to the fact that my spirit had been abandoned by the neighborhood I had so much loved. One thing is certain: Time brings about a change, and whether one is ready to embrace it or not, it will come! I gave Boogalou some gas money to just drive me around the South Side, and we ran across a few people I hadn't seen in a while.

The following week was time for me to start getting my life back on track. My son, my cousin Cindy, who had come by the house the next day, and I walked to the corner where a phone store was at, and I got me a cell phone. The next thing I needed to do was get my driver's license and state ID. I had already sent for my birth certificate and Social Security card before I had gotten out of the joint. The day I was released, I was given my birth certificate at the front gate, and my social was mailed to the house from the Social Security office. It was at the house when I got there.

Everybody was at work, so I called Boogalou and asked if he could take me to the secretary of state. He came and got me and took me to get my state ID without any issues, but getting my license was another matter. As it turned out, someone with the same name and birthdate of mine had racked up a lot of tickets in Pennsylvania, so Illinois put a hold on me getting my license until I was able to get a letter from the secretary of state in Pennsylvania clearing me so I could get my license in Illinois. It didn't matter that I had been incarcerated for the last twenty years and that clearly it wasn't me! I wasn't allowed to get it until I got the letter from Pennsylvania faxed to Illinois Secretary of State.

That was a process of holes and hoops I had to jump through to get that letter, but eventually, I got everything I needed that they wanted me to get them to fax the letter. Once that happened, I was able to take the test to get my license, which I passed. This took about another week in all. With me securing my license, it was now time for me to get a car. I knew somebody who had dealer license and asked him if he could help me get a car at the auction. He took me to the one in Alsup, Illinois, and I purchased my first car for $2,300.

It was a gray '93 Pontiac Grand Prix coupé, a beautiful car. I got so many compliments for it. It was clean and had about 100k plus miles on it. It ran well. I had no issues with it.

I was excited to have my first car. Someone real close to me actually told me I needed to slow down. I was moving too fast. I couldn't comprehend that. I was just doing what I needed to do for myself and wasn't waiting for anybody. They said I could have waited to get me a cell phone and a car! It made me think that the level of achievement was giving me too much independence too soon and that I wouldn't need to be dependent on them! I believe they thought I wasn't going to be able as soon as I was to be doing some of the things I was able to do without their help. They really wanted the credit and be able to always say or one day throw it in my face that it was them who helped me get on my feet. I wasn't going too fast. I had just come off a twenty-year interruption. It was time for me to get to work, and I wasn't waiting for anybody to help me.

The first thing I did after getting my car was gas it up and take a trip to Peoria to surprise my eighty-eight-year-old grandma Ola, my father's mother. I was so excited that I was going to see her. One of the reasons was, as the years progressed while I was away, sometimes when I talked to Grandma Ola, she would say, "Now you know, Lil Billy, Grandma Ola is getting up there. I might not be here when you get here!" I would say something like this: "Grandma Ola, that's nonsense. You going to outlive us all!" So the fact that I had made it out while both of my grandmothers were still here, Grandma Ola was on top of my priority list to go see.

I called my uncle Garry and told him that I was driving to Peoria to come see him and Grandma Ola but to not tell her because I wanted it to be a surprise. He agreed to it. I hit the road and made it to Garry's house. He showed me around a bit and took me to the studio where he did the news at. Then we headed for Grandma Ola's house. When we got there, he told me to wait outside on the porch until he came to get me. I heard my uncle say, "Ola, I got somebody with me that's going to fix that door upstairs." He motioned for me to come in.

When I walked into the living room, my grandmother was sitting in her wheelchair not looking at me but at the TV. I said, "Excuse me, young lady!" She turned around, and for a minute, she had this look of disbelief on her face as if her eyes were lying to her. Then she whispered almost childlike as if she didn't want me to hear in case she was seeing things, "Lil Billy?" I said, "Yes, Grandma Ola, it's me, Lil Billy!" I walked over and hugged my grandmother, and I could feel her whimpering and crying. She was very religious, so I could hear her saying, "Thank you, Jesus. My grandbaby is home. Thank you, Jesus!" It was a moment, to say the least.

We sat and talked for hours. It was a good visit. I needed that day just as much as she did. A dream of mine had come true that day—that I would walk through her doors again. I left the next day, but I would make that trip as much as I could after that. On May 26, 2010, at the age of ninety-four, my grandma Ola had transitioned. The day before, I drove to Peoria to be with her. I was glad I had been blessed to spend that day with her. She continues to live in my heart forevermore.

Chapter 23

Two Weeks in, Two Weeks Out

As I STARTED moving around and getting myself familiar with the environment again, things weren't looking as hopeful between me and my son's mother. I won't go into the details of the issues that started to come between us, but within two weeks of me getting out, I made the decision to move out of her house and in with my first cousin Sherri and her husband, Jeff, and their two young sons at the time. They had a beautiful big house in the south suburb in Sauk Village. Jeff is a good man, whom I loved as if he were my own blood. From day one, he embraced me with the love of family and brotherhood. I promised them both that all I needed was about ninety days, then I would have my own place. This was the beginning of September 2004, and at the beginning of December 2004, I had moved into my very first apartment on Seventy-First and Jeffery, the South Shore neighborhood in this building named the Highland. It was a one-bedroom apartment and perfect for me.

While I was living with my cousins in Sauk Village, I started looking into CDL's programs. The first one I investigated was a program that was close to me in the south suburbs. I found out that Governors State University had a CDL program, but when I went there to find out what I needed to do to get in, they told me it cost around four thousand dollars and that I would have to pay out of my pocket because financial aid wouldn't cover it, and a Pell Grant wouldn't pay for it. I felt dejected, but I didn't give up. I looked into a few private truck driving schools, but basically, the issue was pretty much the same thing, no financial assistance available. I didn't want to go through a trucking carrier company. Although carriers paid for people to get their CDL, they wanted you to sign a contract and drive for them at least two years and mostly over the road. I wouldn't be allowed to do that on parole, so that was not an option.

A friend of mine by the name of Juan, whom I was cool with while we were locked up together and had been doing time in many of the same prisons together, had been released a month before me in July 2004. I saw Juan once I got out, and he told me he was going through this reentry mentoring program that was being run by the Safer Foundation at St. Sabina Church, the same St. Sabina that Father Pfleger was pastor over. I told Juan I really wasn't interested in some faith-based program that the Safer Foundation was running, but Juan was persistent. Every time I talked to him, all he talked about was the mentoring program and how it was helping him. I still wasn't interested in joining, but one day, Juan called me and said, "Billy, Safer has a new program that Mayor Daily is sponsoring to help people just getting out of prison to pay for them to get their CDL, but it's only going to be for people that are enrolled in the Safer Foundation's mentoring program! You need to come sign up 'cause I know this is what you trying to do!" Bam! I was now convinced I needed to be in this program! Juan told me to call this lady named Toni Foulkes. Toni was the case manager and job coach at St. Sabina for Safer. I called Toni as soon as I hung up talking to Juan. Toni is one of the nicest people I've ever met in my life. She really cared for her guys on her caseload and did everything she could to help them. She had this favorite auntie vibe that makes you feel like she has your back. Toni is the type of person who will move mountains for her guys.

When I came in to do my intake, she explained to me the program lasted a year. I had to be a mentee for that amount of time before I graduate. She said after I graduate the program, I had the option of becoming a mentor. She told me to be in compliance with the program, I had to come to mentoring secessions every Wednesday nights. They served food every session, brought in guest speakers, and offered services to help guys with employment, school, and counseling for substance abuse. She told me she would get me into the CDL program, which was a pilot program to help returning citizens get meaningful employment opportunities by driving trucks. She further explained that it was an accelerated program, which meant that once the program started, the written exam would be given two weeks later, and to move forward in the program, you had to pass it.

I knew that CDL manual by heart. Every day for the past six months of me reading it was about to pay off for me. I never believed in luck, but I heard somebody say, "Luck is only preparation that meets opportunity!" So in this case, I'll keep it simple. I was lucky because I was prepared for the opportunity that came my way. Now being a part of the mentoring wasn't a bad thing to do any longer when I had to come there. I still wasn't feeling it. The reason why was because all the mentors who were volunteers were members and churchgoers. I felt these mentors, as well-meaning as they were, couldn't relate to the issues these guys had been through and were going through, who were the guys they were assigned to mentor. They were good Christian people who were giving back, but what they were bringing, with respect to their time, wasn't effective. When I started coming to the sessions, I wasn't getting anything out of them either, so I wouldn't say anything. But in those type of settings, it's hard to stay quiet for long. Soon, I started chiming in; and almost by default, I became the mentor of my group.

About four months into the program, the cohort of guys who were there before me was graduating from the program. I had already successfully gotten my CDL and was driving for a small sanitation company called Castlerock in Addison, Illinois. I was driving around Chicago and its surrounding suburbs cleaning portable toilets on construction sites. I did such a good job for Castlerock that the owner of the company, Fred Kasick, stopped hiring from the tempt agencies I came through and started hiring a couple more people directly from the Safer Foundation. Fred told Safer, "Send me more Billys!"

Although I found my way in Castlerock and did great there, Fred actually fired me after my first day on the job. On my first day, he sent me out to a route with this older white dude named Sunny. When we were done with the route, Sunny misled Fred into thinking I wasn't a safe and good driver. Behind my back, he told Fred I was driving dangerously close by tailgating drivers in front of me. He said I was using my turn signals and basically just lied on me because none of these things were true.

After Sunny gave Fred this false report on me, Fred called me into the office. It was him and this dude named Rubin, who was the route manager and the only black guy working there at the time. Rubin and I would become friends and are friends until this day. Fred said, "Thank you for coming out, but I don't think this is going to work, so we are going to part ways. I'll pay you for today!" Man, I was not expecting to hear that. That caught me off guard. I really needed this job. I couldn't accept this, so I told Fred, "You appear to be a fair man, but I think whatever was said to you about me wasn't fair or true! You don't owe me anything beyond this point, but I just want to ask if you can give me the opportunity to show you who I am and you to get to know me based on what you get know for yourself instead of somebody else's opinion of me that don't know me." Fred looked me in my eyes and said, "You know what, I owe you that much. Report back tomorrow!" I learned later that Sunny was on the verge of losing his job, and I guess he was bad-mouthing me to try and secure his position with the company. Sunny was fired about a month later. I worked for a year and a half for Castlerock before resigning when I got another job.

Let's go back to the graduation for the mentors. Like I mentioned earlier, about four months into the program for me, Toni informed me that she put me on the program to speak at the graduation for the other cohort. I told Toni there was no way I was going to get up in front of a room full of people and speak. That was not what I do. I tried to come up with any and everything I could think of to get out of doing it, but Toni wasn't having it. She told me, "Billy, you have something to say, and these people need to hear it!" So since there was nothing I could do to get out of it, I started thinking about what I would say.

I went home and wrote a speech. Leading up to the day of the graduation and every day from the moment Toni told me I would be speaking, I was a nervous wreck. Finally, the day of the graduation, I was looking at everyone in the room and was just full of nervous energy. As the commencement began, I saw that I was put last on the program to speak. When the time came for me to address the audience, I told myself, "Tell your truth. Speak from your heart and from a position of strength, not fear and nervousness." So right before I was asked to come up to the podium, the speech I wrote that I had in my hands under the table I tore up into little pieces, and I put it in my pocket. I just began by speaking about my journey of incarceration, my focus to overcome the boundaries, what I've faced, and how grateful I was of the support of my family and the Safer Foundation and the resources I have been able to benefit from.

People applauded, and at the end of me speaking, it was a standing ovation. This woman walked up to me and hugged me. She introduced herself. Her name was Jodina Hicks. Jodina Hicks at the time had under her supervision half of all the programs at the Safer Foundation. Eventually, she would become the COO of Safer while reporting only to Diane Williams, who was the CEO and president. Jodina said, "Billy, I'm so glad to finally meet you. I've heard so many good things about you. I like what you said and how you said it!" Jodina became one of my biggest advocates at Safer and also became a friend of mine. From that moment, Safer would invite me to special events, panel discussions, and interviews. I basically became a client ambassador. I hit all the benchmarks of success that the Safer Foundation used to measure their work and the success of the clients they worked with. I continued going to the mentoring program every week and doing good on my job. The Safer Foundation continued to invite me to speak on panels, give interviews, and speak at board meetings on the solutions and effective ways to reduce recidivism.

Because of my involvement in doing these things, it helped me develop and cultivate positive relationships and strong networks within that community in and outside Safer. As these speaking and networking opportunities came my way, my relationship with Jodina and Tony Lowery became stronger. Tony Lowery, whom I consider a mentor, oversaw the housing and policy reform at Safer. Because of this, maybe about fifteen months after Safer helped me get my CDL and job with Castlerock, Tony Lowery told me that Jodina said, "I don't think Billy needs to be driving trucks. He needs to be working with us full-time!" Tony told me that a position as a job coach was going to be available within a couple of weeks and that I should apply. I became a little nervous. I didn't want to disappoint Tony and Jodina and have them lose trust in me because I may not possess the ability to do the job satisfactorily, but then I thought about my ability to interact and connect with people the way I was able to do in the mentoring groups at St. Sabina and also throughout my time in prison. I just knew I had the ability to get along with people. What helped me also were Jodina and Tony's faith and trust in me to do the job. It made me feel more confident that the job was right for me.

So May 26, 2006, I started my career with Safer as a job coach. This was the job I quit Castlerock for. I had a positive departure with Castlerock and left an open door behind me there. I wrote a letter to Fred expressing my gratitude for him giving me the opportunity to work for Castlerock and that my time with Castlerock helped me to grow a lot. I did let Fred know I was putting in my two-week notice. Fred expressed to me that he appreciated my time at Castlerock. He told me he wasn't going to hold me up and that I could take those two weeks off. It was very amicable!

Chapter 24

Safer

WHEN I STARTED working for the Safer Foundation, it was a natural fit for me. I worked in the Sheridan Program. The Sheridan Program was a prison that had been turned into a drug treatment program prison, and everybody there was going through treatment. The Safer Foundation was one of many stakeholders that was contracted to help the men in the program overcome their drug addiction through job readiness so that they would have a better chance of not reoffending and recidivating. As a job coach, one of my responsibilities was to visit Sheridan prison twice a month. That meant I had to get approved to go into the prison. I was hired, and for the first year I worked as a job coach, I hadn't submitted my application for approval to go back inside. I didn't want to ever walk back into another prison even if I was being paid to do so. So I purposefully didn't fill it out and didn't send in the application that had to be submitted to the Department of Corrections in order for me to go in and work inside. Honestly, I didn't think my application would be approved because of my background, so I didn't waste my time going through the process just to be told my application was denied.

Over that first year, the issue wasn't pushed about me getting my approval to inside since all the other job coaches in the program had clearance and were going in already. The manager of the program who managed the inside work at the prison was promoted to director of the department, which meant all the job coaches were now under his direct supervision. His name was Jim Utley. Jim Utley was a former warden who had lost his job when the republican governor George Ryan went to jail and Rob Blagojevich, who was a democrat, became governor. Ironically, Blagojevich ended up going to jail too.

Jim was a good man and told me that he started working for the Safer Foundation as just a transitional job until he could get back into the Department of Corrections so that he could get his time in and then retire and get his full pension. Jim was also a former marine and over all a good guy. I really respected him for his empathy. He had his own views about things, but I found that he had a sincere heart for the work, and he also believed in me. As the director of the Sheridan department, he pushed me to fill out the application and get it submitted, so I did. To my surprise, ninety days later, I was approved. Twice a month, I was going back into a prison to work with my clients before they were released. Once we got into the follow-up stage, I had already come to know them to an extent, at least familiar with their requirements and resources they needed. I excelled in my position, and I loved what I was doing. Jim and I got along well and had a solid working relationship. He supported me in every way.

Also, I had strong allies from the top, including our president and CEO Ms. B. Diane Williams. I appreciated Ms. Williams and respected her vision and advocacy for the fair treatment of returning citizens by working hard to remove the barriers to employment. In 2008, Ms. Williams was the keynote speaker at the White House on the discussion of reducing recidivism and successful reentry for people with criminal records. The discussion was also published in a national publication. Ms. Williams was asked to talk about someone she personally knew who had gone through her program whom she considered an exemplary example of successful reentry as a success story.

I was at home one night watching TV when Jodina called me. I could hear the excitement in her voice as she explained to me that Ms. Williams was at the White House and called her to ask if she thought it was okay to tell my story because they asked her for a success story, and she wanted to tell them about me. Not only was I honored but it was humbling as well. Not long ago, at sixteen, I was being sensationalized as probably the worst human alive. Now my story was being lifted up at the White House as an example of why not to throw away people because they could change and become the example of habilitation. The honor certainly was not in my story being highlighted to the Bush administration. The honor was that Ms. Williams and Jodina wanted to hold me up as an example of what success looked like and that it wasn't my sixteen-year-old mug shot. I definitely agreed to it and appreciated the fact that I was thought of in that way.

When Jim became director of the Sheridan program, we had two offices in the community, one on the South Side, which at the time was on Sixty-Third and Honore, and the other was on our West Side office at 808 S. Kedzie. Safer no longer had the office on Honore but continued to operate on Kedzie. Until then, there was no manager over the program, so Jodina and Jim decided to add a manager to the org chart. Jodina asked me one day at an event we were at how I felt about managing the Sheridan program. I expressed to Jodina that I had never managed anyone on that level, and she basically said, "Billy, you can case-manage with your eyes closed. I know you can manage those that case-manage. Plus, Jim believes in you, and you were his first choice, and he will be there to help you!" So I embraced it and accepted the challenge. Jim got the position approved, and I became initially the interim manager. I had six months to show I could do the job, but only after three months, the interim came off, and I was officially promoted as the manager of the external Sheridan team in 2009, three years after I started working with the Safer Foundation.

My time at the Safer Foundation was very valuable to my professional growth as a person. I was given numerous opportunities in many ways as a client and as an employee. I remember when I was still a job coach, the executive team decided to reevaluate the retention model across the entire organization as an effort to align and promote continuity across the board. They wanted to see what was working and what wasn't and how to make sure the model was consistent within every department. So they decided to convene a retention task force. There were seventeen people within the organization who were asked to work on this task force. One other person and I were invited to be part of the task force, but we weren't on the management and above level. Everyone else were managers, program managers, directors, and a couple of VPs. So it was an honor to be a part of it.

We were told that at least 40 percent of our work would have to be dedicated to the task force but were still expected to carry out our normal duties. They told us if we didn't want to be on the task force, then we didn't have to be, but I knew it would be stupid of me to turn down this assignment. This put me in the game on another level with the organization. I wasn't just seen or, for that matter, was not overlooked anymore as being important to this organization. I jumped at it but was still nervous about being part of the process. I think it took us nine months to do our research and come up with our findings. We were going to present the research at the annual staff gathering when everyone came together as a whole for two days. It was decided that we would present our findings, talk about the challenges, and what we found that worked and how we would use this information to help make the retention model better.

The task force met one day to discuss who should be the presenters at the all-staff meeting. We all decided that there would be four presenters—two to present the findings and two to present how the retention model would be affected by them. I had no intentions of being a presenter. I was trying to disappear in that meeting. Mostly, everyone on the task force were leaders in the organization and many times had been in front of the room speaking. I remember Marketa Ash, a task force member and at the time the HR manager, made the statement, "There are people in this room that the organization needs to hear from, and there are people in this room that the organization always hear from. The people who now should speak shouldn't be the ones that always speak!" I knew then Marketa was pushing me out there. That was how I felt. It was decided the way the presenters were going to be chosen, which would be names pulled out of a hat.

I personally believe mostly everybody in that room put my name in the hat because the first name to be pulled out of the hat was mine.

We were only two months away from the all-staff meeting, so for two months, I promise you, I was a nervous wreck. But when the time came for me to do my part, I did it, and I did good. So many people I worked with came up to me and said how well I had done. Ivette Sosias, the HR consultant who hired me, walked up to me after I finished presenting like she was my own mother. She grabbed me by my cheeks and told me how proud she was of me and said how she remembered the first day I walked into her officer to interview for my job, and now look at me, I was on stage speaking to the entire organization. She really made me feel good about the experience.

Chapter 25

My Special Four

I HAVE TO go back to a year after I was released in September 2005. I was still working for Castlerock and doing well. I was single and enjoying my freedom. I was dating and casually seeing a couple of women but nothing serious. One night, I was hanging out with a friend of mine I had known since childhood. We called him Grunt. He invited me to meet him up at a spot on Seventy-Fifth, right off Cottage Grove. It was dark and well into the evening. I wasn't really feeling the vibe in this spot. It was some hole in the wall. I stepped out to get some air and seriously contemplated not going back in there.

As I stood close to the corner, a white Buick LeSabre pulled up to the light, and the passenger window starts to roll down. Inside was a woman who was cute, and instantly, she caught my eye. She said, "Excuse me, but can you tell me where the 50 Yard Line is?" I said, "I can do better than that. I can show you. I'm parked right here. Follow me!" She became my excuse to leave. I got in my car that was parked right around the corner. She pulled right behind me and then followed as I led the way basically about a mile in the opposite direction to the 50 Yard Line.

When I got there, I parked and waited for her to get out of her car. When she walked my way, I was even more interested and wanted to see if she was going to give me a chance to get to know her better. I asked what her name was, and she said, "Shawnna!" I wasn't expecting her to do what she did next. She boldly snatched the hat I had on and gave me a once-over. I could only assume I won her approval because she asked me what my name was. I told her.

As we walked toward the 50 Yard Line, I was making my move. I asked her if I could get her phone number because I had no intentions of going inside the 50 Yard Line but that I wanted to see her again. She agreed to give it to me and told me to call her in a couple of days because she was going to be busy working twelve-hour shifts because she was a nurse. Two days later, I called the number she gave me, and an older gentleman answered the phone. It turned out to be her father, Gene. He told me she wasn't there but that I could leave a message, which I did.

I found out later that Gene lived with Shawnna and her four kids. When I eventually met Gene, he took a real liking for me, and I also took one for him. I learned later that when Shawnna was about seven, Gene left her, her mother, and her younger brother, Kevin, and didn't come back into their lives until she was in her midtwenties. Because of this, they had a contentious relationship; but in spite of that, Shawnna loved her father tremendously, and Gene loved her. Gene tried his best to make up for lost time by being there for his grandkids. He loved those kids with all his heart and affectionately called them his kids: "Them my kids!"

A few hours later, I got a call from Shawnna. We talked for about an hour. She told me she had just become a nurse two years before and that she had four kids, two girls and two boys. Her oldest daughter, Janitra, was thirteen at the time, her son Stanley was nine, her daughter Ariana was five, and her baby Adonis was three. After talking on the phone several times that week, we decided to meet up. We started seeing each other on a regularly basis. Shawnna was cool and funny as hell. Her personality was upbeat and outgoing. She really loved her kids and proud to be their mother. All she did was talk about them, so much so that I wanted to meet them. Shawnna wasn't having it at first. She told me if I stayed around long enough, I would get to meet them, so I accepted that. We weren't rushing anything. I was still seeing a couple of other women, so it was no pressure at all in any way.

Eventually, when I did meet them, it was like a match made in heaven. Honestly, it was like I was more compatible with her kids more than I was with her. They really took a strong liking for me. I remember one day she brought them to my apartment at the Highland, and I asked them if they knew how to dance. At first, they were acting kind of shy until I decided to offer them money to see who could dance the best. I'll say this. I ended up giving all of them some money. To be so young, they were very talented. These kids impressed me. I had them from that moment on. Her youngest son, Adonis, who was three, we really bonded and developed a close relationship. I mean, all the kids were close to me, but Adonis and I really bonded strong. He wanted to be around me all the time when I came around.

Shawnna shared with me that she was in an eleven-year abusive relationship with her kids' father. He was extremely abusive, both verbally and physically. She was very young when she started seeing him, and he was her first love. Eventually, she found the strength and left him, but that experience really left her traumatized. I think when I met her, she had only been out of that relationship barely a year; so as we started dating and getting to know each other, we had some real challenges. I believe honestly I came into Shawnna's life at the wrong time. It was bad timing! She was like a caged bird recovering from broken wings, and now that her wings were healing and the cage door was open, she enjoyed flying. I was also dealing with Cheryl and some residual feelings of resentment for several reasons. I knew when she found out about Shawnna and me spending time with her and her kids, it became very toxic between us. So my relationship with my son suffered because of this and caused my involvement in his life to suffer. I would say Cheryl interfered with me trying to play my part as my son's father.

It became the classic situation of me now being more involved with someone else's kids than my own. It wasn't because I didn't want to be fully involved in my son's life, but Cheryl made it very hard to do so. Shawnna and I were together from 2005 to 2011. We even got married in 2009. In that time, there were all sorts of things that occurred, good and bad but mostly bad. It's funny because I can honestly say Shawnna and I have always been better at being friends than being a romantic couple. In our relationship, we had issues of insecurities, and infidelity played a role on both sides because I was no longer happy at one point and felt like I deserved to be happy.

Instead of just leaving at first, I continued to stick around because of my love for the kids, so I stayed maybe longer than I should have. In 2011, Janitra, Shawnna's older daughter, gave birth to a beautiful baby girl and named her Zailey! I literally fell in love with my granddaughter. Zailey and I bonded from day one, and she became the apple of my eye. I became her PaPa. I loved her as much as I loved my grandson Cinco, number five, my son's son. Although Zailey isn't my biological granddaughter, I've helped raise her since she's been here. I'm the reason why she's so spoiled too. But only a few months after Zailey was born, I moved out; and officially, my relationship with Shawnna was over. I basically started living my life as if I was a single man while I was still with Shawnna.

Chapter 26

WOA (Work of Art)

IT WAS JUNE 2008. A cousin of mine named Chucky, whom I hadn't seen since we were kids, came to visit me after coming from his son's high school graduation in Maryland. This was his first time back in Chicago since he was a kid. He and his sister Lisa had moved to California with their grandfather after their mother, Linda, passed. Their grandfather, Uncle Leon, was my grandmother Freda's brother.

I was riding back from O'Hare airport after dropping Chucky off, who was on his was back home to Sacramento on a Saturday morning. Driving back from the airport, I decided to go wash my car but didn't have enough money on me, so I went to the Walgreens on Seventy-Fifth and the Dan Ryan where an ATM was. After coming out of Walgreens from using the ATM, I got back inside my car to leave and head for the carwash. As I started to back out of the parking space at Walgreen, I noticed in my rearview mirror a white Cadillac drive by, causing me to have to stop to let it pass by me. My attention was immediately captivated by the woman behind the wheel of that Cadillac. Even from the rearview mirror, I could see how beautiful she was. She had a caramel complexion with a glow that almost blinded me.

Without thinking, I put my car in drive and pulled back into the parking space I was in. I told myself I needed to investigate this situation further. When I got out of my car, I started walking in her direction, now searching for the caramel-skinned queen with the blinding beauty. There she was, coming from around her car as she made her way toward the entrance of Walgreens. When I saw her walking toward Walgreens' entrance, I couldn't believe how fine this woman was! The only thing that rivaled that blinding beauty was her extremely shapely body! She had it, both face and form!

A thought came into my head: "Bro, she's out of your league!" But just as fast as that thought came, it was followed by another thought: "It's time to play in the pros, my man!" I had to give my own confidence a boost before I allowed her to intimidate me to the point where I would punk out and not approach her. This woman's walk should be complimented by a theme song. She was that sexy! As I almost got lost in a trance from watching her walk through the doors of Walgreens, my desire to get to know this woman became stronger than my fear to approach her. I told myself, "Be confident. She too damn fine not to give it a shot!" So I walked through the doors.

I shook off the intimidation and the trance and followed my mind to make my move. I didn't know what I was going to say when I approached her. I began saying shit in my head that didn't make sense and sounded corny. I decided to just be me, introduce myself, and ask her for her name and if I could get to know her! While I was thinking about all this, she walked out of an aisle and was headed in my direction. Our eyes connected. I hoped it didn't look like I was stalking because that was exactly what I was doing, but I didn't want to appear thirsty when our eyes connected. We did exchange hellos, which was a positive boost to my confidence.

I decided to leave the store. I wasn't abandoning the mission. I just decided to call an audible and change up my plan. I thought it would be best if I waited outside for her instead of following her around the store like I was harassing her. When I saw her walk through those sliding glass doors exiting the store, I said, "Excuse me, but what's your name?" She said with a smile, "Shannon!" Her response had me smiling inside. I felt better about my decision. I said, "Shannon, my name is Billy, and I think you are so beautiful.

But if I could, I would like to get to know you better just to see how beautiful you really are. Is that possible?" To my surprise, she said, "Sure. I'm fine with that!" I told her I didn't want to hold her up, so was it okay if I could get her number? She gave me her number. I asked her when the best time would be for me to call, and she said anytime. I called her a little later that day, and we literally talked on the phone for four hours. We had great chemistry and quickly hit it off. Over the next few years, Shannon and I cultivated a great friendship.

September 8, 2007, was Labor Day, only a few months after I met Shannon. Shawnna, the kids, and I drove to Peoria to spend the holiday with my uncle Garry, his wife, Denise, and my grandma Ola. Garry had barbecued, and we enjoyed the day in his big back-yard with other family and friends. When I returned to the city, we dropped the kids off at her mother's house, and Shawnna and I went our separate ways. We planned to meet back up at the house later that evening. There was a block party around the neighborhood I grew up in on Eighty-Fifth and Justine. I went and hung out there on the block with a few people I had grown up with. It was getting late, and that long drive I made earlier to Peoria was starting to take its toll on me. I was getting tired, so around 1:00 a.m., I headed home.

When I pulled up in front of the town house I lived in, I cut the car off and unfastened my seat belt. I hadn't even let my windows up. While I was driving home, I had let them down just to let the breeze blow in my face to keep me awake. It was only seconds after I turned off the ignition when my driver door was snatched open! Before I realized what was happening, I was staring down the barrel of a gun in my face. It didn't even register right away that I was being carjacked right in front of my house. The sound of the voice of the robber brought some clarity to the moment when I heard him say with this gun in my face, "Nigga, get the fuck outta the car. You know what this is!" My mind was still trying to catch up with the moment. The suddenness of what was happening had me stuck. Then I heard a second voice behind me on the passenger's side say, "We not playing with you, motherfucker. Get the fuck outta the car!"

Without thinking, I took the keys out of the ignition and threw them at the one standing by my driver door. As soon as I did that, the individual who was behind me pulled the trigger, and all I saw was the flash of gunfire illuminate the inside of my car. It blew the baseball cap I had on off my head. I felt instant pain behind my right ear. I automatically thought I had been shot in the back of my head. My next move came without any thought as well. Instincts took over, and I ran out of the car, pushing my assailant as I made my escape. As I ran past him, he, too, took a shot at me, and I actually saw the bullet skip off the ground beside me. Looking back on that incident, I know without a doubt that taking my seat belt off saved my life. Had I still had my seat belt on, I would have been trapped in my car; and certainly, they would have killed me. Yahweh blessed me that night again and spared my life and allowed me to escape. I was able to run through a gangway and came out on the next street over where I saw the guys driving away in my car.

I ran back home and went into the bathroom, immediately checking for blood and looking to see if I had been shot. There was nothing, but my head was killing me. There was no bullet wound, but there was a big red bump behind my right ear. I guess the bullet came so close without actually striking me that it left a big knot on my head. That was a traumatic event, and to this day, I never sit in parked vehicles with my seatbelt on. Ever since what happened between me and Benji, I've always felt that I would have to give up something more than just the time I did as a sacrifice for my transgression; and although I came very close that night, I don't think that was it! I was left traumatized by that experience.

A week later, the news reported that a seven-year-old girl was shot in the head and killed by a stray bullet when she was bent down tying her little four-year-old sister's shoe. I have often wondered why her and not me. That baby didn't do anything to deserve what happened to her. I remember when I went back to work after this happened, people I worked with, in and outside the department, showed me nothing but love and expressed how glad they were that I wasn't killed. It made me feel good that people really cared about my well-being.

I had another close call that could have easily resulted in me getting seriously hurt some years later. It was the summer of 2016. Zailey's mother, Janitra, asked me if I would go pick Zailey up from school. I agreed. I had just left Popeyes on Seventy-Fourth and Stony Island. I drove out of the parking lot and onto Seventy-Fourth and then made a right onto Seventy-Third and BlackStone. As soon as I turned onto the block, I noticed there were four young cats standing in the middle of the block. I also noticed that they were paying extra close attention to my car as I started heading up the block toward them. The situation didn't look right, and my instincts told me this could be trouble. The one thing I thought about was to not panic and not make any sudden moves that could possibly be misinterpreted by these young guys and cause them to do something stupid. So I just kept driving forward at a normal speed.

When I finally reached the point where they were standing, I could see three of them were holding guns already drawn, and the fourth was pulling a gun out of his waistband. I thought this could be curtains for me! They had this look on their face like they had just seen their most hated opps and were ready to give me the business, but thankfully, they didn't. I was able to drive away. As I drove away, still feeling the weight of the moment, what crossed my mind was this: I could call the police, but honestly, that wasn't an option. The police weren't going to help. Think about it. These were young black males armed on the South Side of Chicago. Calling the police could have gotten them killed! Or I could have kept going and went about my business, then possibly watch the news later that night and hear that someone got killed over there. Usually, the first thing people say when they hear about senseless killings in the news is that "somebody needs to do something about this!" Well, this was the perfect opportunity to do something! That was why I didn't go on about my business. Instead, I decided to turn back around and drive up the block again; but this time, I rolled my tinted windows down so they could see inside and realize I didn't pose a threat. Not too many people who don't want to see people shooting other people are willing to go confront young blacks carrying guns to talk to them about not doing something that will destroy their lives and the lives of others!

By the time I drove back to where they were standing and caught their attention, I stopped and said, "I come in peace. Can I get out and speak to you guys?" At first, they were still posturing and acting tough; but when they realized I was sincere and meant them no harm, they allowed me to get out and talk to them. After I got out of my car, I introduced myself, and then I asked them their names and how old they were. Two of them were eighteen, one was seventeen, and the other one was fifteen, all very young with guns. I told them about my story, that at sixteen I made the tragic mistake of carrying a gun and using it, resulting in someone dying. I told them I didn't want to see that happen to either of them and that I love them enough to come back and talk to them. I told them they were too young to go away to prison for life or an early death!

I told the fifteen-year-old he was really too young to go away for the next hundred years of his life without really knowing what it was like being with a woman. That would be tragic! I was so glad I went back to talk to those young men. In the end, we actually hugged, and I told them I would be back to check in with them. I've been back at least ten times since then but have never seen them again. I felt good that when I got home and watched the news that night, no one reported that anyone had gotten killed on that block. I would like to think it was because I did something about it!

When I met Shannon, I had multiple things going on in my life at once. I was still with Shawnna, and the relationship was not as good as I would have liked it to be, but my relationship with her kids was growing stronger by the day. They saw me as a father figure while, at the same time, my position as a father to my own son was not as strong as I thought it should have been. Things with Cheryl only got worse as my life moved forward. I was struggling to try and maintain a positive relationship with my son, but honestly, at times, it seemed like our relationship was on life support. A lot of things contributed to the ups and downs we experienced. His mother was having a hard time with him as well, and because I wasn't getting along with her, it seemed like things only got worse with him. We weren't seeing eye to eye at all. I didn't want Billy to have resentment for me because of my relationship with Shawnna's kids, so I made sure that he knew that he was always welcome at my house. He would come over and spend weeks at a time, and any given night, he would be there. Shawnna also loved Billy, and even though she and Cheryl didn't like each other, Billy actually loved Shawnna and the kids, and they loved Billy. They saw him as their big brother. As much as I hoped things could be better with my son, it never got to the point I wanted to see it at.

My friendship with Shannon progressed. We spent a lot of time talking and getting to know each other, but since I was still involved with Shawnna, there were some restrictions that Shannon imposed on me. I honored that and didn't press her or pursue her but made it no secret how I felt about her. My relationship with Shawnna was complicated, for the lack of a better term. I did love Shawnna. She had such a good heart, but it was very heavy with trauma. My patience began to waver. It was hard to just walk away from someone I truly cared about and her kids, so I hung in there as long as I could.

Honestly, Shawnna probably could not have cared less about me leaving because I think she was also feeling like the best thing for us was to not be together. I realized Shannon wasn't going to wait for me when she ended up getting involved with another dude. Our friendship didn't end, but the way we dealt with each other had changed. I respected her situation, and because I really cared about her, if she was happy, I was happy for her. So during this time, Shawnna and I ended up getting married. I really wanted it to work for us, and we tried to push hard past the things that hurt our relationship. It's funny, though. As hard as it was to get over some of the things that went wrong in our relationship, I believe both us never stopped wanting to see the best for each other.

A little over two years after we got married, we separated! That was November 2011. I moved in with my cousin Macafee. Ironically, this was around the time Shannon had broken it off with the guy she had been dating. Shannon wasn't ready to be in a relationship, but at the same time, we started hanging out. We were spending a lot of time together and started the process of building a lasting bond. She still was guarding herself because, unfortunately, she had a previous relationship that didn't work out, and she wasn't ready to go through any more disappointments and heartaches. So I had to be patient with her, and we took it slow. I hadn't completely severed my relationship with Shawnna because although there was no romantic or intimate involvement, we were still tied through marriage and through her kids. I really felt in my heart they had become mine, especially Zailey because I was there since she was born and because the bond that had been established between us was just entirely too strong. To Shawnna's credit, she recognized how important I was to them and them to me. She never got in the way of that, even when we weren't getting along. She never interfered with my relationship with those kids.

Chapter 27

30 for 30

No MATTER HOW my life was going, whether I was in prison or living my life outside, I always thought about Ben Wilson and how that fateful day unfolded. I was at home one August night in 2011 in the apartment I shared with Shawnna, watching my granddaughter Zailey, who was barely two months old, when I got a call from my cousin Cindy. I could hear the excitement in her voice. She said, "Billy, you remember my friend Denise?" I said, "Yeah, why, what's up?" She said, "She just called me and told me her son's father is with some dudes that want to talk to you. They want you to be in some movie!" Because Cindy was so excited, I didn't think she was lying or playing a joke, but what she was saying wasn't making any sense to me because of the way she was delivering the information. She was everywhere with it, so I began to interrogate her. She got irritated and said "Nigga, just call this number. His name is Mike!" and hung up.

I called the number. It rang a couple of times, then someone said, "Hello!" I said, "Hey, can I speak to Mike?" He said, "This is Mike. Who is this?" I said, "This is Billy!" Mike immediately handed the phone to another guy. He said, "Billy?" I said, "Yes, this is Billy!" He said, "Peace, Billy. My name is Coodie, and, man, I want to talk to you about giving me an interview!" He went on to say, "Me and my partner Chika are doing an ESPN 30 for 30 documentary on Ben

Wilson, but I don't want to do it and not give you an opportunity to be in it and tell your side of the story!" It all made sense of what Cindy was trying to tell me after speaking to Coodie. Coodie went on to tell me that Mike and one of Benji's close friends Mario were talking about the 30 for 30, and they agreed that I should be in it.

I initially was apprehensive about getting involved. At this point in my life, I had enjoyed a certain amount of anonymity although Benji was always talked about. The only people who knew my past were those who knew and those whom I revealed it to who may not have known who I was. If you didn't know me, you probably didn't know who I was! So this was a big decision I was being asked to make, to participate in a project that I know could and would reach millions of people. This also was the first time that anybody who had a platform wanted to know my side of the story and gave me the opportunity to tell it and let it be heard by many.

As I talked to Coodie, my instinct told me that this dude was a sincere cat, and I felt he had integrity. We talked on the phone for a few hours, and he told me what his vision was and what the intent he wanted to see come out of this. He said he wanted to help people in Chicago specifically to learn from this and heal from it. Before we hung up, I decided I would do it. After making the decision to do it, I talked to people close to me whom I trusted and often sought out for advice. I definitely told them that I was approached to do this and was ensured the way it was going to be done wouldn't be to hurt me. I told them I was going to do it. I had more than a few of my most trusted people tell me I shouldn't but who, at the same time, supported my decision to do so.

Coodie relied a lot on Mario for context of Benji's character and personality. Mario was very important to the project because he was Benji's best friend. At first, he really had no interest in talking to me, let alone wanting to meet me; but as time went on, me getting to know Coodie and Chika and them getting to know me as well and them working closely with Mario, of course they talked about what they had been learning from me. Mario decided to give me a chance as well as Mike, but it was Mario who called me one day and told me he wanted to meet me and talk. I had no problem with that, so one morning, we decided to meet at the car wash on Sixty-Ninth and South Chicago.

He asked me what happened, and I told him. He told me we were good after he listened to me, and we hugged, and Mario has been a friend to me since that day. I think I had talked to Coodie at least a thousand times since the first phone call conversation to the day we filed my interview a year later in my office at the Safer Foundation, which at the time was on Seventy-Third and Cottage Grove. I also introduced Erica to Coodie. Erica was not only my friend since childhood but she was also very cool with Benji Wilson. It was interesting that the only people who knew that I was in the documentary were Mario and Mike while it was being filmed. I appreciated Coodie and Chika for keeping that a secret. Everybody else in that documentary had no clue that I was in it.

I was glad that I decided to do it. It gave me a chance for the first time to publicly tell my side of the story. I knew that the 30 for 30 was a major platform, and for Coodie and Chika to give me that opportunity to tell my side was major. Over the years, I've heard so many outlets talk about the situation from a very biased standpoint, and I have always questioned why no one ever approached me and asked me why I did what I did, especially since Benji's death has stayed relevant and talked about over the years. Maybe certain outlets didn't think it was important to reach out to me. I have heard the truth embellished so much. For example, Comcast SportsNet did a documentary called "The Legacy 25," which came out in 2009. They said in the documentary I was locked up still in the federal system. That was an outright lie! I had been paroled from the state of Illinois, not the federal system, in 2004. I was used to the truth being stretched, so I was grateful that those brothers gave me my chance to have my say.

Since then, I've had the opportunity to meet people who knew Benji, and I've never had a problem with any of them. I even met his nephew, Benji's namesake, at a restaurant on Seventy-Ninth and Indiana. Shannon and I were ordering food, and a guy walked in and asked the people working in the restaurant if he could leave some fly-ers in there for an event that was coming up. Shannon was standing next to the counter when he put the flyers there. She took one and walked up to me to show me what it was. As he walked by, he saw me looking at it. It was a flyer commemorating the anniversary of Benji's death. He stopped and asked if we knew who Benji was, and I told him I knew who he was. Before he left, he said he hoped to see us at the event before walking out of the door. This encounter took place after the 30 for 30 had come out. He was also featured in it. His father was Benji's older brother. As soon as he walked out of the door, he immediately came back in and walked up to me and asked me, "What's your name?" I said, "Billy Moore!"

At this point, I could only imagine what was going through his mind. Did he have some hostility he wanted to express to me? This was a moment I didn't know what would come out of, so I just braced myself for anything. I positioned myself to have Shannon stand behind me as he stood in front of me. He seemed to be a little shocked. Certainly, I know I was caught off guard. I know he wasn't expecting to meet me by passing out flyers to remember his uncle, and here was the guy who shot him. He said, "I never knew I would meet you!" But as he said that, he stuck his hand out to shake mine. I had no choice. I felt compelled to return the courtesy and shake his hand back. I said, "Me either." The moment ended as fast as it began, and he just turned back around and left the restaurant. I never saw him again after that.

Chapter 28

Like Father, Now Son—Unbreakable Cycle

IT WAS JULY 2009, and my son was eighteen years old. By that time, he had a son of his own. He was two years old, going on three, and living with his mother in St. Louis. We call him Cinco, William Moore IV, my first grandson. Unlike the day my son was born, we were both blessed to be there for that day, September 8, 2006, two years to the day before my close call with death when I was carjacked. My son had gotten in some serious trouble at this time and had gotten arrested for an aggravated battery with a firearm. His case had played out for about three years until he was eventually tried and convicted. At first, when he had gotten into this trouble, I was disappointed because all my life I wanted him to learn from my mistake so that he wouldn't have to suffer the same consequence I had already paid. But at a certain point, I stopped feeling disappointed and just became deeply saddened because I knew what he was going through every day being away. The only good thing I felt behind this was that when I would drive past the block he and his mother lived on, I wouldn't see him because he was away inside. But before he went away and I would drive by the block, whether I saw him or not, I always felt an uneasiness knowing that the probability of him getting in trouble or hurt was becoming more realistic. My son ended up serving six years and nine months in prison.

I fully understood the depth of the suffering of being incarcerated and the depressive spirit it inflicted upon an individual every day they spent inside. Of course I never wanted him to have to experience that. It's so traumatic! For me, incarceration is synonymous with death! I've always felt that the only place lonelier than a prison or a jail cell is a grave. I've never been in the grave, but we all know that's a place you don't want to be. But I have been in a cell, and even people who haven't don't want to end up in one, and never do I want to again! So if being dead is the lowest state you can go, the step above that has to be the jail cell! I never wanted him to experience what life was like under those circumstances. Prisons cells hold the living dead, and that's the best way I can describe it for anyone who has never been there.

For anyone who has done time, only they can relate to the feeling that is hard to understand for those who haven't gone through it. I don't wish prison on my worst enemy. As I lived, I've come to the conclusion that no matter how much you try and tell people what they should and shouldn't do, for them, that advice is never good enough. I guess as people live their lives, for some, it's just the process of learning lessons that the flames of experience have to be touched before they realize for themselves that the fire burns, lesson then learned! But at what price does the experience cost? Hopefully, those lessons won't burn you up and consume your very life!

Chapter 29

Stupid Motherfucker

RIGHT AFTER ZAILEY, my granddaughter, was born, the Safer Foundation had lost the Sheridan program contract with the state of Illinois and the Department of Corrections. I was now facing being laid off. I was glad that Jim Utley had pushed me to submit my allocation to go inside Sheridan prison because I was now eligible to work for the Department of Corrections! I applied for a position to work inside one of two work release centers the Safer Foundation was contracted to run for the Department of Corrections. They are Crossroads and North Lawndale work release centers.

The work release centers are the lowest security level in corrections. They are referred to as community correctional centers, but they are still prisons that fully operate under the Department of Corrections' guidelines and operational procedures! North Lawndale had a CRC-II (correctional residential counselor II) position available. A CRC-II is basically the person that supervises the security staff, the shift commander. This was the position I applied for. To my surprise, I got hired for the position in September of 2011. This was crazy. Never in my wildest dreams did I ever think I would be working as a correctional officer, but I was! I went from prisoner to prison guard within seven years of being released.

I had the best situation going for me. As the person who ran the shift for security, I had a number of things I controlled. For example, I could assign staff where they worked, approve movement, and other things that made sure the shift ran right. I made sure that I consciously treated the men there with dignity and respect, and because of that, they allowed me to do my job without compromise on either side! My father said, "Give a man power, and you will see his true character!"

There was this one staff member who treated the residences like they weren't shit because he could. I didn't like that. I remembered COs like him acting like that when I was doing time, and I didn't have any power to do anything about it, but now I had the power to do something about him. I tried talking to him at first about the way he treated these guys unfairly and without respect. Of course because he thought he had the authority, he could treat them how he wanted to. He used against them his ability to send them back downstate to a prison as his leverage to treat them bad. I told him he should be mindful because unlike asshole correctional officers these guys have dealt with in one of those downstate prisons, he lived on the South Side of Chicago, and the likelihood of him seeing one of these guys was much greater than the likelihood of them running into one of those COs. This dude wasn't that bright, and eventually, I had to write him up for being insubordinate. Much of the staff didn't like him either. I had good working relationship with the center supervisor, Mrs. Johnson, and pretty much everyone else whom I worked with there. The residence also showed nothing but respect for me. This job was surreal for me, especially on a few occasions a couple of guys who knew me from doing time together came to North Lawndale and saw me in that role.

My correctional career was short-lived. When I was carjacked a few years earlier in front of my house and literally dodged a bullet to the back of the head, I made a mistake in judgment and got me a gun for my protection. Unlike the sixteen-year-old who went and got a gun, I didn't carry it on me. Nevertheless, it still was just as stupid of a decision. My reasoning was, I was never getting caught off guard like that again. The night that bullet bypassed my head, it was another moment of clarity with mortality.

One night after I got home from Shannon's house, I pulled into the back of my cousin's house in Englewood where I was staying. I had moved out from Shawnna and was staying with my cousin Macafee. As I parked into the lot in the back of the house, the slick boys—a slang term guys from Chicago used to refer to police specifically in unmarked police cars and plain clothes—pulled into the alley and blocked me in. They put the flashlight on me and then got out of the car and walked up and told me they got reports of shots being fired on the next block and asked if I heard them. I told them no, I hadn't heard any gunshots. They asked to see my license and insurance. I complied. At this point, I knew they had no probable cause to search my vehicle because everything was up to date, but I was still a black man and a murder convict being stopped by white police officers in an alley in Englewood at midnight. The odds weren't in my favor, and I didn't feel good about this scenario. Never have I ever felt good with any police encounter. So when they asked if they could search my car, I felt like it was more of demand than a pseudo request. So, of course, I granted permission.

The search turned up nothing, and I was allowed to go in the house, and they left. What I didn't know at the time was that they were trying to get a name to put on a warrant to search the house looking for weed. The next evening, soon after I got in from work, a search team, including the two police officers from the alley the night before, were all set to kick the front door off the hinges, but Macafee heard them coming up the steps and opened the front door. They rushed past him as they made their way into the house. I was in a back bedroom when they busted in. One of them asked me my name. After I told them my name, he told me to stand up and turn around and proceeded to put the cuffs on me. He took me to the living room where I saw my cousin sitting on the couch in handcuffs. As I was made to sit down next to him, one of the police officers said, "We have a search warrant. Somebody said that weed was being sold out of this house!" I was sitting there thinking who the fucked lied on us. I was working for Safer, and Macafee was an assistant engineer for a large apartment complex.

They searched the house for what seemed like hours, and they did find some weed. There were two small bags that Macafee's baby mama had. The problem was the gun they found in the closet in the bedroom I was in. I had it in the closet and a piece of mail with my name on it. I was fucked! Due to the fact that my name was on the warrant, which they needed a name and was able to get my name from the night before when they asked to see my license in the ally, plus them finding mail in my name, I was arrested. I was charged with unlawful use of a weapon as a felon. I had been out for seven years doing well, and now once again, I was in handcuffs. So now my son and I were in trouble with the system, fighting cases at the same time! What an example!

My uncle had paid bond to get out, and I fought the case for sixteen months. I was able to get unemployment and did security at Washington Park Grammar School. I even got a paper route literally. I would deliver newspapers at 3:00 a.m. until my unemployment was approved. Because of my background, it was going to be hard beating the charge. I challenged the warrant, lost the challenge, and ended up pleading guilty to two years on June 2013. I served eleven months. Those eleven months were harder than the nineteen years and nine months I had done. Every day, I kicked myself in the ass. I thought about what I was able to do and what I had lost. I didn't think I was ever going to get back to the level I had obtained.

Two days after I turned myself, I was in Stateville NRC (Northern Reception Classification). This had not been built the last time I was in Stateville. It brought to life for me what the prison industrial complex had become. When someone went through NRC, for at least four weeks, that person would be locked up for twenty-four hours a day. Once a week, he would get fifteen minutes for a shower and two hours once a week for yard time. It was even worse for someone who got sent there for a parole violation that caught a new case. They could sit in there for years or for however long it took to resolve the new charge if their court dates were less than thirty days apart. If their court dates were beyond thirty days, they wouldn't keep them at Stateville. It was utterly depressing, a hundred times more than it was thirty years ago. During those eleven months, Shannon didn't abandon me. She supported me and helped to make those eleven months a little more bearable.

Finally, the day came when I got out. It was May 14, 2014. This time, I paroled in Peoria and was there with my uncle Garry and auntie Denise. Shannon came to visit me in Peoria and stayed the weekend when I got out. She was so beautiful, and I enjoyed every moment of my weekend with her. I knew that our relationship was headed for another level from where we left off before I had left for eleven months. The weekend went by too fast, and before I knew it, she was headed back to Chicago. I knew my life wasn't in Peoria. It was in Chicago with Shannon. I was there for only two more weeks before I moved back to Chicago. My uncle Garry is my hero. He's always been there for me without judgment!

A friend of mine gave me a security job to secure a site for UJAMAA Construction Company that had built the Walmart Grocery on Seventy-Fourth and Ashland. I showed up early every morning. For the first few weeks, the only thing that happened was, machine operators started drilling holes in the ground. The GC (general contractor) who supervised the site was a guy named Gust. Gust took a liking for me, so by the time work started to install the sewer system, Gust introduced me to the foreman of American Backhoe, a sewer-installing and underground company. His name was Justin. Gust asked Justin to give me a shot, and that was exactly what Justin did. Justin was a hard ass. He pushed the guys who worked for him, but he was a good dude. I learned some things working for American Backhoe, but at forty-six years old, I didn't see construction as a long-term, sustainable career path for me.

During the same year, in August, my boy Big Tony got me a job working on the setup and breakdown crew for New Life Covenant Church. New Life was the fastest-growing church in Chicago at the time under Pastor John Hannah. I did that for about a year and then got the full-time job of cleaning New Life's office building on Fifty-Fifth and Michigan. A few months after I started working for New Life, Big Tony told me he wanted to introduce me to a guy who told him he wanted to meet me. He said that he was connected to Benji's two younger brothers and wanted to bring us together for a reconciliation. His name was Charles Johnson (CJ).

At the time, CJ was the COO of New Life Covenant Church. This was in December 2014. CJ had already been talking with Benji's brothers way before this time. I asked him why he wanted to do this. He basically said the same thing Coodie told me. He believed that the brothers and I could use this reconciliation to help heal our city and teach some young guys how to make better decisions before they make some tragic choices. I definitely liked the idea of the reconciliation. I know he had reached out to some influential people to support this effort. As I got to know CJ, I could see that this brother was a connector and a power broker. He knew people and tried to help people as best as he could. So I believed CJ when he said he wanted to do it for the reasons he gave. He also said he wanted to help us as well. He told me that he wasn't going to do anything without me being involved and that he told the brothers that also. It took some time for these things to come together, but I'm a firm believer in what is meant to be will be!

I stopped doing construction when I started cleaning the office building on Fifty-Fifth and Michigan, but I needed a better job. So I reached out to some people I knew over at the Safer Foundation—to be specific, a VP I had worked in the department of at the time I caught my gun case. His name was Mr. Butler. Butler was a cool guy who gave me more than one shot. I appreciated him for his support. He was the one who approved for me to do my 30 for 30 interview at the office at Safer on Seventy-Third and Cottage. He told me to apply. Two of his departments needed a caseworker. I applied and got hired back working in a program called Train2WorkII that was funded through a federal grant from the Department of Labor.

It was November 2015. My job was to recruit residence from both work release centers and enroll them in vocational training, do case management, and make sure they were transported to their trainings in Schaumburg, Illinois. I met this sister by the name of Teneishae, who was our data manager. She ended up quitting and went to work for an organization I had never heard of but was doing outstanding work in the community called IMAN (The Inner-City Muslim Action Network).

During this time, my relationship with Shannon became serious. May of 2016, I purposed to her, and she accepted. I was engaged to the woman of my dreams. We set the date to June 3, 2017, and while my personal life was going great, things on my job was not going so great at Safer. I was still cleaning the office at New Life overnight too. My relationship with my supervisor at Safer became too much of a challenge. I loved Safer and still believed in its mission. Safer has good people working there, but I could no longer work under the person who was my supervisor, so I decided to quit in December 2016. I still had my night job at New Life Covenant. I wasn't making a lot of money, but I was happy with a peace of mind. That was important to me. Before I left, I started feeling stressed walking through the door at work. I couldn't keep doing it. The day I quit, it got so bad that I literally walked out. I still love that organization and have lifelong friends whom I met at Safer.

Chapter 30

Barely a Season

My son came home on March 24, 2017, a few days after the start of spring. I was so glad for him and glad that that ordeal was finally behind him. I had plans to help him with what he was going to need to be successful with transitioning back into society. I helped so many other men on their journeys back. I knew I could help him as well. I thought about how unfair it was for him to have to grow up for the first thirteen years of life without me. Then after I finally make it out, the next six years we became almost estranged. There were various reasons I believed why, but that won't change anything, and as I look back, none of it was worth it anyway. Then he went away for close to seven years. We never got the chance to be a part of each other's lives.

We had a conversation when he came home. He didn't ask me to help him get on his feet or to help him get a job. He asked me to help him raise his son. I felt honored when he asked me that. For me, his question validated his respect for me. He told me he understood how and why things became what they did and that he held no resentment toward me. There was never a question of his love for me, but before this moment, there was a question of respect. That conversation removed any and all doubts I had about his respect for me. It's never good to have children who have no respect for their parents, but to now know my son respected me, I was grateful he had freed me from that insecurity of not believing he did. I told him I tried to do everything I could to guide him in a different direction but that it became hard because of everything else that had played a role in how our relationship became. Nevertheless, I was so glad to have him back, and I was determined to help him raise his son and help him get back on his feet.

At that time, I was still searching for a better-paying job and was getting ready for my wedding. So I decided to reach out to the sister Teneishae to see if IMAN was hiring because she said they were preparing to expand their Green ReEntry program and would be looking to hire caseworkers. She told me they would doing their hiring soon but did not know exactly when. She suggested I come around to meet the people over at IMAN and for them to get to know me. It was totally okay for me to come around because IMAN has this unique communal environment that is not the conventional working environment.

One day, Big Tony and I were over this brother named Lil Law, who has since passed on. May he rest in peace! I was telling him I was trying to get in with this organization named IMAN! Law said he went through their program when he first came home from prison and spoke very highly of IMAN. While we sat there, he called a brother by the name of Bilal who worked at IMAN. He put me on the phone with Bilal, and Bilal asked me if I could come over to IMAN right then. I left and headed over there.

Bilal was a big and imposing guy. We had similar backgrounds, and we knew a lot of the same people. Bilal had done fifteen years in prison and came home and turned it around. Bilal was a smart guy with an imposing edge but was highly intelligent, humble, funny, and down-to-earth. Bilal was his Muslim name. IMAN is a Muslim-led organization. The word *IMAN* means faith in Arabic. But IMAN is a community-based organization that helps and employs people whether they're Muslim or not. Bilal invited me to come and have breakfast Saturday morning after the Morning Prayer.

I knew it was going to be hard to do because usually I didn't finish cleaning the office building until around 3:00 a.m. But the brothers would meet around 6:00 a.m. I pushed myself that morning and showed up at Cracker Barrel on Sixty-Fifth and Pulaski where they had breakfast at. I met a brother named Shamar, who was a senior director at IMAN. A dark-skinned brother and very intelligent, an expert organizer! He grew up in Moe Town, and his father and uncles were very influential in that neighborhood. They made sure Shamar stayed on the straight and narrow. He went to school and became one of the best community organizers. I met Dr. Rami Nashiashbi, the charismatic and humble executive director and leader of IMAN. I was so tired from working all night. I stayed up to make sure I went to that breakfast.

I didn't say much beyond introductions. I just wanted to come get to know the brother, and they get to know me. As I started coming around, I became a familiar face. I learned that IMAN had operated a community clinic and also an arts and culture department as well as an organizing campaign that was grooming leaders from the community that were directly impacted by things impacting the community. Bilal was over the housing program under Green ReEntry. Bilal told me that IMAN was about to start a partnership with Chicago CRED, Arne Duncan's organization. Arne Duncan's story before leading Chicago CRED had a long history in Chicago as the former head of CPS (Chicago Public Schools). When Obama became president, he picked Arne to be his secretary of education. Now the former cabinet member was back in Chicago, leading the charge to reduce gun violence, a crisis that had gripped Chicago for the last fifty plus years by not seeing anything less than four hundred homicides since 1965. Under his leadership, Chicago CRED was established!

IMAN has been around for twenty plus years, working on the south and southwest side of Chicago, organizing around social justice issues that have impacted mostly black and brown communities—from police accountability to the eco food system and from affordable and accessible health care to behavioral health and artistic expression as well as housing for returning citizens and teaching the brothers the construction trade to obtain meaningful employment. So because of the partnership with Chicago CRED, IMAN was able to expand their Green ReEntry program to include the youth demo-graphic, eighteen-year-olds to twenty-five-year-olds. Until this part-nership, IMAN only worked with a small number of men returning from prison, so since CRED's focus was on eighteen- to twenty-five-year-olds, IMAN expanded. The opportunity to partner with CRED was big. With this expansion, IMAN would have to hire more peo-ple, and I wanted to come and work for them. I felt comfortable being around these brothers. Rami, although he was the executive director, I found to be very approachable and down-to-earth and extremely smart.

The Green ReEntry program is a cohort model designed to teach men one of three construction trades: HVAC, carpentry, and electrical. These skills are taught in the class and then used on prop-erties IMAN purchases to be rehabbed. Aside from that, a heavy focus on the cognitive development of the participant is facilitated through weekly sessions of essential life and soft skills: CBI (cog-nitive behavioral intervention), behavioral health counseling, test-ing and drug counseling. Because of the partnership with CRED, IMAN's Green ReEntry program is now an intergenerational cohort model. The intergenerational model has been invaluable to the pro-gram, bringing together younger men, most of whom have not had a positive male figure in their lives growing up, and sharing the space with adult men, most of whom have spent a significant amount of time in prison and had missed out on helping to raise their own chil-dren. These young men and older men learn from one another. I had hopes of getting my son in the program. He came to my wedding and said, "Pops, I need a job!" I told him, "You been out only two months. Just be patient. I got something for you soon!" This was on June 3, 2017.

June 3, 2017, was the day a dream came true for me. On that day, the woman of my dreams made a promise to love me and be with me until the day I die. This was the day Shannon and I got married. I had prayed for this to come my way, and the Most High blessed me to have her. It was even more of a blessing for my son to be there. Things were looking up currently in my life. I just married the woman of my dreams, my son was home, and I was about to go work for an amazing organization. Shannon and I honeymooned in Jamaica. This was my first time on a plane. It was beautiful.

I was assured by Shamar and Bilal I was being heavily considered for the position for the Green ReEntry team once the contract was signed with Chicago CRED, so I felt good about the opportunity that was right around the corner for me and my son, literally weeks away from happening. Middle to late June, I was interviewed, first over the phone by IMAN's behavior health director, Natali Rehdman, the next day by a panel of senior management, and a week later by Bilal and Shamar, a real good brother whom I had learned a lot from since I've met him, and Rami.

A friend of mine and someone whom I consider a mentor, Dr. Troy Harden, and I were having a conversation one day. This brother Troy was a true Chicago dude. He came up on the low-end hustling and doing his thing in the streets, having his of pitfalls because of the life. Needless to say, he found himself doing a couple of stints in the joint. At some point, though, Troy got it together, addressed some important issues, overcame some personal demons, and went back to school. This brother didn't stop until he put these letters in front of his name: PhD! Now Dr. Harden teaches at Northeastern University. The conversation was him encouraging me to get back in school. He said, "Man, just start taking a few classes!" I had made up my mind that it was the right thing to do, so I did everything necessary to get started. Plus, I knew by doing this I could use it to also help motivate my son to stay focused on doing right. My motivation was sky-high, and I knew once I started, those eighteen months would fly by to graduations.

Around the time I was enrolling, Billy was mad at me because I kept telling him to stop driving his girlfriend's car every time I saw him driving. The main reason why was, he didn't have a license, so we hadn't talked in a couple of weeks. I didn't care if he was mad. I didn't want to see him go back to prison for driving without license while on parole! I even told him that I would take him to go his license, but for whatever reason, it didn't happen. I knew if he got pulled over by the police, he was going back for a violation to the worst place he could be sent to: Stateville NRC and twenty-four-hour lockup! I didn't want to see that happen, but Billy had a hard time listening sometimes to me.

It was July 6, 2017. I started out early that morning because Northeastern was a nice drive far north. It was a beautiful day, warm and sunny. The expressway was clear with hardly any traffic on my way there. I got there at about 11:00 a.m. As I was heading to the financial aid office, I looked at my phone and noticed I had a missed call from my cousin Cindy. I didn't think anything of it, but before I was able to call her back, she called me again. When I answered, it was Cindy's daughter Nikki on the phone. I could hear panic in her voice. I immediately knew something was wrong. She said, "Uncle Billy, Lil Billy got shot!" I wasn't expecting that, and my first thought was, is she serious? I said, "What? He got shot? You sure?" She said, "Yes, Uncle Billy!" My thoughts instantly started battling with one another. Of course I was thinking, *I hope he's going to be okay*. But when people get shot, you know how bad that can get, and those thoughts kept surfacing also.

I said, "Where at and when?" She said they were on their way to Eighty-Fifth and Laflin. I hung up and left the building, racing to my car. My mind was all over the place, trying to avoid thinking of the worst possible outcome. It's never a good feeling not knowing any details beyond the general information. Because I was feeling overly anxious, I called my cousin back; and this time, Cindy answered. I asked her, "Cindy, where is my son?" She said, "He's on Eighty-Fifth and Justin. We just got here!" I was too damn far away, trying to get to the South Side as fast as I could. Now traffic wasn't as kind going back as it was coming to Northeastern. Nikki called me back and said, "Uncle Billy, the police is putting up tape around a car Billy was driving!" I asked her, "Is Billy in the car, Nikki?" She said, "Yes, he's in there!" When she told me he was still in the car while the police were putting the tape up, I knew he was gone. That tape made him now part of the crime scene. A few minutes later, my cousin Sherri called me. When I answered, she was in tears. She said, "Billy, Naughty is over there, and he said MoMo gone!" Naughty was my cousin, Sherri's brother. When Billy was a baby, we used to call him MoMo, and Sherri never stopped calling him that.

When I heard her speak those word to me, I felt an indescribable void that I knew could never be filled! Those words broke my heart. The reality that my son had just been killed was so heavy. It killed all possibility of hope for the best, the moment, for the day. No more hope for him could I pray on. He was gone! As much as I didn't want to, I had to embrace the truth of his circumstance. I was still so far away trying to get there. I called his mother, but she didn't answer. I called Shannon's job and asked them to have her call me because there was a family emergency. She called me back within minutes, and I told her what had happened, and the news left her devastated. She immediately left work and headed to where Billy was at.

When I finally made it there, police were everywhere. I couldn't drive down the street he was on, so I had to come up the alley. When I walked over to the tape and saw the car, there was a sheet draped over it. He was still inside the car. I couldn't see and had no idea what condition it had left him in. There were so many people gathering. I looked over my shoulder and spotted Cheryl and her daughter Chela. She was hysterical and in utter grief. I felt hurt for her. I felt hurt for him. I was trying to hold up and be strong. When I looked at Cheryl, I thought about Mary Wilson, Benji's mother. I could now feel her grief because I now fully understood it. Someone had taken my son away from me, his mother, his son, and everyone who loved him. He was gone, and there was nothing I could do about it. This was the worst feeling ever, ten times worse than when I lost my father and mother. I asked myself if this was my sacrifice for what I had done to Benji and his family. I assumed it was meant for me to feel this kind of pain. I had a full understanding of the type of grief that is brought about through the untimely death of your child. I knew I had to accept what had happened, but understandably so, there was no consoling his mother. I walked over without saying a word, and I just held her.

A detective walked up and said, "Is your son named William Moore?" I spoke for the both of us and said, "Yes!" He asked us to come and sit in the back of his police car. While we were in the car, another police officer walked up to the car and showed us a picture of Billy and asked, "Is this your son?" I said, "Yes!" He said, "Can you confirm his name?" I said, "William Moore!" He said, "So sorry for your loss." He asked us how old he was, and after I told him, he walked away. I asked the detective what happened. He told me that whoever it was, he was seen on tape walking up to the car and proceeded to unload. I asked him how many times Billy was hit. The detective said that information I would have to get from the medical examiner's office, but according to the shell casing they found and the type of gun that was used, there were sixteen that were found. He believed Billy was hit by all of them. As I sat in the back of that police car, I thought about the people who did this and wondered why. One thing I didn't have to wonder about was that I knew whoever did this was lost inside this vicious cycle of ignorance that led them to carry out senseless violence without any conscience. I, too, was lost in it. I knew right then I had to forgive them for what they had done. I remembered when I created this same grief for Benji's family and friends. I wanted their forgiveness.

Chapter 31

IMAN—My Purpose

ONE WEEK LATER, I got a call from Bilal. He said, "Hey, we want to extend an offer for hire!" He said, "Can you attend a weeklong training beginning this Friday?" I said, "Yes, I accept the offer, but I can't come Friday. It's my son's funeral! He was killed last week!" Bilal was in shock when he heard me say that. He offered his condolences. I asked him, "Can I start Monday?" He said, "Let me call you back, but it shouldn't be a problem." About ten minutes later, Rami called me. Rami said, "Billy, I'm so sorry to hear about your son. I understand if this isn't the right time for you to take this position!" Rami spoke with pure sincerity. I knew he meant what he said out of concern. I responded to Rami by saying, "Rami, losing my son has left a void inside of me, and because of what happened to my son, I need to be there working for IMAN, helping these young men find their purpose because working for IMAN is now my purpose!" I said, "I just need to first bury my son Friday, and then I'll be there Monday at training!" He didn't argue with me. He just said, "Okay!"

My son's funeral was on Friday, July 14, 2017, and he was buried that same day. Hardest part of this ordeal was walking away and leaving behind my son's body in a grave. After burying my son, IMAN was just what I needed to get me going and do something meaningful. My career with IMAN started three days later, July 17,

2017, as the case manager of the Green ReEntry intergenerational program. My mission was to use my life experiences as an example to others to not make the mistake I'd made and to honor my son by helping young men who could easily go out and kill or be killed because they lacked hope. I could do this through the work we set out to do at IMAN. In addition to me, two other brothers who had long-standing ties to IMAN were hired as caseworkers, my brothers Ali Kanoya and Gemali Ibherim.

Ali was a brother who was funny as hell. He was a Muslim who lived his life to the best of his ability to his faith. He became our guy who was consistently there early every morning preparing for the brothers to come in. Ali would lead the check and pledge every day. This was something that he took ownership and showed initiative of.

Gemali was also a Muslim who had taught me so much through his walk of faith and principles in life that had helped guide me in my own journey to being a better person. He was the biggest advocate of the participants. He was a witty brother with a sense of humor. His technical knowledge, organizing skill, and facilitating ability had made Green ReEntry a valuable program. Gemali was our lead facilitator of CBI. He had also taken the initiative to organize our trips by putting together budgets, booking hotels, and renting buses. We couldn't be what we were without him. Since starting, our team had grown with two more caseworkers.

Rafiqi and Najm—both brothers were faithful Muslims. Rafiqi was a humble brother who brought with him a positive attitude to work every day. He was someone you could count on. Najm was one of the most thoughtful brothers I had ever met. He also had a way of making the brothers accountable when they were in the space. He took the initiative to make sure attendance was being taken and was accurate. Najm was highly intelligent and dependable. These were my brothers. Balil was our enforcer. We all called on Bilal for advice and leadership. I knew I leaned on that brother. Balil was Green ReEntry. He kept the order.

We all brought our hearts to the work. We shared our stories, exposed them to holistic therapy through art and behavior counseling, brought in speakers who had impacted the community in positive ways, and took them on trips to various states outside their everyday existence. We wanted to create a culture unique to IMAN. One of the brotherhood's—with our younger guys and older men who came from various parts of the city, primarily from the South Side of Chicago—one of the first things we agreed should be done was to come up with a Green ReEntry pledge. While Gemali worked on creating policy and procedures and all the technical documents, which were invaluable to the program, such as softs skill schedules and the various spreadsheets necessary to keep track of important information, Ali and I worked to come up with a pledge that embodied the spirit of Green ReEntry. What I wanted the pledge to define for our participants was their purpose not only at IMAN but also in their community. What was manhood, responsibility, accountability to self, family, and community? This was what we created:

> I am a man. I pledge as a man to be respectful to myself, my family, and my community. I pledge to never take away but to contribute to my community and as a participant of this program. I pledge to give as much as I receive. I pledge to be respectful to both peers and staff. We are a team, one united, one chain. We are only as strong as our weakest link. We succeed by strengthening each another. Failure is not an option, IMAN!

This pledge is recited every morning by Green ReEntry participants and staff to start our day. A motto came out of this pledge by the first cohort: 1 Link, 1 Chain! This has become the motto that now resonates throughout all of IMAN! I'm so proud of this. This is now the unofficial title of the pledge: the 1 Link, 1 Chain pledge! We have a Green ReEntry program in Atlanta too. One of my proudest moments since I've been at IMAN was when our Atlanta participants made a YouTube rap video of the pledge. Please go look it up. It is truly amazing!

Chapter 32

March for Peace with the Secretary

A MONTH AFTER I started working for IMAN, Ali Kanoya introduced me to a guy by the name of Curt. Curt was from Foster Park. He lived on the next block from where I lived, but while I was away doing my time was when he was growing up on the next block. He and my younger cousins were actually gangbanging against one another. Curt had made a name for himself in the streets. Curt had looked up to Benji and admittedly disliked me because of what happened between me and Benji. Curt had his pitfalls along the way and found himself doing a prison stint. Now Curt and I are cool. He was a calm, mild-mannered brother and, to some degree, introspective. I respected that about him.

Fast-forward and years later to the current, Curt was now working with an organization named Chicago CRED. CRED stands for Creating Real Economic Destiny. The founder of CRED is Arne Duncan, former head of CPS (Chicago Public School) and secretary of education under President Obama. Arne came back to Chicago and wanted to reduce the homicide rate and gun violence in Chicago. This is the mission of CRED. CRED is a founder of IMAN's Green ReEntry program. A few weeks after meeting Curt, I attended a march for peace and a call to end gun violence in Chicago at St. Sabina on August 11, 2017. This was a month after my son had gotten killed. I saw Curt. After we greeted each other, Curt told me that Arne Duncan was there, and he wanted to introduce me to him.

There's a back story involving me and Arne Duncan. Arne and Benji Wilson were friends. Arne Duncan was a basketball player, and during his high school days, him and Benji Wilson played together in Chicago tournaments. They played with and against each other in pickup games also. So I was not one of Arne Duncan's favorite people. I assumed Curt told Arne I was now working for IMAN and had also recently suffered the loss of my son, so Arne was willing to meet and talk with me. Curt told me, "Let me introduce you to Arne." Curt said, "Arne, this is Billy!" Arne held his hand out, and we shook. I asked Arne if he was aware of my story, and he said he was but that he wanted to hear it from me. Arne was very casual wearing a jogging suit. This tall white cat, still very athletic looking, was standing there in a matter-of-fact way and with an approachable demeanor. This dude was Obama's secretary of education, a presidential cabinet member, but that day, he seemed like just a regular guy. After I asked him if he was aware of my story and he said he was but that he wanted to hear it from me, I told my story.

I was honest with him, and as we marched for peace, Curt and I explained that we both grew up in this area, and we talked about particular places that we walked past, places either he or myself couldn't go when we were younger. We walked through Foster Park and talked about everything. It was a good event. The heavyweight champion Deontay Wilder even came out and joined the march. I told Arne what happened the day Benji and I had our confrontation. At the end of the march, Arne told me that he would call me because he wanted me to come and talk to the guys in his program in Roseland, the YPC (Youth Peace Center) in Roseland. A couple of days later, Arne called me and asked me if I could come over to YPC. Bilal and I went there, and I shared my story with the young men in their program. When I finished talking, the energy in the room was very emotional. Somebody was cutting onions because there wasn't a dry eye in the room. After that, I don't think Arne ever saw me the same. He was able to now look past my historical mistake and see me for who I was. He realized that I was not the sixteen-year-old kid who tragically made the mistake that caused his friend's life. He knew that I wanted to help young men in our communities not make that type of mistake!

Chapter 33

Steven Ward

WE WERE READY to start recruiting participants for the first intergenerational Green ReEntry cohort. It was early August 2017. I was driving to work one morning, feeling good and motivated about the opportunity to bring in young men into our program who needed the services we had to offer that could help them in multiple ways: cognitive therapy, developing hard skills, and hopefully finding meaningful employment.

It was 8:00 a.m. when I rode past Sixty-First and King Drive. Anybody who knows anything about this area knows this is a hot corner. I figured what was better than to make this corner a recruiting ground for the program. We wanted the high-risk individuals who were most likely to be shot or to shoot somebody. So when I saw the two guys on the corner selling weed and loose cigarettes, I asked them out of my window if they wanted a job. Immediately, they said yes. I pulled over and got out, walked over to them, and explained what we were doing at IMAN and that if they wanted to get into the program, they should come up there later that afternoon. Something in the back of my mind told me I wasn't going to see them again, and I didn't. As I finished talking to them and was about to head toward my car, a woman who had walked out of the store and overheard me telling the guys about the program asked me if her son could join the program. I asked her how old her son was, and she said he was twenty-four. I told her absolutely. She asked for my number so that she could give it to her son because she really wanted to see her son get in the program.

Later that afternoon, while working to get acclimated in my new job, I got a call from a number that wasn't programed in my phone. When I answered, on the other end was a young man's voice. He said, "Can I speak to Billy Moore?" I said, "This is Billy. How may I help you?" He said, "My name is Steven Ward. My mother told me to call you. She said you may have a job for me." This was my introduction with Steven Ward. He sounded eager and motivated. His energy had me excited. For as long as I had worked with young men, I knew in the beginning most of them started out strong in the process; but in the end, they didn't always finish strong. For me, in the beginning, I was always optimistic that most will finish as strong as they started even when I knew some wouldn't. I never wanted to count anyone out. So hearing the excitement in Steve's voice had me feeling good about his opportunity and of what he could get out of our program.

I explained to Steve what the program was about and told him what day he needed to come to IMAN so we could get him signed up. When orientation finally started, Steve was there every day. He was my first recruit. Steve showed up on time, engaging and show-ing a willingness be a part of what we were doing. He also showed a gratefulness that he had this opportunity. Steve told me one day that he, his brother, and his sister basically raised themselves. His father was never around, and his mother had issues. He told me the lady who approached me that morning was not his real mother. She was the mother of his ex-girlfriend who took a real interest in his well-be-ing even after her daughter stopped dating him. His schooling came from his upbringing in Cabrini-Green. Steve was intelligent, street smart, and tough. He wasn't a follower. If he didn't like something, he didn't have a problem letting you know, but he was also one of the most likeable guys in the cohort. Everybody liked Steve. Correction: We all loved Steve.

When orientation was over and the start of the first day of the program came, Steve didn't show up. This was the first time this happened. About an hour later, I got a call from him. I asked him why he wasn't in the space, and he said, "Billy, I got shot last night!" I was like, "What? You got shot? Where are you?" He said, "I'm here at IMAN, walking up the stairs to your office!" I walked out of the office and opened the door to the stairwell, and just as he said it, there he was, hopping up the stairs with a bullet hole on his hip. I could not fathom the resilience of this brother and his determination to be a part of what we had. He said he was there ready to work even with a bullet hole in his body. I told him to go back to the hospital. I was concerned. I didn't want to see him catch an infection. I assured him that he would not lose his spot in the cohort and insisted that he go home.

Within a couple of weeks later, Steve returned and took off in the cohort. He was very competitive and hated to be outdone in the classroom or on-site. During lunch, he and Gemali would play this card game called Casino. He couldn't stand it when Gemali beat him. This dude was funny too. He loved to joke, but he also had a serious side to him as well. He emerged as a leader among his peers quickly. I managed a caseload, and Steve was on it. The one problem I had with Steve was that sometimes he would come late, but I found out it was because Steve's fiancée, Lolita, had a son whom Steve would take to school sometimes, and because they were living on the West Side, it would make him late.

Lolita called me one day to tell me how appreciative she was of the program. She said since Steve joined IMAN, all he talked about was the program. She said he was not hanging out anymore and every night was studying. I didn't know at the time when the program first started that Lolita was a few years older than Steve, but it became apparent it was her maturity level that I believe helped Steve elevate his outlook on life and that influenced him to take things more seriously. She helped him get focused and stepped his game up. Everything wasn't perfect, but over all, Steve was one of my best participants. I would tell the guys we were not there to manage men but to help them learn to put their thinking in front of their feelings, and when they put their feeling first, then they put themselves to be managed by someone else. I didn't have to manage Steve. He did well at managing himself. He used the Green ReEntry program for what it was meant for. He was changing. There were things he valued, things that were meaningful to his life, and he took them seriously.

Every December, IMAN had its end-of-the-year gala fundraiser event. It was an event that invited out the funders and potential funders, partners, supporters, and the community to help celebrate our work over the previous year. The end-of-the-year event came only four months after the Green ReEntry program started that summer. While planning for the event, the Green ReEntry staff debated if we were going to have the cohort participants working with the staff at the event that night. For staff, that was a working event, but we decided to just let the cohort enjoy the night off because it was on a Saturday. I didn't know until later that Steve actually asked if he could work the event, but since it was decided the cohort didn't have to attend, he was told that he didn't have to. The event went off without a hitch, and the fundraiser was a success. It was a beautiful night. Everybody was dressed up in all black.

I went home that night and had a good night's sleep. When I woke up the next morning, I saw I had multiple missed calls, twelve to be exact, and quite a few text messages. They were all made during the hours between 3:00 and 4:00 a.m. I immediately got worried. You don't get that amount of missed calls and texts message at that hour of the night/morning without it being about something serious. I saw the missed calls were from Lolita, Steve's fiancée, and his play mother. The messages only read to please call. My instinct set off an alarm. I didn't want to hear something bad about Steve.

When I built up the courage to call Lolita back, I was bracing myself for the worst. I knew I had to make the call and find out why my participant's fiancée and mother were calling me at such an hour. When Lolita answered the phone, the sobbing in her voice made it clear something was very wrong. Her words confirmed my worst fears when she said, "Billy, Steven was killed last night!" When she said it, I didn't want to believe it. But the sad fact was, I knew it was true. For me, it was only five months earlier when I heard those words about my son. It brought to the surface for me the unhealed pain of having lost my son a few months earlier, and now instantly, my heart was grief-stricken by the loss of my Steve, a participant in the program and my first recruit. Steve was like my firstborn of IMAN Green ReEntry. I was heartbroken by this news!

I was witnessing his change and seeing his greatness manifest, and just like that, Steven Ward was taken away from us! I then called his play mother, and of course, she was emotionally upset. Not much was said beyond the obvious. I had to call Rami and give him the news. Once I told Rami, who was clearly shaken by the news, I reached out to Bilal, Gemali, and Ali. The news of Steve's death erased any positive feelings that the night before gave any of us that next that morning. The news of the day was about Steve. This sent shock waves through IMAN and our partner Chicago CRED. For me, it made me realize how important this work was and how it was necessary that we had the ability to touch more young people as possible to prevent these incidents from continuing to play out. Young men who are changing will never be too far removed from those who aren't. Our biggest challenge is that when those who want to change, the world around them stays the same. Opportunity for change has to become more accessible for more young men caught up in the cycle of ignorance and living in the spirit of doubt and defeat.

When it was reported in the news what had happed to Steve, the media reduced his humanity to the common narrative of a gang member shot to death. This was the way the media explained away our circumstance when we would far too often see play out in urban black and brown communities as if by saying it was gang-related could somehow justify the loss of that life. Rami decided not to let Steve be reduced to a two-sentence byline in the news as a gang member killed in senseless gang violence. We were going to complicate the narrative. Rami and the senior leadership at IMAN decided to honor Steven Ward by producing a documentary of his life at IMAN. Bilal came up with the brilliant idea to name the new youth home building Steve, and his cohort brothers were working on the Steven Ward Resident youth home!

Only two weeks before Steven Ward died, on November 13, 2017, Arne Duncan brought Laurene Jobs Powell to IMAN to show them the program. Laurene's organization, the Emerson Collective, was a funder of Chicago CRED. Arne and Rami were leading a discussion with the participants about what the program meant to them. Steve stood up and talked about how for the first time he really felt he was a part of something that had a positive effect on his life. He said up until that time, nothing went well for him and how he basically had raised himself. He talked about appreciating the way we made sure they were taken care of and how we would stand on them about coming there and being on time. Gemali had the foresight to capture when he videoed Steve, not knowing that only two weeks later, he would be murdered.

Chapter 34

The People, the Work, the Opportunities

THE BEGINNING OF 2018, IMAN had a major spotlight shined on the organization. Our executive director, Dr. Rami Nashashibi, became a recipient of the MacArthur Genius Award, a very prestigious award that the MacArthur Foundation gave to people who had worked to impact the community in a positive way. We at IMAN were very proud of the recognition Rami was given because of this reward. For me, it was a validation of the man I had come to know Rami to be. I had the opportunity to go to fundraisers and events where Rami spoke at. The one thing I noticed about Rami was that he wasn't trying impress us at IMAN when he talked about holding certain people, particularly his own people, accountable in the community where they were making money in black and brown communities but not necessarily giving back or exercising positive relationship in our community.

I witnessed Rami in a room full of his own people and called them out on not being accountable and how they could do more to build positive relationships in these communities that they were making so much money in. He talked about how he identified with the struggles of African Americans in this country, that during slavery, how a slave memorized the Quran to preserve Islam in this country. He talked about the pride he felt in how black men would adopt names like Mahammad, Ali, and Elijah and the shame of how some of his Arabic relatives and those who operated within the business community in those communities, upon coming to America, would change their names to Mikey, Lennie, and Mo. From that day forward, I knew this guy was as real as they come. He had earned my respect. Rami tried his best before any decision he made to be as fair and merciful as he could be. Rami was an individual that you would learn from whenever he spoke.

It was during the summer of 2018, and we had only about two months left to go with our first intergenerational cohort when Arne brought a lady by the name of Debra Gittler, who was the CEO of ConTextos, an organization that had helped people living and experiencing a life of trauma to write their memoirs and to discover their journey to healing through their writing. It was started in El Salvador where they still worked in prisons with groups like the MS13, one of the most notorious gangs in the world. They worked with schools in Chicago, men in Cook County Jail, Division 10, and with Chicago CRED and their affiliates, including our participants at IMAN.

ConTextos had some creditability when it came to helping to give the voiceless a voice to be heard through published memoirs that are complicating the narrative internationally. We decided that a partnership with ConTextos would only enhance our soft skills sessions at IMAN. ConTextos had this motto, which was an African proverb: "Until the lion speaks, the tale of the hunt will always glorify the hunter!" When I first heard this, it spoke to me and to my story. I asked Ms. Gittler if she didn't mind that if I decided to write my story, I would use this proverb for my title. Yes, she said. When we tell our own story, we complicate the narrative. No longer will it be left up to others to tell it. No longer can anyone define who we are when we have the power to tell our own stories. This is what motivated me to begin the process of writing this book. Since beginning this process, I've had an op-ed published in *Crain's*, which is in the September 24, 2018, edition. Here it is:

> In November of 1984, the world witnessed my
> greatest mistake when I killed high school bas-

ketball superstar Benji Wilson. I served twenty years in prison for my crime. Since then, I've been committed to reconciling my past by working to reach young men before they end up on a path to destruction, with a life sentence or early death.

For young African American men in Chicago, the margins of error are small. Many of our young men feel imprisoned in their communities. With high poverty, no jobs, run-down neighborhoods, irrelevant schooling and drug trafficking, they feel trapped without the option of leaving. Survival means embracing the lifestyle around them and accepting low expectations. That's why many of them have guns. To protect themselves, to carry out "justice" the way it's been carried out for decades—without the police. The stress of living under these circumstances is beyond imagination. It's a daily challenge to have to live this way. So far this year, almost 400 people have died from gun violence, but more than 2,000 have been shot, according to city data. And that doesn't count the family members who are directly affected. This is what young African American men in Chicago are forced to live in. These are the margins they are forced to live in. These young men have been told for so long that they are irredeemable, that many have begun to believe it.

There aren't enough programs like IMAN or our collaborative partners Chicago CRED and Chicago Beyond that help young men feel differently about themselves and their communities. Programs like ours build positive networks amongst the same young men who sometimes see each other as enemies. We help develop social emotional skills and attainable goals. IMAN has been doing this work for over two decades. However, in order to reach more individuals who are at-risk, we need more engagement from community members, leaders and businesses to get involved. This means coming together to scale out the efforts and resources to expand our capacity.

This epidemic of gun violence has a residual effect over the entire community. In order to thrive, everyone must get involved. I'm calling on the business community to get involved not just from an economic development standpoint but a moral investment. Creating viable solutions is a heavy lift that requires everyone to come to the table, especially businesses, as we collectively seek to eradicate the cultural norm and cycle of violence in communities. While lives are being lost, revenue is still being generated, but how much of it going towards ensuring the preservation of life and keeping communities safe? Businesses need to be a part of the larger solution by investing more resources towards prevention, like the work happening here at IMAN. We simply can't do it alone.

And we need more men like me engaged in doing this work. Men who have lived these experiences, felt the way these young men do, and come home to reconcile our pasts and improve our communities.

Crain's published this after they sat down and interviewed me and Arne Duncan about our relationship and our reconciliation through the work we were doing together, Chicago CRED and IMAN. Since then, as an ambassador of peace and restorative justice, Arne had invited me to be a part of numerous discussions along with some of the young men in my program around the country as we look for ways to reduce our homicide rate here in Chicago. The city of Chicago hadn't had less than four hundred homicides a year since 1965. Realistically, the work that must be done to get on par with cities like New York and LA, who have as much six times less the rate of homicide but two to three times bigger populations, we will need an 80 percent reduction.

It's not going to happen through a three-year contract to maybe two or three nonprofit organizations doing the work. It's going to take an effort from the city mayor's office and the states to at least create a public safety initiative beyond just putting more money into policing, which is not working. There must be an investment in sustainable outreach, trauma-informed care, preventative alongside intervention, and focus ensuring stronger futures for our children who are starting out within certain margins by working to make sure that spirit of doubt and defeat don't overtake them. I was honored and privileged when Arne Duncan asked me to speak and share my story on February 15, 2019, at the Harris Theater in Downtown Chicago in front of a packed house close to two thousand people. Arne led a discussion with five former mayors from around the nation that day who had similar issues with gun violence and was able to get a handle on it. Here's what I said:

> I know about Gun Violence. At 16 years old, I committed my greatest mistake. I ended the life of Benji Wilson who became the 669 victim of gun violence in Chicago that year as a result of a confrontation that went terribly wrong. I know about Gun Violence. July 6 2017, my only son was shot 16 times and became the 339 person killed in Chicago that year. I became a victim. I then fully understood the grief, pain and suffering of what I inflicted on Benji's family and friends. Today, 15 year later after serving 20 years in prison, I work with IMAN, The Inner City Muslim Action Network. I mentor young men

who have been identified as high risk of being shot and or shooting someone, and older men, many of whom have done significant amounts of time. In spite of the narrative, something remarkable is happening in Chicago. We're making new, deep relationships with each other through mentoring and life coaching, training in essential life skills and drug counseling. We focus on health, wellness and healing. We offer trust and friendship. Why? Because trauma is at the heart of this problem. 80% of our men have been shot, some multiple times. Almost all have lost family members and close friends to gun violence. They don't have the luxury of moving away from these Chicago neighborhoods where they have witness so much death. For them, carrying a gun is more than a choice—it's a necessity of survival. Because only 17% of homicides are cleared in Chicago, young men are in state of hypervigilance, having an effect over their physical and psychological well-being. If we want to bring about a revolutionary reduction in gun violence, more men like myself—men that know gun violence—need to become part of this work, without the discrimination of a background getting in the way. Policy makers should consider outreach as not just a hustle, but as an essential tenant of our city's public safety strategy. There should be citizen oversight in police accountability and the teenage homeless population addresses. What I bring to the lives of these young men is the mistakes I've already made so I can help save them from the consequences I have already paid. It's believed that experience is the best teaching, I would like to challenge that thinking, I believe it's wiser to learn from the mistake others. But if we're serious about reducing gun violence, we need to provide Chicago's young men with more trauma care and mentorship. I think of how the young men I work with would have probably killed each other before joining the program if given the chance, but now because of the program has built life long bonds with one another and now openly profess their love for each other. These stories remind us of an essential truth: the worst thing is never the last thing. But in order to create a new thing, we need to help these young men learn how to manage their pain and emotions. We can't dismiss or penalize and label them for it. Yes. I know about gun violence. But I know there's something even more powerful than a gun—relationships big enough to overcome the worst kinds of trauma We have a choice, we can choose to see these men through that old cycle of violence and trauma, or we can work to create a new story yet to be told. I choose new, I choose peace.

Chapter 35

The Reconciliation

THE ONE OPPORTUNITY I'm most proud of was when Charles Johnson's hard work paid off. He finally got me and Benji Wilson's two younger brothers to agree to sit down to reconcile over dinner. This was an endeavor for CJ that took almost four years to make happen. For myself and Benji's brothers, thirty-four years had passed by before it happened. It was on a mild November evening, November 21, 2018, to be exact, thirty-four years to the day that Benji had passed. I found myself walking into the living room of Charles Johnson's house for the first time facing the brothers of the young man I had been responsible for the life being lost and whom I had taken away from them over three decades before. I invited two people to be there to witness this restorative justice sit-down. My guess were Rami and Arne.

Before I had come into the room, CJ had already talked with the brothers with Arne and Rami. I was brought in last. Everything that I thought it would be didn't prepare me for the moment when time came for me to walk into that room and take a seat across a table in person with these two men. The energy was that of an intense tension inside a room intentionally decorated to provide relaxation and comfort! It was an awkward moment, to say the least. Anthony Wilson, the youngest but the taller of the two, was closest to me.

Before sitting down, I reached out to shake his hand, which he reciprocated by shaking my hand back. When I had extended my hand out to Jeffery Wilson, he respectively declined and said he would wait. I took it to mean I hadn't earned his respect yet, even by agreeing to be there to answer any questions within reason. I understood and didn't push the issue.

Anthony Wilson, in my opinion, was more receptive and open, but I could tell that my very presence conjured real raw emotions for both of them. He was moved to tears for most of the conversation. I felt his pain, and in spite his emotions, I also felt like he was there to find healing for his pain through agreeing to have this conversation. Jeffery gave me the impression that his anger and pain were almost beyond reconciling at first. I got the sense he wanted me to prove to him something he was not willing to believe and accept. Almost everything I had to say wasn't going to be enough to convince him because it couldn't bring his brother back. There was even a moment when I thought it might go far left when for about the longest thirty seconds of my life Jeffery Wilson and I locked eyes and got caught in a staredown that was so intense I could see the pulse beating through his temple. I had to remind myself that I was not there for that. I was there to open up to these men and try and help them heal from the wound I had inflicted on them and the pain I had caused their family.

I decided to humble myself because I could empathize with their pain. I decided not to become emotional but continue to talk through the feelings by trying to find a way so he could understand I felt his pain. I told Jeffery, looking him straight in the eyes, "I didn't come here to be disrespected and tell you how to grieve. I know I don't have that right, but I do feel your pain! I know I'm the reason why your brother isn't here, but you have another brother sitting next to you!" I went on to say, "But for me, I lost my only son, which means if it wasn't for the fact that he had a son, my bloodline ends with him. So trust me, I not only can imagine your pain. I feel your pain also! But for those who killed my son, I won't live with hate inside of me for them because if I did, I would be wasting my time being here hoping that you would forgive me, and I'm unwillingly to forgive them! The difference is that I'm here to ask for your forgiveness. They haven't sought out mine, and I've forgiven them a long time ago!" After I finished speaking, I literally felt the room get lighter. The energy in the room now became conducive to its relaxing and comfortable aesthetics that it was meant to produce. It was as if a heavy weight that seemed to be weighing his heart down was lifted in that moment. Jeffery Wilson stood up and said, "Now I am ready to shake your hand. I just had to know that you were sincere, and I believe that you are. I forgive you, Billy Moore!"

What he did next totally caught me off guard. He looked at me and said that he had something he wanted to give me since the day his brother had died and then asked if it was all right if he could give it to me. I had no idea what it was, but I nodded in agreement to go ahead. He reached in his pocket and took a bullet out and sat it on the table and slid it toward me and said, "I wanted to use this on you from the day you took my brother away from me, but now I don't feel that way, so I want to give this to you in this way!" I didn't see any value in accepting that bullet, so without hesitation, I told Jeffery Wilson, "I don't accept that. I don't touch bullets!" I understood the message behind it, but I was not going to accept that from him. The handshake was enough for me. That would have been like I was accepting the fact that he was now allowing me to live! I couldn't do it. Pride had nothing to do with my decision to decline the offer. I honestly just didn't think it be appropriate for me to accept it.

Anthony told me that it was because of his daughter and mother that he could find within himself to forgive me. He told me, "Because you took my brother away from me, you now have the responsibility of being my brother!" Honestly, when he said that, his words shook my soul. That was so profound and deep. I don't think I could ever be worthy to have that responsibility, but nevertheless, I embraced it.

Anthony Wilson meant what he said. A few weeks later, after he accepted an invitation from me and Rami that was extended to Jeffery Wilson also to our year-end event, when I walked up to Anthony Wilson with his daughter and wife standing by his side, he introduced me to his daughter by saying, "This is your uncle Billy!" Wow, I was speechless, to say the least. At the end of the night, at the reconciliation dinner in CJ's living room, we all embraced and took a picture, which Arne Duncan sent to Common, who in turn posted it on his Instagram page and talked about how this exemplified what forgiveness was about. Shout out to you, Common. Much love and respect, my brother!

The second time Arne brought Laurene Powell Jobs to IMAN, Common was with them in the fall of 2018, a few months before I met with the Wilson brothers. I only had one previous encounter with Common through a brief introduction by Coodie in April 2016 when he was in Chicago promoting the movie *Barbershop: The Next Cut.* Mario Coleman and I were interviewed by Sway from VH1 in the back of the barber shop where earlier Common had done a special with Ice Cube that Sway had hosted. I got the impression that Common still wasn't feeling me. He looked up to Benji as he explained in the ESPN 30 for 30. Even after seeing me in that documentary, I believed Common still wasn't ready to forgive me. But the day Common came to IMAN with Arne Duncan and Laurene Powell Jobs and got the chance to see the work being done there—I happened to be a part of the work, but he had no idea I worked there—he wanted to spend some time in the space and see what we had going on in person. When he walked past me, I knew he immediately recognized who I was, and it seemed to catch him off guard. Apparently, Arne hadn't told him I worked there. As Arne and Rami led the discussion and opened up the discussion with the participants, Rami intentionally wanted to give me the last word after he first introduced me and talked about my role at IMAN in the Green ReEntry program and how I had been working with these young men every day to help them change the direction of their lives.

I told Common that I appreciated him coming to spend time with us. I went on to talk about him and me being in the same documentary, and I also reminded him of one of his first raps and that he was kind of disrespectful toward me in it with his lyrics and how it was somehow parallel to how these young guys used social media to feed hostilities against one another. He was surprised when I said that and asked what was it that he said. I said, "You said, 'My first shot of henny, hit me in the chest like those marks that shot Benji!'" He acknowledged it, and I told him it was not a problem, that I got love for him. I expressed that this was what my life was about. Every day I was working and dedicating my time to helping make a change in our community. Everyone in the room—from Rami, Laurene, and Arne to all the Green ReEntry staff and participants—was focused on us. It was a moment that was special to me because I truly admired Common and so proud of him in how he represented himself and Chicago. I knew he had finally seen my humanity beyond my crime, and he said that.

I walked up to that brother, and we hugged. Through that embrace, I felt the strength of true brotherhood being shared. From that moment on, I knew we were good. It was important to me for a dude like Common to have respect for me and the man I was and what my life was about. The next day, CJ called me and told me that he was with Common earlier that day and that Common told him about the day before and had nothing but positive things to say about what happened.

Chapter 36

Creditability

ONE OF MY participants, who was on probation for a gun case, didn't show up to the program one day. I tried calling him, and his cell phone went straight to voice. So I called his emergency contact, which was his mother, to see if she knew where he was. She told me that his probation officer had him locked up because he was in violation of the conditions of his probation and told me he was going to court the next day. Of course, I was going to go to court to see what the deal was. When I first got to the courtroom, I asked the public defender in the courtroom if she was the lawyer representing him after I explained he was in a program I worked for. She told me she couldn't talk to me because she didn't represent him.

So I just waited there until he was brought out in front of the judge. I was also there to find out if I could advocate for him with his public defender so that they would know he was in our program and maybe tell the judge that. I sat there for two hours before he was finally called from the back and brought before the judge. His probation officer was asking for the judge to violate his probation because for five straight months, he had failed every drug test he was given. Dirty drops had him facing prison time. The judge was becoming frustrated as he read from the report about him and asked, "Why is he on probation?" The states attorney said, "He has a gun charge,

Your Honor!" The judge told my participant that for five straight months, he did not get his drug counseling complete but did the opposite by getting high every day. My participant told the judge in a tone barely legible to be heard that he was working and that he was getting drug treatment through his job. When I heard my participant say this, I became disappointed because, clearly, I felt I had failed this young man in his development because he was not prepared to represent himself when it counted the most, in front of this judge. The judge went in on him and basically asked where he worked. He told the judge he did construction! The judge asked where construction jobs did drug counseling. The judge was very sarcastic in his tone and was all ready to send my guy straight to prison without passing go!

When the judge said my participant wasn't making any sense at all, the public defender whom I spoke to earlier, who said she couldn't talk to, was now representing him and remembered I was there for him. She said, "Your Honor, there's someone here that said my client is in his program. Maybe he can shed some light on what he's talking about!" The judge actually entertained her and said, "Where is he?" She gestured for me, and the judge told me to come forth. I'd been to court several times to support my participants, and never had I been asked to come forth and address the court, but that day was different. I was not prepared to address the court, but I wasn't going to be like my participant. I was going to represent IMAN, the work, and him in the way it should. I told the judge that my participant didn't have a job, that he was in a stipend program that focused on teaching the construction trade. Our program was to transform the thinking of our participants through cognitive behavioral therapy and soft skills. I said that he was doing good but struggled some after getting shot early on in the program with smoking marijuana, so we had referred him to see our drug counselor who was a licensed counselor.

The judge looked at me and said, "If this guy is an example of success of your program, then your program is a failure!" He said, "I hope you are not a state-funded program because if so, my tax dollars are being wasted!" After ripping me, the judge turned to my participant and said, "You have an opportunity that you are wasting. These people are trying to help you, but you act like you don't want it!" The judge turned back toward me and said, "Sir, I understand exactly what you are doing, and I appreciate what you are trying to do, and I'm sure there are people you are helping!" The judge turned back to speak to my participant and told him that because of me, he was not going to violate him but that when he came back to his courtroom a month later, the report on him better be different and that if it was the same, he promised him he was going to prison. The judge thanked me again and ordered that my participant be released.

The more I do this work, the more I cherish my successes, but sometimes the failures become so much. It leaves me feeling sometimes if this thing can really be turned around. Although at IMAN we provide a space for young men to come, to learn a trade, receive cognitive behavioral therapy, get their high school diploma, receive drug counseling, develop social and emotional health, and hopefully in the end, become employed, successes can be defined by these things and so many other things but also not oblivious of the failures that are still lurking around the corner, in the community, the neighborhoods, and in the family. For my guys who struggle every day to change, our communities are not being impacted enough that when they go back to them, what is waiting can be overwhelming by circumstance that can outweigh the achievements they have obtained. Others who haven't had access to these spaces of change are still trapped in the cycle of ignorance that are constantly recycling them deeper into the most fucked up set of circumstances, which makes it that much more difficult as they struggle to make it out. So many of our young men will carry guns to protect themselves, smoke weed, and pop pills to self-medicate their trauma. On any given day or a minute away, they are one bad decision that can place them in a situation that can cost them the better years of their life or, even worse, their very life.

Despite the circumstances they live in that are hardly ever been considered in their favor, the circumstance of the lifestyle is what they are judged and condemned by. It's hard not to be judged by your worst mistake, but I'm here to tell you that you can be far better that it. We can't continue to allow people's perception of who we are to define our reality even when we sometimes fall victim to a flawed system that only focus on punishment and retribution. For some, justice has no flexibility and provides no room for mercy. It's rare that we catch a break, and more times than none, we become victims of our circumstances. No excuse, though. We have to run the race based on how things are. We stop living in ignorance beneath the clouds that hide the vultures waiting to eat us alive!

About the Author

Billy Moore was born on the South Side in Chicago to teenage parents, Vennetta Harvey and William Moore Jr., on January 1, 1968. In the summer of that year, his family moved to the predominantly white middle-class neighborhood of Auburn Gresham on the southwest side of Chicago, Illinois. By the time Billy started grammar school, the neighborhood was totally integrated by African Americans.

Billy came from a loving and supportive family. Although his father and mother had separated when he was around three years old, his father was very active in his life. Unfortunately, when Billy was fifteen, his father died from cancer when he was only thirty-four years old. This was around the time in Billy's life that the cultural pull of the infamous Chicago gang influence began to draw Billy in.

Billy's mother worked hard to support them with the help of their extended family, of his grandparents, but the presence of his father was greatly missed. Only fourteen months after the death of his father, Billy would commit the greatest mistake of his life when a confrontation with a promising and gifted young man named Ben

Wilson would result in the tragic death of Mr. Wilson. Billy would spend the next twenty years of his life in prison.

Billy was determined to not allow the mistake he made at sixteen be what would define him for the rest of his life. He's working to complicate the narrative that had sensationalized his mistake. He believes that people are better than their worst mistake. Since his release from prison in 2004, Billy has worked hard to being better than his worst mistake. Although he knows he could never make up for the one life he took, he has dedicated his life to trying to save as many lives as he possibly can!

CPSIA information can be obtained
at www.ICGtesting.com
Printed in the USA
LVHW032140230421
685340LV00018B/195